Power Under Her Foot

Power Under Her Foot

Women Enthusiasts of American Muscle Cars

CHRIS LEZOTTE

McFarland & Company, Inc., Publishers
Jefferson, North Carolina

Some material in this book was originally published in another form
in *Frontiers: A Journal of Women Studies* and is reprinted here
with permission of the University of Nebraska Press.

LIBRARY OF CONGRESS CATALOGUING-IN-PUBLICATION DATA

Names: Lezotte, Chris, 1949– author.
Title: Power under her foot : women enthusiasts
of American muscle cars / Chris Lezotte.
Description: Jefferson, North Carolina : McFarland & Company, Inc.,
Publishers, 2018 | Includes bibliographical references and index.
Identifiers: LCCN 2018013309 | ISBN 9781476670164
(softcover : acid free paper) ∞
Subjects: LCSH: Women automobile drivers—United States. |
Muscle cars—Women—United States. | Women—United States.
Classification: LCC TL152.3 .L49 2018 | DDC 629.222082/0973—dc23
LC record available at https://lccn.loc.gov/2018013309

BRITISH LIBRARY CATALOGUING DATA ARE AVAILABLE

ISBN (print) 978-1-4766-7016-4
ISBN (ebook) 978-1-4766-3173-8

Front cover photograph by Ivan Kurmyshov (iStock)

Printed in the United States of America

*McFarland & Company, Inc., Publishers
Box 611, Jefferson, North Carolina 28640
www.mcfarlandpub.com*

Table of Contents

Acknowledgments

This book had its origins in a graduate course on gender, technology, and culture at Eastern Michigan University nearly ten years ago. One of the course units focused on the automobile and featured an excerpt from Virginia Scharff's groundbreaking *Taking the Wheel,* a social history of women's early automobility.[1] When I inquired if there was any other automotive scholarship of note focused on the woman driver, I was told there was very little; therefore, it was suggested that women and automobiles would be a fruitful subject to pursue if I had any interest in doing so. Although I have never been what one would describe as a car "nut," I believed my Motor City upbringing, coupled with an advertising career that included writing car commercials, would serve as a good foundation for scholarship devoted to women and cars. When a paper I wrote for that EMU class—on women and the chick car—was published in a highly regarded academic journal without revision, I knew I had found my research niche. Thus my first thank you must go out to the instructor of that course—the irrepressible Denise Pilato—whose energy, guidance, and inspiration led me to this amazing journey on the subject of women and cars. Appreciation is also given to EMU auto history professor Russell Jones, who introduced me to the automotive literature and encouraged my investigation of the muscle car and the woman driver.

After completing my master's degree at Eastern Michigan University, I entered the doctoral program in American Culture Studies at Bowling Green State University. While unfamiliar with automotive scholarship, my peers and professors were intrigued, supportive, and enthusiastic about my subject matter and provided me with the theoretical and methodological tools necessary to conduct stimulating and sound research. I would like to thank the many scholars and advisors at BGSU who guided the various research projects that became the foundation for this book. Thank you to Linda Dixon for direction on the initial project proposal, to Radhika Gajjala for supervision on the ethnographical research that evolved into a journal article, and to my dissertation committee of Vicki Krane, Ellen Berry, Catherine Cassara, and chair Susanna Peña for helping me to rework, revise, and incorporate new data on women and muscle cars into a dissertation chapter. Upon completion of my doctorate (at the age of 66!) I was awarded a one-year research fellowship at the Bowling Green State University Popular Culture Center. The supportive environment—made possible by past and present Department of Popular Culture Chairs Marilyn Motz and Kristen Rudisill—was crucial in the development of this and other women-and-car endeavors. Much appreciation must also be given to the folks at the Browne Popular Culture Library at BGSU for helping me sift through hundreds of old automobile advertisements and promotional material and for entertaining and enlightening me with personal car stories. I would also like to thank the staff at the Benson Ford Research Library and the *Detroit News* for assistance in locating archival materials.

Many individuals outside of the university setting also assisted in this project. Thank you to the editors and reviewers at *Frontiers: A Journal of Women Studies*. Your patience and guidance in the editing and revision process allowed me to frame my research in the original paper—and subsequently in this manuscript—in an effective and intelligible manner. Thanks also goes out to the many auto-minded folks I have met at regional and national Popular Culture Association (PCA) conferences, particularly automotive subject chair Skip McGoun and my fellow car chick Carla Lesh. Your enthusiasm, support, and constructive criticism have made a positive impact on my work. A shout out also goes out to journalist, author, and car enthusiast A.J. Baime, whose unlikely but much appreciated interest in my research encouraged me to think outside of the academic box. I must also thank the director of the local Society of Automotive Historians chapter—and muscle car aficionado—John Jenza III, aka "Top Hat John," for taking the time to look over this manuscript for technical errors as well as for his encouragement and advice. I could not have completed this project without the unwavering support of my husband and resident car expert Alan Kalter, who spent more than one summer helping me track down potential participants at car shows and cruises all over Michigan and Minnesota. Thanks also to my stepson and the other "doctor" in the family, Barrett Kalter, who although somewhat puzzled by my research interests, has been nonetheless supportive of both my research and writing pursuits.

Finally, my appreciation goes out to the countless women who participated in this project by sharing their love of muscle cars with me. I am forever grateful for your honesty, humor, knowledge, and unbridled enthusiasm. Through your funny, sentimental, outrageous, and empowering car stories, you have not only made this book possible but more importantly, you have given the woman driver a much needed voice.

"When I am in my car I feel free, no stress and have so much power under my foot I can't get enough of it."

31-year-old 1968 Plymouth Satellite owner

Preface

Popular representations of the "woman driver" have their foundation in two enduring stereotypes that have existed since women first expressed the desire to get behind the wheel of the gasoline-powered automobile. The original woman driver stereotype was developed during the post–World War I era in an effort to limit women's mobility. As historian Julie Wosk argues, the stereotype grew out of two male fears: first, that female motorists were "abandoning their proper maternal and caretaking roles" and second, that "mechanically skilled women were invading their turf" (xiii). Its most prominent expression was through humor; the woman driver—as nervous, flighty, mechanically inept, and accident-prone—quickly became a frequent subject of cartoons, editorials, burlesque, comedy routines, and popular jokes. In the decades following World War II, the woman driver was recast as a mother whose vehicle reflected her household responsibilities and caretaking role. This stereotype originated in the auto industry as a means to divide automobile use by gender and thereby reassert the association of mechanical expertise and automotive skill with the male driver. It relied on the cultural assumption that women's "unchanging biological natures" resulted in a gender-wide preference for practical, safe, and reliable cars perfectly suited for the transportation of kids and cargo (Scharff 116). Both constructions of the woman driver have persisted into the twenty-first century. Old woman driver jokes have received new life in cyberspace as memes, online videos, and Facebook pages. And despite the plethora of automotive choices, the auto industry continues to recommend primarily family vehicles to female motorists.[1] The association of women with a particular type of vehicle and driving experience; the assumption that women lack automotive expertise and mechanical ability; the belief that women's interest in the automobile is centered primarily on safety and reliability; and the notion that women get behind the wheel mainly to fulfill the role of family caretaker and chauffeur collectively contribute to dominant and rarely challenged representations of the woman driver. While the family vehicle—e.g., station wagon, minivan, hatchback, small SUV, or crossover—is valued by millions of women for its serviceability and dependability, its ubiquitous association with the female gender in advertising, the media, and popular culture effectively obliterates any other automotive possibilities for the woman behind the wheel.

As a Detroit native, aging second-wave feminist, and former advertising copywriter/

WHEN WOMAN DRIVES

Cartoon: "When Woman Drives." While the woman driver was often portrayed in a humorous manner, such images stemmed from very real societal concerns over the effect of women's automobility on long-established ideas and practices (William G. Steward, Library of Congress, Washington, D.C., 10 August 1915).

art director on the Buick account, I have always been troubled by the lack of attention awarded to the automotive needs and desires of women who do not fit the "soccer mom" mold. I suspected that women who possess a passion for cars, are excited about the driving experience, and who view the automobile as an integral component of their identity were more common than the auto industry and the media would have us believe.

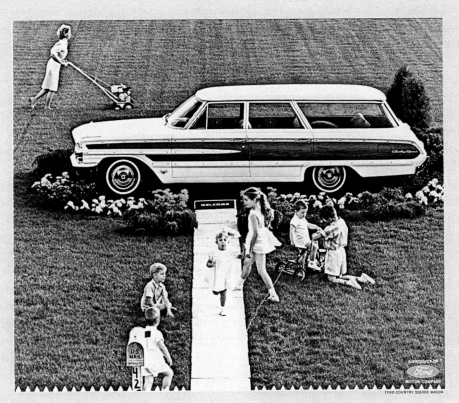

She had so many children she didn't know what to do
–until she got a new FORD wagon.
Designed by America's station wagon specialists,
Ford wagons come in 13 different models,
the biggest choice there is.
Only one thing worries Mom now;
It'll take two more kids to fill this wagon up!

TRY TOTAL PERFORMANCE
FOR A CHANGE!

FORD

Falcon · Fairlane · Ford · Thunderbird

11269
This advertisement appears in
Look—November 19, 1963

Ford wagon advertisement: "She had so many children she didn't know what to do." The end of World War II marked the beginning of the massive baby boom. It was an era in which, historian Stephanie Coontz notes, "people married at a younger age, bore their children earlier and closer together, [and] completed their families by the time they were in their late twenties" (26). The nine-passenger station wagon became the vehicle of choice for growing (and growing) families (*Look*, November 19, 1963. From the Collections of The Henry Ford).

Therefore, I thought it would be interesting—and illuminating—to conduct an examination of female motorists who own and drive vehicles rarely associated with the woman driver. I believed such an endeavor would not only cast doubt on the legitimacy of existing woman driver stereotypes, but would also provide a much needed forum for female car enthusiasts whose voices have historically been silenced.

While I have addressed a number of these automotive categories—chick cars, classic cars, and pickup trucks—in previous research, I decided to focus this particular project on the American muscle car and the woman who drives it for a number of reasons. The first is the muscle car's longstanding association with masculinity and the male driver. The muscle car was developed during the early 1960s by rising automotive stars specifically for the young male baby boomer market. It has repeatedly been called upon in film, literature, and song as a marker of male identity. The qualities ascribed to the muscle car—powerful, loud, brash, and reckless—are often applied to the young man who drives it. Therefore, women who prefer high-performance Mustangs, Camaros, and GTOs challenge gendered prescriptions surrounding car choice and use reinforced by carmakers, the media, and popular culture for over a century. Secondly, the muscle car has a strong connection to the Motor City. It was inspired by street racing youths who congregated on Detroit's Woodward Avenue; conceived by auto execs who traveled down Woodward to GM headquarters in downtown Detroit each day; and built in Detroit auto factories by proud blue-collar Detroit workers. Women of Southeastern Michigan who came of age during the muscle car era—whether or not they actively participated in the culture—were no doubt aware of and influenced by the presence of noisy muscle cars on city and suburban streets. As such they represent a significantly large population of informed and enthusiastic female muscle car enthusiasts in a concentrated auto centric area. As an aging boomer who hails from Motown, I felt I possessed a unique opportunity to speak with local female car enthusiasts about their past and present involvement with the American muscle car. Thirdly, in the twenty-first century, the muscle car—of both the classic and modern variety—has quietly yet steadily become popular with female motorists. I observed this phenomenon not only at the numerous car shows I frequent each summer in Southeastern Michigan, but also in the automotive press, which has reported on more than one occasion about the growth of modern muscle car ownership among the female driving population.[2] And finally, while during the 1960s and early 1970s young women engaged in muscle car culture on the periphery as passengers and spectators, participation in street racing and cruising was off limits to women as drivers. Consequently, I believed an examination of women's integration into muscle car culture in the twenty-first century—the strategies women employ, the vehicles they drive, and the identities they assume as part of this historically masculine fraternity—would add an important and necessary insight into what we know and do not know about the relationship between women and cars.

What we currently know about women and cars can be found primarily in recent scholarship, automotive advertising and promotional material, and the popular press. Until the late twentieth century, automotive history focused almost exclusively on the male driver. If women were included, it was primarily as influences on male automotive purchases and as secondary drivers of the family car. Feminist historians—particularly Virginia Scharff and Margaret Walsh—were instrumental in recovering the woman driver from the automotive archives. This groundbreaking research not only argues that women were more involved in the driving experience than reported in prior automotive accounts, but also provides context for women's ongoing struggle to become recognized as involved, accomplished, and informed drivers.

Automotive advertising and promotional materials tell us how the industry positions the woman driver and what strategies are employed to appeal to the female consumer. In the early days of the motor age, the woman driver was most often presented as an individual interested in style, comfort, cleanliness, and ease of operation.[3] In the post–World War II era, the female automotive consumer was reimagined as a busy and conscientious suburban mom.[4] However, because of the complicated relationship between automakers and the female consumer—a reflection of the automobile's historical association with masculinity and the male driver—it is difficult to determine whether these portrayals are in fact accurate or if they are a reflection of how automakers wished the woman driver to be perceived. While advertising and marketing is certainly grounded in extensive research, as my own experience suggests, it has the potential to ignore women's car use and experience that does not conform to the prevalent male-dominated automotive narrative.

Major news publications with weekly automotive sections focus much of their space on the car review. Given the tendency of the car culture to divide car use by gender, is not surprising that vehicles rated as appropriate for the woman driver are most often those with an emphasis on functionality, safety, dependability, and family-friendly options. Occasionally a news outlet will publish a human interest story centered on a woman and her unconventional car.[5] However, the majority of media sources tend to focus on the practical—rather than personal—aspects of women's automotive experience.

While these varied resources provide both the background of women's automobility as well as factual data on women's current automotive practices, they lack the human aspect to women's relationship to cars. They do not take into consideration the emotional attachments women form with their automobiles, the ways in which a particular vehicle can contribute to a woman's identity, the meanings women ascribe to cars in general and their own in particular, or how the automobile can influence women's well-being and sense of themselves. Because these information sources rely on historical archives, quantitative data, cultural prescriptions, popular culture representations, and auto industry influence rather than the voices of today's female motorists, they fail to provide a complete understanding of the woman behind the wheel.

As an ethnographic endeavor relying on participation, observation, and interview, this project adds to the current literature through the incorporation of women's real life driving experiences into the automotive archives. It offers firsthand accounts of the passion, involvement, attachment, connections, influence, and empowerment the automobile contributes to women's lives. The focus on a specific category of vehicle—the American muscle car—brings attention to how the longstanding association of powerful cars and masculinity has served to limit women's car use, impede women's recognition as legitimate car enthusiasts, and reinforce gender stereotypes about the woman driver. Developed from conversations with women who own and drive all generations of muscle cars, this project acknowledges that not all women are interested in cars for practical reasons; that women's relationship to cars differs from—but is not less than—that of men; that fast and

Sheryl Neibert purchased her 2012 Chevrolet Camaro SS 45th anniversary edition as the means to become more involved with the Eastern Michigan Camaro Club. She loves taking her 6-speed, carbon flash gray metallic convertible on road trips, to car shows, or just around town with the top down in good weather. She especially enjoys the power and performance of the 6.2 liter V8 engine; as Sheryl exclaimed, "I am woman; hear me roar" (courtesy Sheryl Neibert).

powerful cars are not the sole province of male drivers; that women have the means and ability to challenge gender stereotypes through car use; and that women view muscle car ownership as an important contributor to their identity, relationships, and quality of life.

This project is the culmination of time spent with 88 female American muscle car enthusiasts. It reflects their passion for the automobile, the pride they take in owning a piece of American automotive history, and their efforts to make muscle car culture accessible to the woman driver. While some of the more conservative women I encountered were hesitant to share their car experiences with a research scholar, the majority of female auto aficionados I ran into were surprised and delighted that someone, anyone, was interested in what they had to say about cars and opened up their hearts (and car hoods) to me. In the pursuit of this project, I found myself enlightened, entertained, and enriched by the stories told by this group of muscle car–loving women. It is my hope that you will, too.

Introduction: Muscle Men to Fast Women

Muscle Men

Between 1964 and 1973, the muscle car emerged as a "dominant icon in car culture America" (Heitmann 177). Though a serendipitous intersection of circumstances—post–World War II prosperity, baby boomer youth culture, illegal street racing, and young auto execs poised for greatness—the muscle car was produced and introduced to great acclaim and unanticipated success. Most commonly defined as an American two-door, rear-wheel-drive, mid-size car equipped with a large, muscular V8 engine and sold at an affordable price, the muscle car was inspired by the young working-class men who congregated in Detroit neighborhoods to engage in illegal street racing. As auto historian John Heitmann notes, the muscle car soon became the vehicle of choice for male baby boomers of driving age with "money in their pockets looking for excitement" (17). The 1964 Pontiac GTO, the brainchild of young GM executive John DeLorean, is often recognized as the original muscle car. The enormous success of DeLorean's GTO inspired other automakers to quickly follow suit, with offerings that included the Dodge Charger, Plymouth Road Runner, and Chevrolet Chevelle. In order to take advantage of the muscle car phenomenon, automakers expanded the category to include beefed-up pony cars such as the Ford Mustang, Chevy Camaro, Dodge Challenger, and Plymouth Barracuda, as well as full-sized cars and compacts packed with massive engines.[1] "Earsplitting and shamelessly macho," writes auto journalist Lawrence Ulrich, these "power-crazed machines" came laden with hood scoops, racing stripes, and shiny mag wheels, and were available in a variety of high impact colors such as Panther Pink, Grabber Blue, Plum Crazy, and Top Banana ("Plymouth"). By the mid–1960s, Detroit area streets were rumbling with the loud, powerful, colorful, and relatively inexpensive automobiles that, as auto historian Mark Foster exclaims, "reeked attitude!" (76).

The enthusiastic response of male teenage drivers to the American muscle car was often echoed by the adult male automotive press. Jim Campisano, former editor-in-chief of *Muscle Cars* magazine, exclaimed, "Muscle cars are about screaming big blocks revving to the redline. They're about full-throttle power-shifts at the drags. [...] They're about cruising on a warm summer night with your buddies or special someone" (8). *Automobile* magazine founder David E. Davis depicted the muscle car driving experience as "losing your virginity, going into combat, and tasting your first beer all in about seven seconds" (qtd. in Mueller 17). Male automotive scholars reacted in a similar fashion. Writes Heitmann, "with a standard 325 horsepower engine, optional tri-power performance, and a Hurst 4-speed, this light, fast, and inexpensive car resulted in a thrill with every ride" (177).[2] In his research into the muscle car era, William McKinney suggests these vehicles provided male youth with the means and opportunity to "do what most young men want to do the most … pick up girls!" (11). As such remarks suggest, the muscle car was the perfect vehicle, both literally and figuratively, for a coming-of-age male market "with discretionary cash and an urge to express their rebellious identity through the automobile" (Gartman 194).

The muscle car reigned on Detroit area streets, and across the nation, for nearly a decade.[3] In the production and promotion of the muscle car, the auto industry not only fulfilled the demands of a newly affluent male youth market, but also used the opportunity to reinforce gender roles through the determined association of power, strength, and performance with masculinity. As Orval Lofgren notes, modes of driving arise out of "a specific time and place, and they have often developed in contrast to each other. They tend to have a history of both gendering and class" (49).[4] The muscle car entered the automotive landscape in the early 1960s, before the women's movement questioned and challenged traditional female gender roles, and before it was acknowledged that women's pay should be equal to that of men. Taking these cultural restrictions into consideration, it is not surprising that young women's participation in 1960s muscle car culture was limited at best. As auto historian Margaret Walsh suggests, during the 1950s and 1960s, "teenage 'auto culture' looked backwards rather than forwards in terms of gender equality" ("Home" 10). While teenage girls may have expressed an interest in muscle cars, the cultural prescriptions and financial limitations young women faced during the 1960s and early 1970s prevented all but the most adventurous from driving loud and fast muscle cars of their own. While she desired to cruise with friends in fast cars, as a 46-year-old 1968 Firebird owner remarked, "all I had as a teenager was my parents' station wagon." When recalling the Mustang she coveted as a teen, a 55-year-old CPA exclaimed, "I wanted to buy it so bad but I wouldn't even presume that that would have been appropriate. So it was like I wanted to but I couldn't." As a vehicle specifically developed and marketed to the young male population, that embodied characteristics—power and performance—often conflated with male identity, the muscle car was deemed altogether masculine and therefore inappropriate for the young female driver. Consequently, most young women participated in muscle culture vicariously; they borrowed the car of a family member or boyfriend, stood on the sidelines with girlfriends, or dated young working-class men with hot cars. As Robert Genat notes, the woman's role in Detroit muscle car culture was most often confined to that of passenger or "avid spectator" (47).

The oil embargo of 1973, the implementation of strict emission requirements, and a growing emphasis on safety brought the American muscle era to an abrupt halt less than ten years after it began. Over the next twenty-five years, automakers made numerous attempts to reestablish the muscle car and rekindle the passion that accompanied it. That goal was ultimately achieved at the dawn of the twenty-first century. The introduction of

1973 Dodge Charger Rallye.
For the hard driving man.

If you're the kind of man that responds to the pulsating beat of a performance car, grab hold of Charger Rallye. Charger's got the low, lean look that tells you exactly what it is—a performance machine that enjoys being on the road. Go ahead, get in. Settle your frame into Charger's optional, soft bucket seats. Turn the switch on this beautiful baby. Charger's new Electronic Ignition System will give you surer starting because it delivers up to 35 percent more voltage to each spark plug. Then pop the clutch on Charger Rallye. That optional floor-mounted, four-speed Hurst shifter and 440 four barrel will let you put this Rallye through its paces. Charger's rugged Torsion-Quiet Ride and front and rear sway bars can take it. This go anywhere, do anything Charger Rallye can be an expression of whatever you want it to say. And those no-nonsense Rallye instrument gauges say a lot about the car and the man who uses them. When you take off with that power bulge hood and those raised white letter tires, there's one thing sure, you'll be remembered . . . as the hard driving man.

Extra care in engineering makes a difference in Dodge...depend on it.

Dodge Charger Rallye Advertisement: "1973 Dodge Charger Rallye. For the hard driving man." Classic muscle car advertising often linked the characteristics of the automobile to the man who owned it. As the copy in this ad suggests, the man behind the wheel of a Dodge Charger Rallye will be remembered as no-nonsense, performance driven, and hard-driving (*Motor Trend*, November 1972).

reimagined retro versions of classic muscle cars created a new and intense demand for fast, powerful, and performance driven American made automobiles. While classic muscle cars have been reclaimed by members of the original muscle car generation—aging baby boomer men—as both an investment and a paean to the past, the new generation of muscle cars has not only attracted those who grew up with Chargers, Challengers, and Camaros, but also a new and emerging market that includes Generation Xers, millennials, and a growing population of women drivers.

Fast Women

While American automakers would spend the last 25 years of the twentieth century striving to develop a fast and powerful muscle car without sacrificing economy, safety, or fun, American women were seeking power of their own. The women's movement of the 1970s, a revolution that would, writes Ruth Rosen, "irreversibly transform American culture and society" (xiii), not only resulted in increased opportunities for women in many facets of their lives, but also provided women with the resolution and means to pursue individual dreams and desires. To many women, that dream was often realized through the acquisition of an American muscle car. No longer satisfied "going along for the ride" in the muscle car of a boyfriend or husband, these women called upon newly acquired autonomy—and spending power—to purchase Mustangs, Camaros, and Challengers of their very own.

While the relaxing of societal gender norms and the rise in women's paychecks over the past forty years has awarded many women the ability to purchase a car of their own choosing, acceptance as muscle car drivers has been less than forthcoming. As automotive historian Virginia Scharff writes, "the auto was born in a masculine manger, and when women sought to claim its power, they invaded a male domain" (13). The strong association of the American car with masculinity and the male driver, accompanied by the persistent efforts of automakers to direct women toward practical vehicles, has often served to limit—if not obstruct—women's entrance into American muscle car culture. As a teenager, a 47-year-old 1972 Plymouth Barracuda owner desired to be part of the muscle car scene. However, as she explained, "They told us that you're not supposed to be in it; girls aren't supposed to be interested in cars and engines and all that kind of stuff." As noted in an earlier project, women who develop an interest in vehicles intended for the male market are often admonished as technologically suspect, questioned about their femininity, marked as sexual deviants, and berated as women drivers.[5] However, women's growing presence at classic muscle car events, as well as the increasing popularity of twenty-first century retro muscle cars among the female population, suggests that female motorists have developed strategies to effectively and determinedly enter the historically male dominated world of American muscle cars.

Calling on the testimonies of 88 female motorists who own and drive all generations of muscle cars—classic muscle cars, retro muscle cars, and the generations in between—this project uncovers the ways in which women have successfully and enthusiastically infiltrated American muscle car culture and in the process, established themselves as knowledgeable, passionate, and legitimate muscle car enthusiasts. It explores women's

AMC Pacer advertisement: "When she gave in to practicality, she didn't give up her individuality." Prior to the introduction of the minivan in 1983, vehicles that promoted practicality, comfort, and functional cargo space were marketed to the woman driver. This 1978 ad recognizes that when partners become parents, it is most often the woman who is obligated to trade in the fun car for a family vehicle (from the Collections of The Henry Ford).

relationship to the automobile through attention to the meanings women ascribe to cars; it reveals the ways women call upon the muscle car as a source of identity formation; it brings attention to women's unacknowledged car savvy and expertise; and it expounds on women's passion for cars and the driving experience. Perhaps most importantly, it examines how women's involvement with the muscle car has the potential to alter common perceptions of the woman driver.

The American Muscle Car and the Woman Driver

While much has been written about the American muscle car, in scholarship as well as in popular culture, the primary focus is on its function as a source of masculine identity formation in the young male driver. When women do appear in the literature, it is in the margins, as passengers, ornaments, or bystanders. However, as the growing number of female muscle car enthusiasts suggests, women have embraced the muscle car not simply as a means of transportation, but rather, for how a muscle car makes them feel and what owning a muscle car says about them. They call upon the unique qualities of a muscle car—style, power, acceleration, and exhilaration—to construct new identities as women drivers. In doing so, these muscle car–driving women have reclaimed the iconic symbol of American youth, virility, and masculinity and invested it with new meanings. Writing about women's early automotive experiences, historian Georgine Clarsen asserts, "Women's active engagements with automobiles were not simply paper copies of men's, but were constitutive of what a car is and how it might be used, and of the social meanings and bodily experiences of femininity" ("Gender" 240). Considering Clarsen's assertion as a call to action, this project contributes to the existing literature through an examination of the relationship between everyday women drivers and the American muscle car.

In his 1983 review of the critical automotive literature, Charles Sanford remarked, "women are conspicuously absent where they should be most present" (137). In the 35 years since Sanford's critical assessment there has been a small but significant incorporation of the woman driver into automotive scholarship. Historians Virginia Scharff, Ruth Schwartz Cowan, and Margaret Walsh have, over the past few decades, recovered the woman driver from the masculine repositories of automotive history.[6] Literary scholars Marie T. Farr, Deborah Clarke, Deborah Paes de Barros, and Alexandra Ganser, and film scholars Jennifer Parchesky and Katie Mills, have called upon representations of the woman driver in fiction and cinema to demonstrate the significance of the automobile to women's lives in a series of geographical, personal, and spiritual locations.[7] Essays, short stories, and poetry that uncover women's varied and complex relationships to the automobile, penned by distinguished female authors including Jayne Ann Phillips, Eudora Welty, and Flannery O'Connor, have been gathered into eclectic collections for academic and popular culture libraries.[8] The exceptional woman driver—defined in scholarship and popular culture as an individual who has overcome significant gender obstacles to gain recognition in an automotive pursuit associated with men—has been chronicled in accounts by Iris Woolcock, Joanne Wilke, Curt McConnell, and Georgine Clarsen.[9] Autoethnography has provided an opportunity for female journalists and racing enthusiasts—including Lesley Hazleton and Denise McCluggage—to reflect upon their own automotive experiences.[10] And social historians Kathleen Franz and Georgine Clarsen, as well as American studies scholar Cotten Seiler, have, through their attention to women's reconfiguration of masculine machines, provided important insight into women's active engagements with technologies generally considered male.[11]

While the existing scholarship provides a number of avenues in which to consider the woman driver, there is a discernible absence of real women's voices. Relying primarily on historical sources, fictional representations, popular culture, and biography, the current body of research is missing the everyday experiences and perspectives of women behind the wheel. There have been a few inroads made; the ethnographical projects of Karen Lumsden and Sarah Redshaw—while focusing on male youth driving cultures—include the first hand experiences of young women.[12] In my own work, including past research on women with chick cars, classic cars, and pickup trucks, I have drawn on interviews with women in various automotive locations not only to reveal their complicated relationship to the automobile, but also to disrupt the notion that the authentic American automotive experience is inherently white, heterosexual, and male.[13] This project builds on and expands my previous work on a specific population of female boomer and post boomer classic muscle car owners to include multiple generations of women who own and drive all generations of American muscle cars.[14] Rather than address women drivers in the abstract—as historical figures or protagonists in fiction and film—it focuses on the experiences of contemporary women in order to obtain new knowledge about the role of the automobile in women's lives, and to consider women's automotive experiences not in relationship to those of men, but as significant, valuable, and legitimate in their own right.

The Women Who Drive Muscle Cars

This project began as an ethnographic investigation of female classic muscle car owners in Southeastern Michigan, a study that eventually became an article in *Frontiers: A Journal of Women's Studies* and a chapter in my dissertation.[15] As I discovered when conducting the original study—through participant-observation at classic car events, as well as interviews with nearly 50 female classic muscle car owners—the women who participate in classic muscle car culture are a very homogeneous group. They are primarily aging baby boomers and post boomers; i.e., women in their 50s, 60s, and 70s, who are white, Christian, middle class, heterosexual, and overwhelmingly conservative in ideology. In the initial project I argued the women embodied a conservative feminism as a means to construct an acceptable place for themselves within the masculine confines of American muscle car culture. The growing popularity of the twenty-first-century retrostyled versions of classic muscle cars, particularly among the female driving population, prompted me to expand the project to include all generations of muscle cars—the old cars, the new retro cars, and the generations in between—and the women who own them. I imagined that this expanded project would not only encompass a more diverse population of women, but would also reveal new information regarding women's muscle car ownership—and the woman driver—over time. Thus I spent the summer of 2015 at local and out-of-state car events, car club meetings, and on online forums collecting new data from

While Susan Glass enjoys driving and exhibiting her 2014 Chevy Camaro 2SS/RS, the most rewarding aspect of owning a muscle car is getting together with others to raise money for important charities and causes. Through membership in local car organization, states Susan, "I have met some of the most kind and generous people in my life" (courtesy Susan Glass).

close to 40 additional women who own and drive the older but not classic version (what I will hereafter refer to as pony cars) as well as the modern or retro American muscle car.[16] My goal was to find out who these women were, and how they compared to the women in my previous studies not only in terms of demographics, but also in the meanings they ascribe to the muscle car, the strategies they use to enter muscle car culture, as well as the ways in which they call upon the muscle car to reimagine what it means to be a woman driver.

As the women in the additional groups skewed somewhat younger than those in my earlier studies, I expected to see a shift in ideology. I assumed that younger women, who have reaped the benefits of the "feminist revolution," would be more likely to lean left than those of older generations.[17] However, I was surprised to discover that, while the number of women who identified as "moderate" increased slightly, those who claimed the liberal label remained few and far between in all generations of female muscle car owners. In fact, of the 79 women in this project who declared an ideological preference, 86 percent identified as moderate or conservative. In the original project, which focused on women whose cars were produced in the 1960s and early 1970s, I noted the connection between classic car culture's link to a nostalgic automotive past and the association of American automobile ownership with patriotism as a way to understand the conservative ideology embraced by the majority of—both male and female—classic muscle car owners. However, as I discovered when pursuing this new group of muscle car owners, the link between conservatism and domestic automobiles is not limited to cars, or individuals, of a particular generation. When I embarked on the original project, I was puzzled as to how I—a liberal second-wave feminist—might frame a project focused on women who identify as conservative yet recognize gender inequality not only in muscle car culture, but in the world at large. Conservative feminism proved to be useful and effective framework through which to explain this dichotomy. Therefore, much as I did in the original project, I considered the embracement of a conservative feminist ideology to be a crucial factor in how women constructed their relationship to the automobile and positioned themselves as participants in muscle car culture.

Consequently, this project uses the framework of conservative feminism to consider how women develop effective strategies for inclusion, as well as material culture theory—particularly the concept of objectification—to understand how women call upon the muscle car as a source of identity and meaning-making. While the women in this project did not openly identity as feminist, they often exhibited behaviors and attitudes that suggest a conservative feminist worldview.[18] The conservative feminist lens also contributed to the ways in which the majority of women in the project attributed meaning to the American muscle car.

Conservative Feminism and Women in Muscle Car Culture

Rebecca Klatch was one of the first scholars to consider the possibility of the conservative feminist. In her research centered on women of the New Right, Klatch suggests that, although many conservative women eschew feminism as being anti-family and pro–big government, there is a faction within the movement that espouses viewpoints that could be considered feminist. The laissez-faire conservative worldview, writes Klatch, "actually shares part of the feminist vision" (119). Unlike her "social conservative" sister, the laissez-faire conservative woman upholds individualism as an ideal, views both men and women as autonomous actors, and recognizes the presence of gender inequality and sex discrimination in American society.

Katherine Kersten echoes the sentiments of the laissez-faire conservative woman in her 1990 conservative feminist manifesto published in *Policy Review*. Kersten bases her "self-consciously conservative feminism" on three premises: "first, that uniform standards of equality and justice must apply to both sexes; second, that women have historically suffered from injustice, and continue to do so today; and third, that the problems that confront women can best be addressed by building on—rather than repudiating—the ideals and institutions of Western culture." While the first two assertions are reminiscent of a liberal feminist ideology, Kersten parts ways with classic feminism through her conservative vision of Western ideals and institutions, particularly those that focus on family.

Kersten writes, "The conservative tradition incorporates a view of human nature, and of justice and equality, that offers a useful starting point to women who seek fulfillment in a world of limitation." This "limitation" is the obligation women have to family and community, which Kersten views not as a burden, but rather a moral duty. As Kersten argues, women's identity and sense of purpose is produced through a connection to others; therefore, women have a duty to promote the public welfare by strengthening the institutions that promote communal values and by "shaping her community's vision of justice and equality."

Much like her conservative feminist sister, Elizabeth Fox-Genovese advocates for the importance of conventional social forms—i.e., traditional marriage, motherhood, and sexual morality—as contributors to women's well-being. And because feminism should promote women's well-being, Fox-Genovese argues, "feminism should protect and promote conventional social forms" (Baehr 102). Unlike liberal feminism, which condemns the sexist hierarchy in gender norms and recommends social transformation, conservative feminists such as Kersten and Fox-Genovese believe it is important for women to embrace such norms because "their well-being and the well-being of others depends on it" (Baehr 106). Thus while individuals who identify as conservative feminists advocate for gender equality in terms of individual pursuits and opportunities, they believe that such attainments should not be made at the expense of conventional social forms.

The women who own and drive muscle cars subscribe to a conservative feminism in a number of ways. While they often assume gendered roles in the muscle car community, they do not consider these duties as representative of gender inequality, but rather, as important contributions they make as women. They believe equality for women within muscle car culture is to be obtained not through critique of its inherent sexism but rather, through women's demonstration of automotive knowledge, care for the automotive community, and passion for American muscle cars. They do not view the inclusion of women into the historically masculine muscle car culture as a triumph in women's rights, but most often consider it a personal accomplishment or realization of a lifelong dream. The women who participated in this project construct muscle car culture as a community that recognizes and pays homage to the American auto industry. They view their participation in muscle car culture, and the gendered roles they assume within it, to be reflective of core American values that the "made in America" automobile represents.

Looking at women's participation in muscle car culture through the lens of conservative feminism provides an opportunity to not only understand the meanings women ascribe to the muscle car, but also to reflect upon how conservative women are able to construct a legitimate place for themselves within a historically masculine culture.

The Muscle Car as a Vehicle of Meaning

Simply stated, material culture is "the world of things that people make and things that we purchase or possess" (A. Berger 16). The discipline of material culture studies

Laura Pasicznyk-Holt purchased her 1969 Mustang 302 coupe in 1987 from her brother for $250. Over the past 30 years it has served as her drive to college car, work car, dog transportation car, bike racing car, show car, and ice cream run car. As Laura remarked, "he's a warrior. He's a workhorse. He does everything" (courtesy Laura Pasicznyk-Holt).

has traditionally investigated what objects reveal about the societies in which they are found as well as the impact such objects have had on these societies. As Jules Prown suggests, objects made or modified by man "reflect, consciously or unconsciously, directly or indirectly, the beliefs of the individuals who made, commissioned, purchased or used them and by extension the beliefs of the larger society to which they belonged" (1). Technology scholars such as Judy Wajcman, Ruth Schwartz Cowan, and Phillip Vannini have incorporated elements of material culture theory into technology studies to illustrate how social practices and cultural beliefs are embedded not only in technological development, but also in technological choices.[19] Nina Lerman, Arwen Mohun, and Ruth Oldenziel pay particular attention to the relationships between gender and technology, noting the central role of gender ideologies in human interactions with technology, as well as the crucial influence of technology "to the ways male and female identities are formed, gender structures defined, and gender ideologies constructed" (1). Car manufacturers have a tradition of incorporating certain elements into vehicles to mark them as male or female; accordingly, it is expected that women and men will choose those vehicles that reinforce cultural gender roles. As automotive history reflects, the American muscle car was manufactured and marketed to a very specific male audience. Consequently, the meanings attributed to the muscle car have traditionally recalled and reinforced its function as a location for the production and performance of masculinity in the male driver.

Vannini is interested in the interactions between technological objects and subjects, particularly the ways in which "humans shape, and are shaped by, the materiality of life"

(2). Through processes of "objectification," Vannini argues, material objects become concrete embodiments of things other than themselves. In the women-car relationships examined in this project, the muscle car is often transformed into something other than what the manufacturer originally intended. It is not simply a means of transportation, nor is it a way to display or reinforce a prescribed gender identity. Women's use of a particular vehicle changes how it will be perceived in car culture, and in turn, alters the way a woman views herself as a driver. In his discussion of objectification, Christopher Tilley writes, "material forms do not simply mirror pre-existing social distinctions, sets of ideas or symbolic systems. They are instead the very medium through which these values, ideas, and social distinctions are constantly reproduced and legitimized or transformed" ("Objectification" 61). The meanings attached to the original muscle car were stable for nearly a decade due to effective marketing, dismissal of the female driver, and the homogeneity of its young target male audience. However, the past 50-plus years have witnessed a transformation in the age as well as gender of the muscle car driver; consequently, the meanings ascribed to the Mustang, Challenger, and Camaro have altered as well.

Daniel Miller suggests that cars are not just material objects; rather, they act in "objectifying personal and social systems of values" as they form "highly personal and intimate relationships" with human beings ("Why" 2). Thus objectification—a wholly reciprocal process in which "object and subject are indelibly conjoined"—provides a fitting framework from which to consider women's relationship to the automobile in a variety of contexts; i.e., the social scripts surrounding women's automobile consumption and use; the ideologies and gender politics that regulate or influence women's engagement in various car cultures; and the possibilities for negotiation or reconfiguration as women drivers through the assumption of new car uses and meanings (Vannini 16). It allows for consideration of alternative meanings of the muscle car, founded in the automotive and life experiences of women that differ from those of the male driver. Conservative feminism provides a lens through which to consider how such meanings are produced, projected, and personalized.

Women and Muscle Cars in Southeastern Michigan and Beyond

The primary investigation of women and American muscle cars was conducted over three summers (2011, 2013, 2015) in Southeastern Michigan. A trip to Minneapolis for a wedding—and a subsequent visit to local car shows—added a few Minnesotans to the mix. The project involved both participant-observation at car shows, cruises, and club gatherings as well as interviews with female muscle car owners and/or drivers. Detroit's muscle car heritage, combined with the short season of good driving weather in Michigan, provided an abundance of car events in a concentrated geographical area in which to examine women's participation in muscle car culture and to talk to women about cars.

The selection of the Detroit metropolitan area as the primary site of this investigation is significant. While the production of the classic muscle car was curtailed after the mid–1970s oil embargo, the love affair with the muscle car—of all generations—remains alive

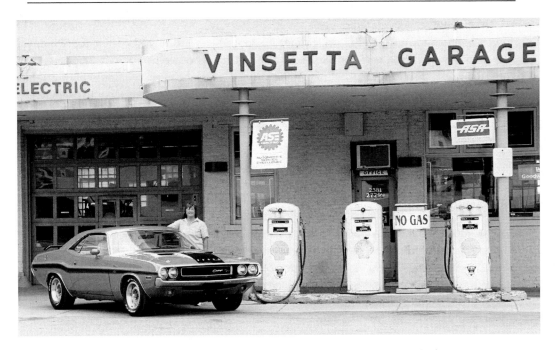

Annie Mott is pictured with her 1970 Dodge Challenger Hemi R/T parked at the historic Vinsetta Garage on Woodward Avenue. This iconic landmark—and oldest garage east of the Mississippi— opened in 1919 to service Model T's, and was a popular stop for teenagers during muscle car's heyday. It closed its garage doors in 2010, but has been reinvented as a restaurant replete with classic car memorabilia (courtesy Annie Mott).

and well in the southeastern part of the state. As the center of the automotive industry during the twentieth century, a significant percentage of the metropolitan Detroit population was involved with automotive production in some capacity. Many of those now involved in various car cultures in the area either worked in the car industry or knew someone who did. Despite the loss of automotive market share and industry jobs, the pull of the automobile remains very strong in Southeastern Michigan, especially to the baby boomer generation. As a 56-year-old 1968 Chevy Camaro owner remarked, "It's a part of who we are. Michigan is car proud."

While other areas of the country can be identified with fast cars—e.g., Southern California and hot rods, and the southern states and NASCAR—the muscle car was not only produced in Detroit, but the inspiration for its creation was illegal drag racing on Woodward Avenue, the street that divides the city into east and west, and connects the affluent northern suburbs to the downtown urban area. The annual Dream Cruise, billed as the world's largest one-day celebration of car culture, with more than 1.7 million visitors and over 40,000 muscle cars, street rods, custom collector, and special interest vehicles, has taken place for the past 23 years on eight miles of Woodward Avenue.[20] Daniel Miller writes, "the car's humanity lies not just in what people are able to achieve through it, [...] but in the degree to which it has become an integral part of the cultural environment within which we see ourselves as human" ("Driven" 2). In Southeastern Michigan, an area whose rise and fall can be attributed to the automobile, a good number of individuals identify themselves by the cars they make and the cars they drive.

As the owner of a classic muscle car (1967 Ford Mustang Shelby GT350-tribute), I had the opportunity to investigate women in muscle car culture as both a participant and an observer. This provided the opportunity to observe women as owners, drivers, and members of automotive organizations, as well as to examine women's interaction with other car owners and interested spectators. Of particular interest was the influence of gender on women's participation. Whether or not women drove their own cars, did their own repair work, had single or joint club membership, participated in club events alone or with a partner, sat at club events with women or men, or engaged in knowledgeable conversation with car buffs and event attendees was duly noted. I also paid close attention to the racial and class composition, sexual orientation, and age range of muscle car owners—to the extent that I could determine those characteristics—while attending various automotive events.

Women's automobiles were also part of the investigation. The paint color, accessories, engine size, and condition were noted, as were artifacts—i.e., trophies, dash plaques, newspaper clippings, owner's manuals, restoration scrapbooks, decals, historical paraphernalia, etc.—placed within or outside of the vehicle. While on site, I asked for permission to take photographs of women's cars. I also encouraged those contacted online to forward favorite car photos. In order to expand the number of possible participants, I relaxed the automotive qualifications to include vehicles with the monikers, but not necessarily the horsepower, of the original muscle cars.[21]

While the primary site of this investigation was regional car events, I also recruited women through snowball sampling as well as on online forums devoted to a particular automobile.[22] This allowed me to contact women who were not active in car events as well as individuals outside of Southeastern Michigan. Due to the recruitment method—i.e., car events, car clubs, and automotive forums—the majority of women I interviewed were not casual car owners, but rather, were more likely to possess a fair amount of car savvy than the average car owner and often used their vehicles as more than daily drivers.

The primary ethnographic method used in this project was the interview. Potential participants were approached at car shows and other events; if they expressed an interest they were provided with a consent form and a self-addressed, stamped envelope in which to return it. Those who responded to inquiries posted on club discussion groups, websites, and Facebook pages, or through the snowball process, had the consent form sent via email. Respondents were given the option of an in-person, phone, or electronic interview.

The interview questions were arranged in three general categories. The first set requested general car information, such as the make, model and year of car, history of the car, and personal stories about the vehicle. Female muscle car owners were encouraged to provide a narrative of their own car histories, as well as to provide personal reflections on their relationship to the car and the meanings cars in general hold for them. The second group of questions focused more specifically on muscle car ownership. Interviewees were asked to provide a personal definition of the muscle car, as well as to reflect on the significance of the muscle car historically and to their own lives. Lastly, those who belonged to car organizations or participated on car forums were asked to reflect on those experiences.

Women Get Muscle

Since the Model T first rolled off Henry Ford's assembly line in 1913, automakers have employed numerous strategies to separate women's automotive experience from that of men. These marketing ploys were developed not only as a means to sell more cars, but also to maintain the gender hierarchy in a changing society. As Michael Berger writes, "the automobile threatened to restructure the social status of women and the meaning of family life in America" ("Drivers" 257). Concerned that women's growing influence as automotive consumers would devalue the very product they were trying to sell, automakers adapted a strategy they trusted would appeal to the woman driver without alienating men. Calling on what they believed to be men's and women's unchanging and inherent biological natures, automakers applied gendered meanings to particular types of automobiles in order to keep the technologies, and sexes, separate. Thus, as Judy Wajcman notes, the "powerful, large car [was] destined for the male head of household" ("Feminism" 135). Women, on the other hand, were assigned the pedestrian, utilitarian "second" car suitable for carrying kids and cargo. While these strategies were initially developed in the early twentieth century as a means to construct women's driving experiences as less than those of their male counterparts, the considerable influence of these tactics remains today. Despite women's significant workplace participation over the past half century, automotive advertisers continue to designate the family car—i.e., minivans, hatchbacks, crossovers, and small SUVs—as most appropriate for the woman behind the wheel.

Therefore, women who own and drive American muscle cars—vehicles deeply ensconced in a masculine tradition—are interesting subjects of study for a number of reasons. Research focused on muscle-car-owning women forces us to confront—and reconsider—the gender stereotypes that surround women's relationship to the automobile. It brings attention to the myriad of ways women use the automobile that have little to do with its function as basic transportation. It makes visible a group of female car enthusiasts rarely considered in automotive scholarship, by automakers, or within American car culture. It causes us to consider how women call upon the automobile as a source of identity that isn't connected to motherhood. By focusing on females of a certain age, it reveals how the invisibility of older women in American society may be challenged through ownership of vehicles that are loud, powerful, colorful, and attention getting. It demonstrates how the muscle car provides right-leaning women with the opportunity to challenge barriers to women's muscle car use while remaining true to conventional social roles. And perhaps most importantly, it uncovers how ownership of an automobile associated with power, speed, and American ingenuity can provide the woman driver with an entryway into a historically masculine culture.

This project is divided into four sections. Chapter 1 provides a brief muscle car chronology, and divides the muscle car—and the women who drive them—by generation. As the initial objective of this project was to compare the women who own newer vehicles to classic muscle cars, this section examines what characteristics—auto and human—determine women's connection to a particular generation of muscle car. It considers how a muscle car generation—classic, pony, or retro—inspires particular meanings, engages

Full-time van. Part-time baby-sitter.

Capability has a kinder, safer, gentler side.

Aerostar can haul six kids to school in the morning and turn around and tow a two-ton boat to the lake at night.* It's also capable of providing for the comfort and safety of its occupants on a full-time basis.

New this year are optional integrated child safety seats that actually incorporate a 5-point belt system.** There's a driver air bag to supplement lap and shoulder restraints.† Every outer seat has a 3-point safety belt. Rear anti-lock brakes also come standard. And electronic "full-time" four-wheel

Standard Driver Air Bag.†

drive is available.

What's more, Aerostar offers you a host of amenities in a comfortable interior with available leather seating surfaces.

Aerostar from Ford. Designed for your comfort...and peace of mind.

AEROSTAR

Have you driven a Ford...lately?

*When properly equipped.
**See your dealer for availability date.
†Air bag effectiveness depends on wearing your safety belt, so always buckle up.

Ford Aerostar Advertisement: "Full-time van. Part-time babysitter." Chrysler's introduction of the minivan in 1983 forever cemented the association between mothers and practical, economical, and safe family vehicles. As evidenced here, other auto manufacturers quickly followed Chrysler's lead (*Sunset*, September 1993, courtesy of Fordimages.com).

women in different ways, offers unique driving experiences, serves as a source of identity formation, and alters how women present themselves as drivers.

While each population of drivers calls upon particular strategies to gain entrance into muscle car culture, many of these tactics are shared across generations of cars and women. In Chapter 2, I present these strategies as roles women assume within muscle car culture in order to be acknowledged as legitimate muscle car owners and to create new woman driver personas.

Considering the relationship between women and cars through the theory of objectification, Chapter 3 examines the various meanings women ascribe to the muscle car across generations of women and automobiles. It considers not only how such meanings differ from those of the traditional subject of muscle car history—the male driver—but also how they reflect the muscle car's significance to women's lives and serve as important contributors to women's subjectivity.

Women driver stereotypes and popular representations of women in muscle car culture have long influenced how women are regarded in the muscle car community and American automobile culture at large. Chapter 4 examines these enduring and ubiquitous representations and reveals the inventive strategies called upon by the women in this project to disrupt, replace, and reinvent them and—in the process—reimagine what it means to be a woman driver.

1

The Generations

Although the original muscle car era lasted just under a decade, various incarnations of the muscle car have been imagined, produced, critiqued, and driven for the past half-century. While most auto aficionados are in general agreement as to the years that constitute the classic muscle car era, the categorization of subsequent generations is often fiercely debated among enthusiasts and the automotive press alike. For the purposes of this project, the decision was made to divide American muscle car generations—and the women who own them—into three distinctive groups. The classic muscle car group is composed of women who own vehicles produced from 1964 to 1973. The pony car group includes women who own automobiles of 1974 to 2004 vintage. Those in the retro muscle car group drive Mustangs, Camaros, Chargers, and Challengers that came off the assembly line between 2005 and the present. While many of the qualities that distinguish the muscle car from other vehicle types are shared by multiple generations, there are particular characteristics that differentiate one muscle car group from another. The same can be said about the women who drive them. What follows, therefore, is a brief historical summary of each category of muscle car, accompanied by an in-depth examination of the women who have fallen in love with a particular generation.

The Classic Muscle Car: 1964–1973

ORIGINS AND PRACTICES

Legend has it that Woodward Avenue, the four-lane thoroughfare that divides the Detroit metropolitan area into east and west, was the birthplace of the original American muscle car. During the postwar era, Woodward was the site of two popular activities that not only led to the muscle car's development and production, but also established it as an important component of 1960s American teenage culture. These practices were street racing, which gave young male drivers the opportunity to test their vehicles, display driving acumen and skill, and impress whoever might be watching, and cruising, a social event on wheels in which teenager boys hooked up with friends, picked up girls, and showed off their loud and powerful automobiles.

Woodward Avenue circa 1970. Cruising on Woodward Avenue was an every night occurrence in the northern Detroit suburbs during the 1960s and 1970s. Automotive engineers would "unofficially" test their cars on Woodward when returning from work downtown, often consulting with local teenage "experts" along the way (courtesy the *Detroit News*).

While cruising was a national phenomenon, it took on special significance on Woodward Avenue due to the thoroughfare's proximity to Detroit automobile manufacturers. As Barry Dressel, manager of the Walter P. Chrysler Museum, remarks, "What drove the cruising era in Detroit was the contact with the automobile engineers who privately or quasi-officially, participated in cruising as well" (qtd. in Ambrosio and Luckerman 7). During the 1950s and 1960s there was an unofficial, but acknowledged, exchange of knowledge, skill, and parts between designers, engineers, and teenage street racers. Engineers often "tested" their ideas on Woodward Avenue after dark, despite the illegality of the practice. In addition, drag racers on Woodward often received parts and support "under the table" from engineers in a "quasi-official" interaction at local hangouts (Ambrosio and Luckerman 92). As Sharon Luckerman and Anthony Ambrosio note, "What [the engineers] learned was not lost on the local teenage dragsters and cruisers. Nor did the car companies overlook the youngsters' creative 'tinkering' to enhance their cars, giving them parts and exchanging advice" (7). This exchange process resulted in the incorporation of a number of "subversive" automotive innovations—pioneered by Detroit street racers—into mainstream automobiles (Gartman 190). The illegal drag racing community—which congregated nightly on Woodward Avenue—not only benefited from the knowledge of automotive designers and engineers who mingled among them, but in turn, also inspired the development of the American muscle car.

As the major thoroughfare that links the affluent northern suburbs to the downtown urban area, Woodward Avenue during the 1950s and 1960s was often the daily route of auto executives who travelled from their palatial homes in Bloomfield Hills to General Motors headquarters in downtown Detroit. One of the individuals who made the trip—and witnessed the illegal street racing taking place—was the mercurial John DeLorean, who is most often considered the individual responsible for launching the muscle car era. John DeLorean joined the General Motors Pontiac team in September 1956. The Pontiac brand had become stagnant, stuck in the past, burdened with the "old lady's car" moniker. DeLorean's task was to transform the "metal behemoth" that conveyed assurance and stability into a model that would attract the growing niche of teenagers and college-age car buyers (Fallon and Sroldes 42). DeLorean and his mentor, Semon Emil "Bunkie" Knudsen, were determined to develop a vehicle that would combine the sportiness of imports with bigger and more powerful American cars. The growth of racing in the United States inspired the team to test out new models in the development stage on local dragstrips and city streets. Thus engineers and design executives, under the tutelage of Knudsen, DeLorean, and GM head honcho Pete Estes, were encouraged to put innovative designs or test equipment on standard models and drive them home down Woodward each night. As Fallon and Srodes remark, "Detroit's teenagers became used to having their homemade hot rods challenged by older men (in their forties), pulling up to stoplights in dull-looking sedans" (44). Soon the "dull-looking sedan" was replaced by a smaller—and much faster—car, introduced as the Pontiac Tempest. Designed by DeLorean, and launched as a 1961 model, the Tempest was named the 1961 *Motor Trend* Car of the Year.

By 1963, the popularity of the Tempest had waned, and the Pontiac division was operating under a "work-with-what-you-have" strategy. Under company cost-cutting measures, GM designers and engineers were forbidden to produce new chassis or engine designs. However, the potential of an ever-increasing, affluent baby boomer market, and the desire of young drivers for a quicker, more powerful vehicle—as demonstrated each night on Woodward—convinced DeLorean to push for faster cars. "Working-with-what-he had," DeLorean realized that a 389-cubic-inch V8 engine had the same shape as the larger 1964 Tempest's optional 326-inch V8.[1] The bigger, more muscular engine fit under the Tempest's hood, while delivering forty-five more horsepower.[2] To keep the car lighter—and faster—as well as to keep the price affordable for the young male buyer, DeLorean removed all the optional equipment and extraneous body trim, while adding stiffer suspension and heavy-duty brakes.[3] The result was the Pontiac GTO, named after the Ferrari coupe, Gran Turismo Omologato.

Yet before the GTO could be introduced, there was a significant obstacle to overcome. In 1963, a marked increase in drag racing accidents created reluctance on the part of GM officials to promote performance cars. However, DeLorean, with fellow engineer Pete Estes, went around GM management and released the car as a $300 option for the LeMans series (Levin 45). Introduced in the fall of 1963, the Pontiac GTO officially launched the muscle car era. The success of the GTO inspired other American automakers—with offerings that included the Dodge Charger, Plymouth Road Runner, and Chevrolet Chevelle—to follow Pontiac's lead.[4] Soon Detroit streets, suburban highways, and rural roads all over the country were rumbling with the quick, powerful, and relatively inexpensive muscle cars. The muscle car became the most popular form of transportation of young American men for over a decade. However, events of the early 1970s—rising gas prices, insurance industry demands for safer cars, government regulations on emissions, and competition from foreign manufacturers—contributed to its eventual demise (Falconer 233).

As this brief origin story suggests, the muscle car's history is a thoroughly masculine one. It was inspired by young male driving practices, developed by rising male prodigies, endowed with characteristics—power, speed, and performance—conflated with male identity, and produced specifically for the male baby boomer market. Since the muscle car's introduction, men and their muscle cars have been repeatedly celebrated in song ("Little GTO" by Ronnie and the Daytonas; Wilson Pickett's "Mustang Sally"), cinema (*Vanishing Point, Dirty Mary Crazy Larry, Gran Torino*), and popular culture (TV series *Nash Bridges* and *The Dukes of Hazzard*), further solidifying the identification of the muscle car as a masculine machine. In the annals of muscle car history, much has been made of the experiences of young male muscle car owners, the identities teenage boys claimed through muscle car culture participation, and the role of the teenage street racer in the imagination, creation, and production of the muscle car.

The tough young muscle car men who came of age during the 1960s and 1970s are now entering their golden years. They take part in classic muscle car culture today as a means to share old car stories, congregate with fellow car buffs, and to reminisce about the days "when men were men, women weren't, and fewer rules ruled" (Mueller 18). Yet while men of the muscle car era have one story to tell, the growing presence of female classic muscle car owners today suggests there are alternative narratives to explore. As accounts of women's participation suggest, the role of the female driver in muscle car culture was contradictory. While some teenage girls willingly assumed the prescribed gender role of passenger or "avid" spectator, others attempted to participate in the same manner and on the same streets as young men.[5] However, most young women did not have the opportunity to participate at all, but had to wait nearly half a century until they had the means, confidence, and societal permission to obtain and drive muscle cars of their own choosing.

This short examination of the conditions that led to the production of the classic muscle car—drawn from automotive history accounts, popular culture sources, and narratives of male participants—provides a rudimentary understanding of how the muscle car served as a site for the construction and performance of masculinity and a means to a collective male identity. In order to understand the meanings the muscle car holds for female drivers—often invisible in the historical and cultural records—it is necessary to recover their stories. As we begin this examination with the classic muscle car, we look at the women who have chosen these vehicles and explore the means by which they have entered classic muscle car culture on their own terms.

> I was a child of the '70s in Detroit—where cars were king (or queen as the case may be). I was lucky enough to have a boyfriend whose father owned a Ford dealership and gave his son a new Mach 1 Mustang every year. So of course, I left the boyfriend at home and took his car out on Woodward Avenue (the main drag on the East side of Detroit) every Friday night with the girls. We would race from light to light—one-mile runs. I lost to a Porsche but won every other race—the guys didn't think a girl knew how to drive. It was all in fun.
>
> —56-year-old 1965 Ford Mustang owner

Women and the Classic Muscle Car

The muscle car was an integral part of American youth culture for the baby boomer generation for nearly a decade. It is not surprising, therefore, that the majority of classic muscle car owners today are aging boomers and post boomers in their 50s, 60s, and 70s and who experienced muscle car culture—whether actively or vicariously—as teenagers during the years of the original muscle car's production and popularity. Although many of the women who contributed to this project were not active participants in auto culture as teenagers, it was hard for them to ignore the presence of loud, powerful, and colorful muscle cars (and the boys who drove them) in the cities, suburbs, and small towns in which they spent their high school years. Because of this connection to the personal past, these women constitute an older population—75 percent were over the age of 50—than those who own and drive more recent generations of muscle cars.

The women with classic muscle cars were not only older as a group than those with cars from newer generations, but also leaned further right. Of the primarily white, Christian, and heterosexual women in this group who claimed an ideology, 90 percent identified as either moderate or conservative. The age of the classic muscle car owning women and the traditional values they embraced differentiated them from those with newer cars not only demographically, but also influenced how they participated in muscle car culture and how they viewed themselves as women drivers.

Karen LaButte's 1969 Mustang Mach I was "a piece of junk" when she purchased it in 1999, but after extensive restoration it is, in Karen's words, "a great diamond." Karen enjoys taking her car to shows, not to win trophies and awards, but "to show off with it." As she noted, "I'm just a peacock; I'm very proud of my car" (courtesy Karen LaButte).

Marriage and the Muscle Car

The majority of women (75 percent) interviewed for this project were married or in long-term relationships. While marital status is not significant enough to distinguish women of one automotive generation from another, it is an important component to the ways in which women enter and participate in classic muscle car culture. Marriage to a fellow car enthusiast provided classic-muscle-car owning women with relatively easy access into what has historically existed as a masculine fraternity. Consequently, over two thirds of the women with first generation muscle cars entered classic muscle car culture as part of a couple. To the women in this project, entering muscle car culture through marriage had two major benefits. The first was greater acceptance by existing male members; the second, considered paramount, was the opportunity to strengthen relationships with spouses through a shared interest in cars.

Most women in the classic muscle car group had a passion for fast and powerful cars as teenagers. However, as cultural and financial limitations prevented all but the most adventurous from driving cars of their own, many sought entrance into 1960s muscle car culture through relationships with car-owning boyfriends. A 52-year-old 1969 Plymouth Road Runner owner confessed, "We all dated guys with fast cars. I guess I thought they were cooler." These cool guys with hot cars often became their husbands. However, while the men continued to tinker with cars after marriage, women were required to put aside their passion for cars to focus on child rearing and domestic responsibilities. As a 52-year-old 1969 Dodge Super Bee owner remarked, "When you've got kids, you know. He'd go to a car show and I wouldn't go." Now facing life as empty nesters, the women take on ownership of classic muscle cars not only to fulfill a lifelong desire to have fast automobiles of their very own, but also to spend more time with their husbands.

As teenagers, young men often objected to women's intrusion into what was considered the hallowed masculine environs of muscle car culture. However as balding senior citizens, male muscle car owners are likely to welcome, if not encourage, women's participation. As a 1969 Mustang 429 Cobra Jet owner observed of men who attend car shows unaccompanied, "they're always saying 'I wish my wife would come with me.'" Husbands often prompt their wives to participate in muscle car culture not only to rationalize their own automotive "habit," but to also foster a common spousal interest beyond childrearing. A 65-year-old retired interior designer came into ownership of a 1970 Chevelle after her husband—who had four old cars of his own—suggested that she "go pick out what I want." While at a car show, the husband of a 51-year-old 1969 Mustang owner told her to "tell me what you like, and so we went looking around." Men also purchase or restore muscle cars for their wives—as a gift for a birthday or special event—as a way to cultivate enthusiasm for the classic car hobby. Remarked the owner of a 1967 Plymouth Satellite, "My husband gave me the 'Chocolate Kiss' as a graduation gift in 1993 when I completed my RN." A man who enjoyed fixing up automobiles could justify time spent tinkering in the garage by designating one of the restored vehicles as his wife's car. And if his car obsession resulted in multiple vehicles, a husband could "discover" an appropriate vehicle for his wife's use. A 55-year-old registered nurse mentioned that when her daily driver was totaled, "we purchased another Road Runner that needed restoration to 're-incarnate' my lost car. This was to be a project my husband completed for me."

While most husbands were in full support of women's participation, others needed a little prodding. As the 60-year-old owner of a 1971 Dodge Charger Super Bee remarked, "I've always wanted an old car. And my husband said we had no place to put it. So he put up a pole barn and I bought the car." Tired of accompanying her husband to automotive events as a "tag-a-long," a 51-year-old 1969 Mustang Mach I owner explained, "We were at a car show and I said because you have a car, I need a car."

The post boomer participants—women in their 40s and 50s—were more likely to have owned and driven muscle cars before marriage. As a 39-year-old automotive engineer exclaimed, "I won the high school drags with the Dart. I still remember going to the drive-in and fireworks shows in the old cars." In contrast to women of the previous generation, these post boomer women often had the financial resources and cultural permission to have muscle cars of their own. Many grew up in households with "car crazy" brothers or dads who encouraged them to develop an interest in automobiles. As a 51-year-old 1969 Mustang Mach I owner revealed, "I've always been a car person 'cause I was brought up with three brothers. So I just love cars." Most either sought out men with a similar interest in cars, or encouraged their partners to become involved in muscle car culture after tying the knot. A 1970 Dodge Charger R/T owner remarked, "My husband and I, when we met, it was on our first date we started talking cars." And as a 39-year-old engineer mentioned, "the Barracuda was purchased primarily to get my husband into the hobby." However, while age may influence the level of muscle car experience and interest married women possess, women of all generations agreed that a shared interest in cars contributed to strong and stable relationships.

Participating in muscle car culture—at classic car shows, drag races, swap meets, and cruise-ins—offers an opportunity for husbands and wives to enjoy an activity together. Working alongside husbands on a classic muscle car—whether changing the oil, replacing a radiator, or simply shining it up before a classic car event—provides women with an opportunity to get to know their husbands better. As a 56-year-old 1973 Dodge Challenger owner related, "I'm not afraid to get my hands dirty. It's always a project together; we do everything together." Classic muscle car culture provides women with the opportunity to step outside the confines of domesticity to engage in what has been traditionally considered a masculine pastime alongside their husbands. Many of the women spoke of how a shared interest in classic muscle cars brought them closer to the men in their lives. As a 31-year-old 1968 Plymouth Satellite owner remarked, "My husband and I have been together for eleven years. Since we have been together he has been drag racing his car and I have always just helped him out. Now we both race and I feel that our relationship is stronger because of the bond we share." Talking about the time spent with her husband restoring her 1968 Plymouth Barracuda, the 50-year-old owner reflected, "I feel blessed that he was able and wanted to put the time and effort sharing something that he does that I could do, too."

The women intimated that accommodating a husband's interest in cars through joint participation in classic muscle car culture was important to marriage stability. Joining their husbands in the muscle car hobby in lieu of other pursuits was not considered a sacrifice, but rather the means to stronger family ties and connection to others in the classic car community. Kersten argues that a woman's acquiescence to her husband's interests does not mean that she denies her own needs and desires to please others, but rather "the conservative feminist knows that it is impossible to forge an identity for herself outside a social context" (4). Many of the women demonstrated support for their husband's muscle car hobby by switching automotive allegiance after marriage.[6] A 52-year-old 1969 Plymouth Road Runner owner remarked, "I always drove Camaros. But he liked the whole Mopar thing.[7] So whatever he could tinker with he felt more comfortable with, that's what we got." A 65-year-old 1970 Plymouth Superbird owner disclosed, "I came from a Chevy family, but my husband had a [Plymouth] Road Runner when we married in 1972."[8] A 53-year-old automotive engineer, who had always been a "GM" person,[9] now drives a 1971 Dodge Challenger because "it holds fond memories for both of us because [my husband's] sister actually had a Challenger."[10] A 41-year-old mother of two had always driven Mustangs, but switched auto loyalty after marriage.[11] She remarked, "After I met my husband I quickly decided I liked Chargers." To the married woman who owns and drives a classic muscle car, giving in to a husband's automotive preferences is a small price to pay for involvement in what has traditionally been a male-dominated pastime. Many of the women feel privileged to take part alongside the men, and believe a shared interest in classic muscle cars is the glue that keeps their marriage intact.

As Daniel Miller argues, automobiles act in "objectifying personal and social systems of value" ("Driven" 2). While the original muscle car was produced to reinforce masculinity in the male driver, it has taken on new meanings in the hands of women behind the wheel. Women call upon classic muscle cars to reinforce conventional social forms, but not in the way auto manufacturers originally intended. Rather, the women in this project view the classic Camaro, Mustang, and GTO as means to solidify relationships and celebrate traditional marriage.

AMERICA'S AUTOMOTIVE PAST

The American muscle car has a unique place in the automotive archives. A product of the postwar era, it was developed and introduced during a time of unparalleled American power and prosperity. As auto consultant John Wolkonowicz exclaims, "look at American cars from the '50s and '60s and you see that swagger, an unabashed, almost naïve confidence. That's the way the country was back then" (qtd. in "Muscles," Naughton). As the brainchild of ambitious, charismatic, and audacious "young Turks" of the auto industry, the muscle car represented American energy, ingenuity, and technological savvy. Auto writer Jim Campisano recalls, "The muscle car was a mirror of the sixties. America was a leader, not a follower. It was also a bit of a bully around the globe. The muscle cars reflected this" (8). The muscle car's demise also signaled the end of American auto industry dominance. Rising gas prices triggered by the 1973 oil embargo, the passage of the National Traffic and Motor Vehicle Safety Act spurred by Ralph Nader's *Unsafe at Any Speed*, the introduction of Clean Air Act legislation designed to control lead emissions, and the growing influence of Japanese makers of small cars created a crisis in American auto manufacturing from which the industry has only recently recovered. Consequently, aging boomers often embrace the classic American muscle car not only as a means to recapture or reimagine one's youth, but to also recall a time when the muscle car represented American industry, power, and exceptionalism. As a 58-year-old 1970 Ford Mustang owner asserted, "[muscle cars] represent the power of that time, the importance of what cars were back then." The women with classic muscle cars—of which the majority are of the boomer and post boomer generations—view muscle car ownership as way to honor America's illustrious automotive past.

While not all of the classic-muscle-car owning women participated in muscle car culture as teenagers, most recognize the important role the vehicle played in 1960s American culture and the Detroit auto industry. As a 43-year-old business consultant noted, "[The muscle car] is a part of American ingenuity. Most people between 35 and 65 look back at the muscle car era and smile because they have a connection to it." A 73-year-old 1964½ Mustang owner remarked, "Well I think [American muscle cars] did a lot for the automotive companies. They got the attention of everybody and they were the cars to own." Whether they were teenagers during the 1960s, or had parents who owned fast cars back in the day, these women view their participation in classic muscle car culture as an opportunity to own a piece of American automotive history. As a 27-year-old marketing coordinator, who inherited her 1971 Pontiac GT-37 from her father, remarked, "[the muscle car] symbolizes a time period in history as well as the automotive advances in technology of that time." As many of the women have a strong connection to the American auto industry—as daughters and wives of autoworkers or as industry employees themselves—they consider it a privilege to own cars that automakers, in the words of a 49-year-old 1969 Dodge Charger owner, "pushed it to the limits to see how powerful they could go with cars."

The majority of classic muscle car owners in this project hailed from Southeastern Michigan and adjoining auto-centric states. Most had strong ties to the auto industry in some capacity. Although not every woman worked in an auto-related field, most had a connection to someone who worked at the Big Three.[12] Whether residents of Southeastern Michigan (home of the mass-produced automobile) or Auburn, Indiana ("Home of the Classics"),[13] the women took pride in owning and driving what they consider to be an important component of America's automotive heritage. When asked about the significance of the muscle car, a 58-year-old 1970 Pontiac GTO owner replied, "It shows the love of the American people with cars over history."

Whether they owned a Ford Mustang, Dodge Charger, or Pontiac GTO, the women with classic muscle cars were very aware of their particular model's technological and cultural contributions. Of her Vitamin C Orange 1970 Plymouth Superbird Road Runner, a 51-year-old auto industry manager exclaimed, "I mean it's a classic, with Petty winning the Daytona 500 and stuff with it. I mean it's just very iconic. It's kind of the epitome of muscle cars in a way, just because it stands out so much." A 58-year-old 1970 Dodge Hemi Challenger owner remarked, "The Challenger was built to compete with the Camaro and Mustang. It was bigger, badder, and faster than the Camaro and Mustang." Speaking with a fair amount of pride, a 62-year-old 1964½ Mustang owner declared, "Well it's pretty special to me, especially coming next year when the Mustang will be 50 years old. And that's kind of tickles me because not everybody has a 50-year-old classic car to drive around." The women often view themselves as historical actors, contributing to the exhibition, preservation, and celebration of the iconic American muscle car.

Auto journalist Keith Naughton suggests that a renewed interest in the classic muscle car is a reaction to America's current global standing. As he writes, "In light of the world's hostility toward the United States, we're banding together and embracing things that remind us of a time when American power was celebrated" ("Muscles"). Although many of the women in this project were not active in muscle car culture during this decade of American exceptionalism, they feel a responsibility to bring public awareness to the muscle car's celebrated and symbolic past.[14] They accomplish this through the construction of women's classic muscle car culture participation as a patriotic act. As overwhelmingly conservative in ideology, the women in this project often express love of one's country through their cars. Bruce Frohnen writes, "Conservatism being concerned greatly with love of the familiar, it contains within itself a disposition toward love of one's own, and not least of one's country" (106). The connection between patriotism, conservatism, and classic muscle car ownership was especially notable among the women who resided in Southeastern Michigan and the surrounding auto-centric environs.[15] When attending classic car events, women decorate their Mustangs, Camaros, and Barracudas with patriotic symbols; stuffed American eagles are often perched on car hoods and American flags can be spotted flying from car antennas. A 56-year-old auto dealership biller finalized the purchase of her 1973 Dodge Challenger on September 11, 2001. As she explained, "when I display [the Charger] I have a flag that I put on the car and my husband works for a tire store, and one of the companies that he was dealing with at the time had hats made that said 'Remember 9/11' so I keep one of those on the air cleaner when I display the car at car shows." A 45-year-old pharmacist describes her 1967 Mustang GTA Fastback as "a sweet piece of Americana." As a hobby with a solid conservative fan base, it is not surprising that these women link ownership of a classic muscle car to patriotism. As Tilley notes, "personal, social, and cultural identity is embodied in our persons and our things" ("Objectification" 61). Classic muscle car culture provides these women with the opportunity to promote American strength and resourcefulness through the display of fast, loud, and powerful made-in-the-USA muscle cars.

THE WOMAN DRIVER'S PERSONAL PAST

If the attendance at car shows in Southeastern Michigan is any indication, the classic American muscle car is experiencing a resurgence of popularity, particularly among members of the baby boomer generation. Tim Falconer attributes the recent surge in classic car ownership to nostalgia. He writes, "The cars have particular appeal for baby boomers with the money to once again own the models they drove back when they were young, or who now finally have the money to afford what they couldn't afford in those days" (233). Auto writer Douglas Sease notes that for aging baby boomers "who got their first driver's licenses when the Beatles were making music," the acquisition of a classic muscle car provides the opportunity to "recapture a vestige of their youth." In his review of the most over-the-top "macho-mobiles" on the road, auto writer Peter Cheney of *The Globe and Mail* notes that classic muscle cars like the 1970 Plymouth Road Runner "take a man back to the time before emission controls, stunt driving laws, and sexual equality changed the world." The muscle car experience on which aging auto journalists fondly reflect, and which became part of American legend as it inspired books, songs, movies, and television shows, was a masculine one. As such, it is most often told through the perspective of a greying man recalling or reinventing a rebellious and adventurous youth. Most often excluded from muscle car culture as drivers, it is not surprising that women's memory of the experience differs considerably from that of male peers.

Unlike the aging boomer men who make up the vast majority of the classic muscle car hobby, the women in this project who were teens during the muscle car era rarely had cars of their own. Some satisfied their need for speed through borrowing the cars of brothers or boyfriends. A 58-year-old 1970 Dodge Challenger owner exclaimed, "I grew up in Royal Oak, Michigan, just two blocks off of Woodward. We would cruise regularly and it's something, I guess, we took for granted. I learned how to drive a stick shift in my brother's 1966 Pontiac GTO, with a Hurst shifter, on Woodward Avenue." When she first started dating her husband, a 65-year-old 1970 Chevelle owner recalled, "well we were, you know in high school, and in the middle sixties, and not everybody had cars like they do nowadays. But he was one of the few who had a job and a car and I liked his car. So I'd take him to work then take his car and run around all day." Others experienced muscle car culture vicariously, standing on the sidelines or spending time with car-owning friends. Back in high school, stated the 47-year-old owner of a 1972 Plymouth Barracuda, "the people I hung out with … were always into cars. And so I just followed along." A 54-year-old 1967 Pontiac LeMans owner noted, "About all I did was cruise with my friends, although I wasn't old enough to have been a part of the major action in the '50s and '60s. I always thought I was born too late, and should have been a part of the *American Graffiti* generation." As sites for cruising and street racing in the Detroit metropolitan area were plentiful, the women who grew up in Southeastern Michigan often made a point of hanging out where muscle cars—and their young male owners—congregated.

However, most young women did not have the means, opportunity, or permission to spend time around cool boys with hot cars. Thus they had to make do with dreams, thinking about what cars they might own, and imagining what kind of experiences such a vehicle would offer them. As a young girl, a 63-year-old 1966 Mustang owner would study new car advertisements and picture herself in the featured automobiles. As she reflected, "Oh my gosh! I remember looking at the pages of new cars every year in the *Saturday Evening Post* and *Life* magazines. I could always spot cars and the make and model when I was on the highway when we were on a trip." The 62-year-old owner of a 1964½ Mustang coupe collected photos of her favorite muscle cars from magazines. As she noted, "I kind of liked to look at them in magazines. In fact I made a little scrapbook when I was in high school, a scrapbook of little sports cars and different muscle cars; I cut them out of magazines and made it look like a little scrapbook." As a young girl, a 73-year-old 1973 Mustang owner would stop by her local dealership on the way home from school and look longingly at the cars through the windows. As she reminisced, "Once in a while I'd go in and the salesmen, sometimes they'd chase me out, sometimes they just let me meander around or sit in the cars." As a 13-year-old, a 58-year-old retired occupational therapist developed her love of Mustangs behind the wheel of the hardtop Mustang belonging to her best friend's mom. As she recalled, "I could not reach the pedals because my legs were too short so my girlfriend used her legs and I steered the car." As teenagers unable to participate due to financial and societal restrictions, the women often called upon their imaginations to create an alternative and welcoming muscle car culture.

While the classic-muscle-car-owning boomer women came of age in an era when young girls were discouraged from knowing too much about cars, women of subsequent generations had more opportunities for an automotive education. Many developed a love of fast and powerful cars as teenage girls through time spent with the men in their lives.

The influence of car-loving fathers, brothers, and other family members often inspired a lifelong appreciation for American muscle. As the 51-year-old owner of a 1966 Chevrolet Impala remarked, "I've always had an interest in cars. I helped my dad work on whatever he was working on. I loved being in the shop." A 32-year-old nurse practitioner now drives the 1968½ Shelby Mustang she restored with her father. As she noted, "Whether it was working on the Shelby with my Dad or on one of the 'daily-drivers,' I've always wanted to help." Now living in Michigan, a 22-year-old college student grew up in a Colorado town in which car culture was not very prevalent. She gained an appreciation for muscle cars through family automotive projects. As the 1966 Mustang owner noted, "I have grown up with cars. My entire family (mother, sister, dad, and me) typically work all winter on a project and then in the summer we go to rod runs, drag races, and other car related events." A 39-year-old engineer developed an interest in muscle cars by helping her father in the garage and accompanying him to local drag races. As the 1967 Dodge Dart owner recalled, "My Dad has owned many muscle cars over the years. I love driving them all. One week for school I drove a different car each day of the week. I had to borrow my uncle's to do it, but I'll never forget that week." A 43-year-old veterinarian purchased a 1966 Dodge Charger to replicate and commemorate the car in which she spent her childhood. As she reminisced, "My car means a lot to me. I have a lot of memories of riding in his car as a daily car; I came home from the hospital after I was born in a '66 Charger." While the post boomer women in this project were too young to experience the classic muscle car culture of the 1960s and 1970s first hand, their experiences as the daughters, nieces, and sisters of muscle car enthusiasts created a desire to own the classic American muscle cars of their fathers, uncles, and brothers.

More so than the women with newer vehicles, women who own classic muscle cars have a deep and abiding connection to a personal automotive past. For post boomer women, that connection is often a car-loving father, brother, or uncle who introduced them to the exhilaration and excitement found behind the wheel of a classic muscle car. For women of the baby boomer generation, it is the memory of cruising in someone else's car, or the recalling of a young girl's car dreams. As Tilley writes, "the meanings and significance of things for people are part and parcel of their lives" ("Objectification" 61). Whether they participated in muscle car culture as drivers, tagalongs, or observers, or simply imagined what driving a powerful machine might be like, these women recall the joys and thrills muscle car culture promised, and have taken the opportunity as adults to own the cars they have desired for a lifetime.

MAKING THE INVISIBLE VISIBLE

Writing about ageism, Baba Cooper observes, "somewhere in the fifties, anxieties about the increase in rejection and invisibility become crucial" (74). Journalist Deborah Orr reflects upon older women's eventual state of invisibility. As she exclaims, "as our skin grows slack and our hair grows grey, we fade into the background, seen but not heard." Feminists have often considered aging in American society as a "form of cultural non-recognition" (Ainsworth 596). In American society, a woman's worth is often based on physical attractiveness. Thus an aging female body is considered deficient and of lesser status. As Margaret Cruikshank remarks, "the judgment that old women's bodies are unattractive is so pervasive to be almost inescapable" (148). The disdain for the older woman is not exhibited through mockery but rather, complete disregard. Women of a certain age are ignored as if they are not present; they become, in fact, invisible.

The majority of women who own classic muscle cars fall into the over–50 crowd. Many have spent a great portion of their lives on the sidelines, as wives, mothers, and caretakers. As overwhelmingly conservative, these women are, for the most part, accepting of traditional gender roles and the silencing of self that often accompanies them. As Kersten notes, the conservative feminist "does not conceive of obligations to others as burdens, but as duties, the performance of which renders one a moral being" (8). Consequently, for the married women in particular, the decline into invisibility brought upon by aging was considered a natural, if not acceptable, process. For the unmarried women, the encroachment of invisibility was less welcome. Without familial obligations to safely shield them, they were more likely than their married counterparts to experience the cultural critique of aging on a regular basis. As single women often seeking companionship, the invisibility brought on by getting older was considered detrimental to personal goals.

Yet whether married or single, a classic muscle car provided the means to the attention often missing in older women's lives. Getting behind the wheel of a roaring Panther Pink Dodge Challenger or rumbling Grabber Blue Ford Mustang guaranteed visibility to 50-something women, even if only for a short period of time. As a 61-year-old 1970 Chevrolet Monte Carlo owner exclaimed, "If you want attention, all you've got to do is drive the cars." Speaking of her 1973 Mustang with a loud 351 Cleveland Cobra engine, a 73-year-old widow remarked, "White Thunder commands attention. And maybe that's what we like." Noted the 47-year-old owner of a 1969 Mustang, "you can't drive this car and expect people to ignore you." Accustomed to going through daily life without being noticed, these women call upon the classic muscle car to draw attention to themselves in an acceptable, and often rejuvenating, way. As participants in muscle car culture, they are expected to drive cars that are noisy, colorful, and head-turning. As a 62-year-old retired Ford employee attested, when she drives her candy apple red 1971 Gran Torino GT down the highway, "everybody beeps at you and tries to get your attention to give you a thumbs-up. And it's just amazing."

The attention directed toward women driving classic muscle cars is often accompanied by an element of surprise. The muscle car's longstanding association with masculinity leads to the assumption that the driver of a classic Barracuda or Camaro will be male. Thus when a Vitamin C Orange Superbird burns rubber down the highway, the last thing most folks expect to see is a grey-haired woman behind the wheel. As a 73-year-old 1973 Mustang owner explained, "I have a feeling that when some people pass me it's like they arch their eyebrows and say 'a woman's driving that car.'" The 56-year-old owner of a black 1973 Dodge Challenger remarked, "I think a lot of times when a guy pulls up beside me they're shocked to see that it's a woman driving and not a man." As the 57-year-old, five-foot-one-inch owner of a 1966 Chevrolet Impala related, when others watch her drive by, "they're always surprised to see little old me at the helm." Although in everyday life the women are content to perform traditional gender roles graciously and quietly, ownership of a classic muscle car provides them with the opportunity to disrupt such expectations in an acceptable and enjoyable manner. As a 56-year-old 1971 Pontiac Firebird owner attested, "It's always a kick because you always don't expect girls to drive cars like this. Guys turn around and look and go wait a minute, there's a girl driving that car."

Some of the women indicated they were a bit uncomfortable with the attention directed toward them when driving a loud and colorful classic Camaro or 'Cuda. A lifetime of reticence due to family responsibilities and domesticity often made them unfamiliar with such unsolicited interest. As Cruikshank writes, "family responsibilities, work pressures, constraints imposed by sexism, and the expectation that they juggle many things at once without complaint all hamper women's self-development" (19). A 55-year-old 1973 Mercury Cougar XR7 owner confessed, "to be honest, I really don't care to be on stage. So I'm not necessarily out there driving to make people look at me." As a 55-year-old 1973 Plymouth Road Runner owner remarked, "I've always been more of a typical female and like typical female hobbies like sewing, quilting, scrapbooking [and] knitting. I don't like to draw attention to myself." Others are concerned with the impression driving a muscle car might give to others. A 63-year-old retired support manager, who purchased her recently restored Plum Crazy 1970 Dodge Challenger when she was 19 years old, asserted, "These days if I drive, I find out that some, if they see a woman driving a car like this, or another kind, sometimes they get the wrong idea. Like you're a snob or something." "I don't think I'm better than anyone else," remarked the 67-year-old owner of a 1966 Mustang. However as she noted, "But it is really fun when the kids go, 'wow, neat car!'" Cruikshank suggests that in order to combat the perceived inevitability of invisibility, it is often necessary for women to reinvent themselves. This is especially important, she argues, in women "who may not have been able earlier to express their full individuality" (19). The women who contributed to this project often discover new versions of their old selves behind the wheel of a classic muscle car.

While often uncomfortable as the center of attention, many of the women noted how the classic muscle car has inspired conversations and connections they may not have had otherwise. Of her red 1965 Mustang convertible, a 47-year-old analyst remarked, "it gives people a better opportunity to have a conversation with me." As women who have often been homebound for much of their lives, ownership of a Plum Crazy 1971 Challenger can provoke questions and comments from admiring spectators. As a 39-year-old engineer reflected, "Owning my muscle car and the experiences has certainly offered an interesting conversation point in interviews and icebreaker moments." Others shared some of the more interesting exchanges they have experienced when cruising in a muscle car. As a 1970 Dodge Hemi Challenger R/T owner explained, "It's great fun when [spectators] yell compliments, hold up scorecards that say 10, and ask questions about the car." The classic muscle car provides older women with the opportunity to emerge from the background of domesticity to make new acquaintances and add memorable experiences to their lives. As a 53-year-old Panther Pink 1971 Dodge Challenger convertible owner explained, "the car becomes a little part of your personality."

If invisibility is a reflection of old age, visibility, particularly when achieved behind the wheel of a muscle car, can make one feel young. Many of the women noted how driving a Charger or Camaro gave the impression they were younger to their peers. As the owner of a 1973 white Mustang convertible proclaimed, "And I'm so enthusiastic about my car, you know it's a lot of who I am. The little old ladies that are 70, 71, you know I'm going to be 74 in three months, people say because you've got that car you don't seem that age."

Of her chili pepper red-with-black-stripes 1970 Chevelle, a 65-year-old retired interior designer commented, "it makes me feel young again. And I like to light up the tires and rev it up." Despite the uneasiness some of the women experienced due to the unfamiliar attention they received, they all acknowledged that ownership of a classic muscle car assured that they were no longer invisible aging women on the sidelines. Tilley writes, through using, consuming, interacting, and living with things "people make themselves in the process" ("Objectification" 61). When behind the wheel of a Firebird, Gran Torino, or Cougar, the participants in this project assumed personas as confident, competent, powerful, and very visible woman drivers.

FRIENDS AND CARS

During the 1960s and 1970s, the muscle car was often a young man's daily driver. However, while it served as a noisy and powerful source of everyday transportation, one of the muscle car's most important functions was the means to an active and lively social life. Before the days of cell phones, laptops, and social media, the muscle car brought teenagers together. Whether engaging in street racing, cruising for hours on end, or hanging out with friends at the local drive-in restaurant, the muscle car, writes Grace Palladino, "opened up a world of aimless amusement that was completely beyond a parent's reach" (166). As Margaret Walsh concurs, "having wheels meant escape from prying eyes, gaining 'street cred[ibility]' among high school or college peers, and access to the local automobile culture" ("Life"). Although teenage girls were often excluded from muscle car culture as drivers, many enjoyed being part of the muscle car scene. They might not drive, writes Walsh, but "they did wish to be seen" ("Life"). While young women rarely had cars of their own, they borrowed the cars of parents or friends because, notes Genat, "They just wanted to be there" (44).

The baby boomer women who own classic muscle cars today often remember this era with great affection. As a 63-year-old retired store manager reflected, getting behind the wheel of her 1970 Dodge Challenger "brings back so many fun memories. When you didn't have a care in the world, but you went to work and then Friday nights, Saturday, and Sunday you went cruising. And met up with, and met a lot of people, you met a lot of young new people friends who all had different kinds of muscle cars. And they were fun." Of the 1960s muscle car scene, a 54-year-old 1967 Pontiac LeMans owner added, "I always thought they were the coolest cars and I liked to be a part of the cruising culture." For many of the women in this project, participating in classic muscle car culture today is a way to recreate and relive the easy sociability of the past. For others, it is a way to experience participation in a community centered on cars for the very first time. However, whether new or old to muscle car culture, the majority of women interviewed for this project enjoy the social aspect of participation; i.e., the opportunity to make new friends outside of their family circle, to take on roles within the classic muscle car community, and to work with like-minded folks for a favorite cause or charity.

For married women, muscle car culture provides the opportunity to participate in an activity with husbands and make new friends as a couple. Many of the women had been homebound for much of their lives, focusing time and energy on family, and rarely making an effort to pursue interests or friendships on their own. Attending car shows and other auto-related activities allowed them to establish a new, and often unfamiliar, social circle. As a 47-year-old 1965 Mustang owner remarked, "I think everybody that puts their car in a car show would have to admit that they like the social aspect of it, meeting new people." Car shows, a 58-year-old 1970 Dodge Challenger R/T owner added, "are a great place to meet people with the same interest and just in general. You get to look at other cars. It's just a fun, social time." As most folks exhibit their cars at shows within a reasonable driving distance, it is not uncommon to run into the same vehicles and their owners time and time again. Noted a 50-year-old 1969 Mustang Cobra Jet owner, "We go to different car shows, especially the local ones, and we meet up with people that we've, we always see. And we sit with them." Many of the friendships made at car shows carry over into other aspects of women's lives. As a 50-year-old 1969 Barracuda owner explained, "You know we go have lunch together, you know we go look at cars, and then maybe we'll go out to an event after, like eating a meal, so, it's a social thing." A 58-year-old 1972 Mustang owner added, "the women have gone on yearly outings without our significant others; the men have gone on outings, also, without the women over the years. We have become more than acquaintances; we are friends." For those who travel to out-of-state events, car shows often serve as a reunion of sorts. Commenting on her yearly trip to an automotive event in Alabama, a 65-year-old 1970 Plymouth Superbird owner proclaimed, "It's like a family. We call it our family reunion; we're related by automobile. And the cars have become second fiddle or whatever, they've become second place to what everyone's doing and how their lives are going." In the 1960s, the muscle car provided teenage boys with the means and opportunity to escape the restrictions of home and family to hang out with peers and impress young women. In the twenty-first century, the classic muscle car allows aging boomer women to drive away from domesticity and gather with like-minded friends to talk about cars, family, and the car community.

For the divorced and widowed, the social aspect of muscle car culture takes on added meaning. After the death of a husband, women often find solace and comfort among those who share an interest in cars. Regarding her involvement in the classic muscle car hobby, a 58-year-old 1970 Pontiac GTO owner reflected, "My car provides an opportunity to see and go places I wouldn't necessarily go. It gives me a chance to make new friends and explore other cars with friends. The club has been involved in each other's lives and when my husband died the club drove the cars to the graveside in a line." Of her membership in a local car club, a 61-year-old widow remarked, "I've got a life line, a lifelong membership with these people. I have a lot of friends in there and I've made a lot of friends over the years." Divorced or widowed women often find companionship in muscle car culture, as single men with an interest in cars are often looking for a female companion with a similar passion. Some of the women found new husbands, whereas others remain hopeful that the right car-loving guy will come along. As a divorced 73-year-old 1973 white Ford Mustang owner declared, "I would really like to have a car guy in my life. Man, it would just, you know to have a guy, park his car, we got White Thunder, park behind our cars and just talk to people as they go by. And that would just be really cool." At an age when widowhood and divorce are not uncommon, newly single women often discover support, empathy, and companionship within the classic muscle car community.

Many of the women who contributed to this project cited the opportunity to meet new people from different backgrounds as a benefit of classic muscle car participation. However diversity—particularly in race, social class, sexual orientation, age, and religious practice—is uncommon within the majority of classic car organizations. Classic muscle car culture in Southeastern Michigan is composed of individuals who are almost exclusively white,[16] Christian,[17] middle class,[18] and heterosexual, who are of the baby boomer or post boomer generation, and who identify as moderate to conservative. While there are certainly significant populations of African American, Latino, Asian American, and gay and lesbian car enthusiasts, they are more likely to participate within automotive subcultures that cater to a specific identity group.[19] In this group of classic muscle car participants, 90 percent were white, 96 percent were heterosexual, and over 90 percent identified as either moderate or conservative. Thus, while female classic muscle car owners express an interest in meeting new people "from whole different spheres," they do so within a culture composed of individuals very much like themselves.

It is not surprising, therefore, that those outside the mainstream—whether through age, race, or sexual orientation—are less likely to view participation in classic muscle car culture as a positive social experience. Young women often feel ostracized or dismissed by older members; women of color fear rejection by the muscle car community; those who identify as lesbian are more likely to find fellowship in LGBTQ car organizations. And while the majority of white, Christian, straight, boomer women are accepted in classic muscle car culture, there are those refrain from joining car organizations due to the perception of clubs as cliquish or political. As a 56-year-old 1973 Dodge Challenger explained, "I think car shows are too political; they get to be political, and I don't want no part of that." Preferring to hang out with a group of car friends, a 62-year-old retired nurse stated, "Car clubs are too political and clicky [*sic*]." Others noted the underlying misogyny of some car clubs and its effect on female members. When competing with her 1973 Ford Mustang at car events, a 73-year-old retired storeowner exclaimed, "The good ole boys don't vote for me." Yet while membership in a classic car organization was not to everyone's liking, the majority of women enjoyed the fellowship of other car enthusiasts and the possibility of expanding their social circle through ownership of a classic muscle car.

Women who own muscle cars—whether classic, pony, or retro—have much in common. However, as aging women with traditional values, classic muscle car owners separate themselves from women with newer cars in meaningful ways. The importance of participation with a husband or partner, the tie to the personal and automotive past, the significance of visibility, and the culture's role as a crucial social outlet not only influence how they participate in muscle car culture but perhaps more importantly, how they view themselves as women drivers.

The Pony Car: 1974–2004

The American Automobile Loses Its Muscle

In 1974, the muscle car lost its power and its luster. The times were a changing, and disregard for safety, gas mileage, emissions, and speed limits were no longer acceptable auto industry practices. While American muscle cars roared down main drags burning gas during the 1960s and early 1970s, Japanese automakers quietly introduced small, fuel efficient, and practical cars for American consumption. The U.S. auto industry, rather than embrace the small car market, attempted to refit the fading muscle car into other automotive categories. Some models converged into personal luxury performance cars. Others, like the Dodge Charger, made a short-lived appearance as a subcompact. Many brands offered sport appearance packages; Plymouth's "vinyl and decal option" promised the appearance of speed without the power to back it up. As Mike Mueller writes, "fast looks sell almost as easily as real speed, even more so when real speed is no longer available" (23). Curbed by the new emission controls, rising gasoline prices, and a newly instituted 55 mph speed limit, American automakers switched their focus from performance and speed to appearance and accessories.

While the intermediate sized muscle cars faced extinction, pony cars—that included the Ford Mustang, Chevrolet Camaro, and Pontiac Firebird and Trans Am—returned to their origins as fun, stylish, and sporty cars with more style than power. The 1976 Camaro, for example, was promoted in print and in dealerships as Chevrolet's "sensibly sporty small car" (Flory 252). Automotive advertisers replaced descriptors such as fast, tough, hissin', made-to-move, and shot-from-a-cannon with terms such as colorful, good-looking, pleasurable, and high-spirited. Some pony cars gained new popularity as popular culture icons, often taking on starring roles in television and film. The 1977 Trans Am of *Smokey and the Bandit* fame—with its infamous "flaming chicken hood" (Perez), the 1978 Trans Am "rocket car" driven by Burt Reynolds in *Hooper*, and "KITT," the 1982 Firebird that served as David Hasselhoff's ride on the TV show *Knight Rider*, became popular car choices among the post-boomer set. Mueller notes, "as the '70s progressed, true performance machines were unceremoniously replaced by 'tape-stripe' imposters." Referring to the cars featured in a popular television show of the time, Mueller adds, "those 'Starsky and Hutch' Torinos of 1976 weren't muscle cars. Not even close" (23).

The pony cars of the early 1980s were forgettable at best. As auto journalist Jeff Perez remarks, "following in the footsteps of some of the best cars imaginable, the '80s sort of floundered in the muscle car department" (boldride.com). Two fuel crises had made gas economy the primary objective of auto manufacturers. As computerized engine management was in its infancy, high horsepower and torque numbers were nearly impossible to achieve within the new restrictive automotive climate. However, as the 1990s approached, the introduction of electronic fuel injection, turbochargers, and overdrive transmissions resulted in more powerful cars, but not without a price. Investments in technology invariably increased the sticker price; writing in 1997, Mueller notes, "the average '90s young blood can't even come close to affording the automotive muscle his more carefree counterpart could've back then" (190). Whereas the original muscle car—produced in a less regulated era—was built to be an affordable choice for the young male market, ownership of a newer muscle car often required a solid middle-class income.

While Mustangs, Firebirds, and Camaros of the late 1990s harnessed some of the power and performance of the original muscle cars, there was, as Mueller laments, something missing. He writes, "Detroit revived the body but lost the soul" (190). The cars from this era appealed to a more affluent customer. They were not the toys of a younger generation, but represented major investments on the part of up-and-coming young men.

With Camaro, you can be practical. Or go bananas.

If you can restrain yourself when it comes time to order the extras, you can move into a handsome 1974 Camaro Sport Coupe for less money than you might imagine.

That's one approach. Approach "A" we'll call it.

There's also Approach "Z". The renowned Camaro Z28 package. All the basic good things plus a 350 V8 with 4-barrel, a dual exhaust system, special sport suspension, Positraction rear axle, sport mirrors, F60-15 white-lettered tires and more. If you *really* want to go bananas you can add spoilers and those bold new Z28 hood and deck stripes.

(There's a third approach, comfortably in between: Camaro Type LT with its sumptuous interior and other elegant touches.)

Camaro. The way it looks is the way it goes.

Chevrolet

Camaro advertisement: "With Camaro, you can be practical. Or go bananas." Although 1974 was the beginning of the end of the muscle car era, auto advertisers remained committed to marketing practicality to women, and the suggestion of power—via sporty appearance packages—to the male driver (*Road & Track*, April 1974).

The original muscle cars were stripped down macho machines that frequently served as an extension of a male teenager's personality. As Mueller writes, they conveyed a "far out, groovy feeling of self-gratification and individual freedom" further enhanced by the "female companionship commonly included as optional equipment" (191). Of the third and fourth generation machines, Peter Henshaw remarks, "these are not muscle cars in the spirit of the sixties. They are too high-tech, too expensive, and too competent" (24). Although the stylish and streamlined pony cars of the 1990s ran fast and handled the curves much like their predecessors, as Mueller explains, "the attitude, the spirit in the machine" that made the muscle car a true American icon was absent (191).

The pony cars of the late 1970s, 1980s, and 1990s lacked the innovation, excitement, and rebelliousness—and some would say masculinity—of the original muscle cars. And while, during this time, advertisers continued to market Mustangs, Camaros, Firebirds, and Trans Ams primarily to men, women began to appear—albeit occasionally—in advertising and promotional material for these vehicles, particularly when the emphasis was on style, design, and sensibility rather than performance. The pony car—especially of the non-muscle variety—had always been considered an appropriate vehicle for the female driver. When introduced in 1964, the Mustang was promoted as a fun, stylish, sporty and affordable vehicle intended to capture "the free spirit and youthful imagination of a changing America" (Clor 7). Mustang advertising had traditionally divided the car's appeal by gender, promoting its high performance, stick shift models to men, while attempting to sell the female consumer on its less powerful, more economical six-cylinder version, promoted in some circles as the "secretary's car." Despite the fact that this sales strategy was undertaken primarily as a means to unload a surplus of six-cylinder models with automatic transmissions, the notion that women were important Mustang consumers was not lost on female pony car admirers. While driving a full-blooded 1960s muscle car could be considered a rebellious and unfeminine act, choosing a fun-to-drive, sporty, and attractive pony car allowed women to unassumingly participate in muscle car culture without disaffecting men. It provided them with an alternative to the ubiquitous minivan that, after its introduction in 1984, became synonymous with the woman behind the wheel. It is not surprising that the overwhelming choice of the women in this project—no matter what generation—was the pony car. Its popularity also suggests that one of the reasons the pony car survived when the original muscle car did not is that it had a loyal consumer base in the woman driver.

> See, mine is different than what most people think is a muscle car. I think, what I perceive people thinking is like big engine, fast cars, something like that. That's what I would say a muscle car is. But to me it doesn't matter. I just like the look of that car.
>
> —43-year-old 1998 Pontiac Trans Am owner

Women and the Pony Car

The lack of power and performance in the pony cars of this era weakened the association between the muscle car and masculinity, at least temporarily. Thus the women in this group were less concerned than classic muscle car owners with challenging gender prescriptions regarding car choice and car use, and more involved with remaking the pony car—physically as well as metaphorically—into something personal and powerful.

Six
and the single girl.

What makes a quiet, sensible girl like Joan fall in love with a Mustang? Not simply Mustang's steely good looks or smooth, racy lines. Not even the hard-to-resist features like adjustable bucket seats, wall-to-wall carpeting, sports steering wheel, and floor-mounted shift.

What really broke down Joan's reserve was the solid practicality of Mustang's deep-breathing Six. She knew she could trust this husky, suave brute of an engine to squire her around town, drive her to the mountains for a weekend, even drop her off for dinner with the girls (who will never guess how little Mustang costs her to own and run). Extraordinarily considerate of a girl's feelings . . . and her pocketbook.

Stop in and see your Ford dealer. Take a test drive and see if you should give in to Mustang because of sheer Six appeal. Smart girls do.

Ford Mustang advertisement: "Six and the Single Girl." The surprising popularity of the V8, manual transmission Mustang among those looking for a performance-driven pony car resulted in a surplus of six-cylinder automatic models. Ford subsequently developed a marketing campaign promoting the economy and sensibility of the lower powered Mustang to young single women. Through playing off the provocative title of Helen Gurley Brown's blockbuster advice book, Ford encouraged "quiet and sensible girls" to purchase the modest six-cylinder Mustang for its "solid practicality" (*Life*, March 11, 1966, courtesy Fordimages.com).

Michele Dozeman leans against her modified 1974 Plymouth Barracuda. A self-proclaimed gear-head, Michelle performed many of the upgrades on her beast of a Barracuda herself. A woman with a penchant for muscle, Michelle also has a newly restored Hemi Orange Metallic 1971 Dodge Charger Super Bee parked in her garage (and noted on her sweatshirt) (courtesy Michele Dozeman).

The women who owned these cars skewed a little younger than the owners of classic muscle cars, with 80 percent of participants over the age of 40. They did not lean as far right as classic muscle car owners—75 percent identified as moderate or conservative—and as a group were more likely than those with classic or retro cars to be single (33 percent). As many of the women were too young to have experienced 1960s classic muscle car culture first hand, they were not as tied to the automotive past as owners of older vehicles. Because these women were less traditional overall than the owners of both classic and retro muscle cars, they differed from those groups in their reasons for choosing a pony car as well as how they chose to participate in muscle car culture.

Making It Personal

In classic muscle car culture, an automobile's value is often determined by the degree to which it is "original." As automotive writer Avrid Svendsen notes, the intrinsic value of a classic automobile is based on "provenance, a car's origin story: How many of this particular model were built, how it was equipped when it came off the assembly line, and what (if anything) has been done to it since then." The claim of authenticity—verified by the presence of original equipment in good condition, factory approved replacement parts or re-fabrications, and proper documentation—is crucial to a classic automobile's success as a show car or on the auction block. Car shows and swap meets are replete with parts and accessories of every possible make and model for sale or barter, and are perused . by individuals determined to restore their classics to original off-the-showroom-floor condition. Exhibitors at car shows will often present scrapbooks that contain photos of the restoration process as well as paperwork that details each change made to the vehicle by every individual who owned the car. Owners hunt down documentation of VINs, RPO codes, date codes, parts numbers, casting numbers, and the transmission and rear end tags in order to verify authenticity.[20] Nothing is more sacrilegious to car buffs than the discovery of a Chevy engine in a Ford product; such a desecration lowers not only the value of the car but the reputation of the individual who owns it as well.

The classic muscle car has a unique place in the automotive archives. Authenticity is pursued among classic car collectors as a means to honor the muscle car's celebrated past and to establish oneself as an important preserver of automotive history. The pony car of the post-muscle era does not claim nor does it possess such an illustrious past. Consequently, the majority of women in this project who own these vehicles were not interested in maintaining them in a manner to preserve authenticity. And because there was little under the respective hoods of late 1970s and early 1980s pony cars that could be considered exceptional, most women had few qualms about changing parts, replacing original equipment, or modifying engines to their own specifications. Rather than focus on authenticity, these women took the opportunity to remodel and recreate Mustangs, Camaros, and Firebirds in a way that reflected their own preferences and personalities.

A 43-year-old business consultant purchased a 1974 Plymouth Barracuda that had modifications completed by the previous owner. As she remarked, since the vehicle was no longer stock, "I decided to make the car into how I wanted it to be." While some of the changes were mechanical, the most eye-catching were alterations made to the car's exterior. She explained, "I had purple 383 billboards painted on the sides, installed a rear gull wing, added rocker gills and fender gills, replaced the rally hood with a shaker hood (with scoop painted purple to match the billboards). I also added air shocks for that old-school tough look." The result was a car that, while harking to its automotive past, was distinguished by its owner's distinctive stamp. As the Kent City, Michigan, resident proclaimed, "This car is my dream muscle car. It has character and I love driving it." A 23-year-old pharmacy technician purchased a stock 2002 Mustang as a project car to work on with her father. As she remarked, 'I then installed rims, a lowered suspension kit, and exhaust system to personalize it." These women viewed the pony car not as a reminder of a less than stellar era of automotive manufacturing, but rather, as a framework on which they were able construct a better version of the car and themselves. As the women's narratives suggest, these reconstructed automobiles are not just material objects. Rather, as Tilley et al. write, "persons make and use things and [...] things make persons" ("Introduction" 4).

Other women in the project acquired mediocre second and third generation pony cars and transformed them into racing machines. A 37-year-old Dearborn Heights, Michigan, resident purchased a 1974 Chevy Nova with the intention of rebuilding it with her father to race at Norwalk. After her dad passed away unexpectedly, the car sat for a long time until friends came to her aid and helped her complete the project. While she wasn't a Nova fan originally, she enjoyed the opportunity to reconstruct the car to her own specifications. As she mentioned, "You can have two of the exact same cars and they'll be totally different. 'Cause there's so much you can do to them. And your own personality kind of comes out." A 38-year-old physician receptionist purchased her 1982 Mustang as a daily driver when she was 17. She spent the next twenty years modifying, rebuilding, and upgrading the vehicle with the intention of taking it to the local dragway. While racing the car was the ultimate goal, she also wanted the car to reflect her personality and her hard work. As she remarked, "I didn't want to have a car like everybody else had. So I wanted my car to always be unique and different." A 49-year-old human resources manager acquired a stock 1988 Mustang GT because, as she noted, "Fox bodies are very easy to convert to racing and to do different things with them."[21] Although it originally pained her to modify a fully stock original vehicle, as she exclaimed, "I'm very excited to get it back out on the road."

While some women upgraded or boosted the vehicle's mechanics to increase power and performance, others made changes to the car's exterior. These alterations were often undertaken as a way to both express and introduce oneself after a life crisis or change. After a painful divorce, a 31-year-old color analyst purchased a 1991 Firebird. She had the surface repainted—pink on the driver's side and blue on the passenger side—and made changes to the exterior that included Lamborghini-style vertical doors "that go straight up into the air." As she noted, "I was just obsessed. And to get all these different pieces, from all the different generations, or all the different years that I liked and do a kind of compilation so I could customize the car, to get what I wanted in a car." The process of recreating a vehicle out of disparate components represented how she put life back together after her divorce and in the process, evolved from victim to empowered person. As she declared, the transformation of the Firebird "was the start of a new chapter in my life." A 48-year-old massage therapist was discouraged from getting a Mustang by a controlling husband. Once her divorce became final, she not only purchased the 2003 red Mustang convertible she had always wanted, but decorated the front hood with flames and an emblem composed of a superman logo, flames, and the words "super bitch" superimposed on it. As she revealed, "for some reason that 'super bitch' emblem became me. Because all of a sudden people would get out of my way." The super bitch emblem—adhered to the hood of her shiny red Mustang for all to see—became a personal declaration of independence. As the Sioux City, Iowa, resident asserted, it represented "freedom from a bad marriage. And freedom to go wherever I want to."

In his work on car modification culture, Dag Balkmar notes that the culture has recently embraced the American muscle car "as a popular car to re-shape, tune, and personalize in style" (150). While Balkmar focuses his research on male car enthusiasts, many female pony car owners have embraced the notion that an automobile may serve as a starting point for a personal identity project. Kathleen Franz writes, "cars have provided fertile ground for personal and community expression, and consumers often used the automobile to promote their own agendas, reshaping the machine to fit their needs and desires" ("Automobiles" 53). Whether they choose to increase power under the hood, or use the exterior of the car as a canvas for personal expression, the women have rejected the notion of "authenticity" to create a vehicle that is both personal and powerful.

SHARING THE EXPERIENCE

As vehicles that have hit the half-century mark, classic muscle cars rarely serve as daily drivers. Rather, they are most often garaged six months of the year, dusted off in the spring, and taken out on summer weekends to cruise or exhibit at sponsored automotive events. Authentic muscle cars—i.e., vehicles that have provenance or that have been restored to original quality—often spend the car show season as "trailer queens"; i.e., they are hauled to events rather than driven. The monetary value of classic muscle cars, the difficulty in obtaining replacement parts, the reluctance to add mileage to the odometer, and the unreliability of 50-year-old Chargers, Road Runners, and GTOs means they are driven sparingly, if at all. Consequently, while women enjoy the experience of owning classic muscle cars, they are often hesitant to spend too much time behind the wheel.

Many of the women with post–muscle era pony cars—particularly those who have invested time and money in automotive restoration—are equally cautious about their vehicles. However, most of the women in this group purchased pony cars with the intention of enjoying them, and take advantage of every opportunity to do so. One of the ways in which this is accomplished is through sharing the pony car experience with friends. Many women choose pony cars that are convertibles, and take pleasure in putting the top down on a warm summer night with a good friend or family member in the passenger seat.

A 71-year-old retired teacher inherited her husband's prized 1994 Z/28 Camaro after he passed away from a sudden illness. Although she had never driven the car while her husband was alive, she found getting behind the wheel of the Camaro provided the opportunity to adjust to life without him and to spend time with friends. As she remarked, "I think I was so overwhelmed with all things I had to do, now I think I'm ready to have some fun with it." She not only takes the Camaro to car shows with family, but offers her friends rides as a way to celebrate a birthday or special occasion. As she noted after one of these outings, "I just feel so good, especially on these beautiful nights, to be out with this car. And I know my friend that I drove on Saturday; she had both arms up, and then she saw a police car and put both arms down thinking oh no are they going to stop us because she did that. But she was really into it. She said […] 'you took ten years off my life.' So it's kind of fun to make someone else feel good, too. I mean that joy is contagious." A 46-year-old special education teacher believed the thrill of driving a 1996 Mustang convertible should be shared. She exclaimed, "I gave a lot of people rides. And I let a lot of people drive it so they could have the experience of driving a Mustang. It was fun." A 50-year-old postal worker is uncomfortable letting others drive her 1997 Mercury Cougar, but welcomes their company as passengers. She remarked, "If I'm going to go shopping with a girlfriend, we might take that for the day." A 17-year-old high school student who comes from a muscle car family enjoys participating in car events such as the Woodward Dream cruise, and taking her friends along for the ride. As she explained, "For Woodward and that, I always take my friends with me. And they have a fun time and so do I."

Many of the women loaned out their vehicles to family members for special occasions such as weddings and proms. A 71-year-old retired teacher gave the keys of the 1997 Camaro to her son for his wedding at the Henry Ford Greenfield Village. As she recalled, "My son took the car there, and then after the wedding they both drove in it, they drove downtown, that was just theirs to use for the evening, until the next day. So that was kind of fun to see them; they were real excited about it." A 46-year-old special education teacher loaned her 1996 Mustang convertible to her children on more than one occasion. She remarked, "You know I was a mom at the time with teenagers so that was a pretty cool thing, for them to have a mom with that car. It went to a few proms. Two with one son and one with another." To these women, having a pony car is more fun when it can be shared with friends.

Those who are around children on a regular basis—as parents or teachers—often take the opportunity to share the pony car experience with the younger set. A 47-year-old elementary school teacher who owns two Camaros celebrates the 1989 car's birthday each year with her students, complete with a Camaro-themed cake. She also uses her cars as a teaching tool, dividing her second grade class into groups by Camaro colors. As she explained, "the kids think it's really cool and the parents will come in and it's like oh my gosh. The first thing we hear about you is 'my teacher is really cool. She's got these cool cars.'" The children of a 46-year-old educator enjoyed riding with mom in her 1996 Mustang. As the Holt, Michigan, resident remarked, "I did some after school activities with my kids so I would drive them in my car which was always a big hit. I drove my kids to camp and that was always fun because other kids liked to see the red convertible come up." Sharing their love of cars in the classroom, on the road, and in the school parking lot not only has the potential to impart a little bit of "coolness" on middle-aged moms, but may also instill an interest in and passion for automobiles in the next generation of drivers.

As Jerry Passon notes, the automobile is often "seen and depicted as the sign of our alienation from nature or humanistic values" (20). However, rather than calling upon the automobile to create distance between themselves and others, the women in this project view the pony car as a means to bring people close through friendship, family time, and fun.

CELEBRATING POPULAR CULTURE

As *CarFax* blogger Aaron Turpen laments, the 1970s witnessed the "near-death" of the muscle car. In 1970 the federal government passed the Clean Air Act, which led to the requirement of smog controls on domestic automobiles. The OPEC oil embargo, which resulted in price controls and gas rationing, soon followed. During this time, in order to accommodate surcharges to policies on high-risk, high-powered automobiles, insurance rates accelerated to record levels. These conditions, writes Turpen, "made muscle cars too expensive or impractical for most buyers."

Faced with decreasing sales and defection to imports, U.S. automakers sought ways to keep the public interested in the struggling pony car. One of the more successful strategies was to create a personality for the car through popular culture. Using a signature car to define a character in a television show or film helped bring attention to a particular model and in the process, create a desire for the product. Some models—such as the 2001 Bullitt Mustang inspired by the character played by Steve McQueen in the 1968 film—were recreations of iconic cars created years after the fact in order to take advantage of a nostalgic cinematic moment. However, during the late 1970s, a slew of road "outlaw" films not only immediately popularized the featured pony car—specifically the Pontiac Trans Am—but also created a car cult following that exists to this day. The film most responsible for the 1970s and '80s Trans Am phenomenon was *Smokey and the Bandit*.

The premise of *Smokey and the Bandit*, writes William Krause, is "a 90-minute, stunt-filled chase scene" (50). The Bandit, played by Burt Reynolds, drives his 1977 Special

Edition Pontiac Trans Am across the South pursued by sheriff Buford T. Justice (Jackie Gleason) as part of a bootlegging scheme. The success of the film, notes Krause, helped to double Trans Am sales; the big-screen antics "helped make the Trans Am into one of the most popular cars in the United States" (53). The car that became a popular culture icon in the 1970s has experienced a surge in popularity in the twenty-first century. In fact, the Pontiac Trans Am is the choice of many women who participated in this project. They chose this vehicle for its notoriety, the opportunity to participate in "Bandit Runs"—an annual reenactment of the journey portrayed in the film—and the "good outlaw" status awarded the individual who gets behind the wheel of a Pontiac Trans Am or Firebird.

A 53-year-old store manager purchased her 1977 Pontiac Trans Am brand new straight out of high school. As she remarked, "when the *Smokey and the Bandit* movie came out with Burt Reynolds, that was just the cool car to have." When she takes the car to shows today, it is proudly exhibited alongside her collection of *Smokey and the Bandit*

Smokey and the Bandit II **promotional photograph, 1980. Modern day Bandit Runs differ from that portrayed in the infamous film in two important ways. First, while today's drives still take place on the winding roads featured in the original movie, the driving methods are considerably tamer. And second, while in** *Smokey and the Bandit* **the woman never moves beyond the role of sidekick, in today's Bandit Runs, the woman driver is often found behind the wheel of her very own Trans Am (Photofest).**

memorabilia. As she noted, "not too many people can say my car was in a movie." Like the protagonist of the infamous film, the Williamston, Michigan, resident considers herself a bit of a rebel, both on the road and in life. As a teenager with a Trans Am, she engaged in a little street racing, one of the few young women in her crowd to do so. As an adult, she believes her Trans Am has helped her break some barriers in American car culture. As she exclaimed, "I'm breaking through the stigma of men and their muscle cars." Film scholar Katie Mills notes the misogyny that underlies many of the outlaw movies. These genre films, writes Mills, serve as a "backlash against the social rebellions of hippies and feminists" (168). The women in these films are most often sidekicks, unwilling passengers, or damsels in distress who need rescuing. However, rather than identify with *Smokey and the Bandit's* female co-star—a runaway bride played by Sally Field— the 53-year-old woman inhabits Burt Reynold's "good outlaw" persona as she gets behind the wheel of her 1977 Pontiac Trans Am.

After participating in the annual Bandit Run with a friend, a 43-year-old optician came home and declared, "I have to get my own car." The purchase of a gold 1998 Pontiac Trans Am—aka "Goldie"—provided her with the opportunity to participate in a cruising event that has taken place for almost 20 years and has, in the process, become an important component of Trans Am culture. Owning a Trans Am allows the Grand Rapids, Michigan, native to escape from domesticity, meet fellow Trans Am enthusiasts from all over the country, and drive on some incredible American roads. As she noted, "I went on this run, and just fell in love with the people. I could not believe that so many people would come together, for a whole week, once a year, just about a car." Although she takes the car to local car events, the highlight of the year is the annual Bandit Run. In their analysis of 1970s "road outlaw" movies, Jack Sargeant and Stephanie Watson suggest that the protagonists "often desire to live outside of society [...] and the automobile becomes their symbol of freedom and unrestricted movement" (128). As an individual whose daily driver is "the carpool car; it has kids in it; it's filthy," this 43-year-old mom of two enjoys the time spent with hundreds of other Trans Am owners driving twisty roads in the guise of the mythical and rebellious Bandit.

The Trans Am also had a starring role on television, as KITT (Knight Industries Three Thousand), the talking sidekick of problem-solver-for-hire David Hasselhoff in the campy action-adventure series *Knight Rider* (Krause 126). Loaded with a vast assortment of special equipment—molecular bonded shell, voice synthesizer, electronic jamming system, olfactory sensor, grappling hook and winch, and flame thrower, to name a few—KITT's role was that of a crime-fighting crusader and protector of "human life at all costs" (K.I.T.T.). Because the instrument panel of her 1987 Pontiac Trans Am GTA resembles that featured on *Knight Rider*, a 17-year-old student from a muscle car family refers to her vehicle as "Kitt." However, as her mother mentioned, "the guys in the Mopar club started calling it 'Kitty.'" Although the older men in the muscle car organization to which her parents belong attempt to diminish the young woman's automotive credentials by calling on a diminutive term to describe her vehicle, the 17-year-old remains steadfast in her decision to identify with the "crime-fighting-crusader" of TV fame through defiantly ascribing the label KITT to her 1987 Trans Am.

Sargeant and Watson suggest that the travelers in road movies such as *Smokey and the Bandit* often take on the mythic stature of early pioneers, "leaving behind the confines of established civilization in order to live life on their own terms" (128). While the women who own iconic Pontiac Trans Ams leave civilization only temporarily, they call upon the vehicles of television and film to construct themselves as female outlaws in a culture shaped by masculinity and dominated by male drivers. To the women in this project, the lack of power in the 1970s and 1980s Trans Am is inconsequential; what is important is the sense of empowerment they achieve when taking the wheel.

EXPERIENCING DRIVING PLEASURE

One of the underlying claims in popular motoring magazines, argues Catharina Landström, is that women are unable to understand the pleasures associated with cars. In these publications, Landström writes, "women are represented as inherently different, rational and impassionate, unable to truly love a car for its own sake" (47). The representation of women's relationship to the automobile as emotionless and uninspired—in motoring magazines, automotive advertising, and popular culture—is based on the perception that women's interest in cars is centered in practicality. This notion originated in the auto industry as a means to separate women's car use from that of men. Its continued reinforcement over the following decades was fueled by the fear that an association with women and femininity would devalue a car and therefore negatively affect its sales among male consumers. This logic, which Landström refers to as a "gendered economy of pleasure," dominates car culture and obscures women's actual relationship to cars. The time-worn focus on the functionality of women's car experience supposes that women's emotional needs in automotive use are met through the car's role as a domestic technology rather than a source of pleasure.

The women who participated in this project disrupt this longstanding assumption. Their cars of choice—a 1980s or '90s pony car—fulfill no practical function. As primarily coupes (cars with two doors), Mustangs, Camaros, and Firebirds are problematic for transporting children; the small trunks have little room for shopping bags; the unremarkable fuel economy makes them impractical for long trips or commutes. Yet as voiced by the participants in this project, what makes a pony car special is the sheer joy women feel while driving them. Of taking the wheel of her 1998 Pontiac Trans Am, a 43-year-old optician exclaimed, "There's just no other feeling like it. It's wonderful." Although the pony cars of this era do not have the power of their predecessors or successors, they have the ability to enhance and embellish women's lives in ways that daily drivers simply cannot. Contrary to what popular motoring magazines and automotive advertisements would have one believe, it is possible for women to experience pleasure through driving. And for this group of women, that pleasure is obtained when behind the wheel of a stylish, sporty, attention-getting, and altogether impractical pony car.

As the participants repeatedly demonstrated, the pony car has the ability to alter how a woman feels about herself. In her prescribed role as mother, wife, and caretaker, a woman can frequently feel overworked, unappreciated, and taken for granted. However, as the women in this project indicated, those culturally ascribed identities often disappear when driving a throaty Mustang, bright red Camaro, or sleek Firebird. As a 42-year-old 1982 Ford Mustang owner declared, "Ah, that's where life begins to me. I mean it's just excitement, the thrill of it, kind of being a whole different person when I get in that car."

A 31-year-old color analyst noted that driving her 1991 Firebird "reminds me that I'm a strong woman in this world." The pleasure derived when behind the wheel of a Mustang or Camaro allows women the opportunity to think of themselves—albeit temporarily— as something other than what society expects them to be. While in their daily drivers they often feel responsible, dependable, and bored to tears; when in the driver's seat of a pony car, the women feel sexy, badass, cool, and fun. As a 43-year-old 1998 Pontiac Trans Am owner proclaimed, "I don't have the movies going; I don't have the kids screaming. It's just completely different."

The pleasure associated with pony car ownership often translates into feeling significantly younger than the age on one's driver's license. A 60-year-old accountant recently purchased the car of her dreams. As she exclaimed, when in the driver's seat of her yellow 1993 Ford Mustang convertible, "I feel carefree and reckless and young." A 60-year-old 1993 Mustang convertible owner disclosed, "I think people think I am a young-thinking person because I have a sporty car." When she pulls up in her 2001 Mustang, folks are apt to consider a 67-year-old office manager in a different light. As she explained, "You know, look at the old lady driving a sports car. You know you're only as old as you feel." There is also a sense of freedom that accompanies pony car ownership. Of her 1991 Pontiac Firebird, a 31-year-old color analyst attested, "It's like a sense of elation, for me. Like, just being free being me." A 71-year-old retired teacher, who inherited a 1994 Camaro Z/28 convertible upon the death of her spouse, remarked, "I just feel so good, especially on these beautiful nights, evenings, being out with this car. I just feel free."

The women were in agreement that the pleasure associated with the pony car often serves as an effective antidote to depression. Taking the wheel of a pony car provides them with the opportunity to temporarily leave problems behind and develop a positive outlook. As a 53-year-old 1977 Pontiac Trans Am owner remarked, "When I get depressed, I can jump in my car, everything goes away. Just the drive in the car will get me out of the pressure of the daily stuff that I'm doing." When seated in her 1998 Trans Am, noted a 43-year-old mom, "you just get this different feeling; like nothing in the world is wrong when you're in that car." A 60-year-old professional dog handler exclaimed, "when I'm driving the Mustang I'm just very proud to be seen in it, to be driving it. It's just uplifting to my spirit." The pleasure the women experience while driving convertible Mustangs and Camaros on warm summer nights was palpable in their enthusiastic responses. As the 49-year-old owner of a 1988 Mustang GT declared, "just having a convertible on a really nice day and putting the top down. There's nothing better."

Whether women upgraded their pony cars with performance options, or appreciated the Mustangs, Camaros, and Trans Ams for style rather than power, they were unanimous in the description of their pony cars as "fun to drive." These women experience pleasure simply by taking the wheel. Of her 1996 red convertible Mustang, a 46-year-old special education teacher proclaimed, "I loved driving it. I absolutely loved driving it." Of her 2002 Camaro Z/28, a 60-year-old data analyst exclaimed, "If the weather is nice I'll drive it just to drive it. I love driving this car." A 47-year-old teacher from Ionia, Michigan, will sometimes take her 1989 Camaro RS to car shows, but as she noted, "I drive it around town cause it's a just a fun little car to have."

A few of the women expressed guilt over the pleasure they experienced through ownership of a pony car. As a 46-year-old 1996 Mustang convertible owner revealed, "there came a point when I would be stopped at a light and people would be looking at me that I almost felt guilty, for having that, I can remember that really strongly. There were times when I thought I don't know; why am I feeling badly about this?" Comments such as this suggest that on some level, women have internalized the common assumption that it is improper for female drivers to experience the pleasure associated with cars. However, despite the guilt-ridden feelings that plagued a few of the women from time to time, they possessed the ability to shake them off when behind the wheel of a Camaro, Mustang, or Firebird.

In her work in transportation studies, Mimi Sheller argues that debates about the future of the car and road system will remain superficial—and policies ineffectual—until they take into consideration the emotional investments people have in the relationships between the car, the self, family, and friends. As Sheller writes, "car consumption is never simply about rational economic choices, but is as much about aesthetic, emotional, and sensory responses to driving, as well as patterns of kinship, sociability, habitation, and work" (222). The historical practice of considering women's automotive consumption primarily in functional and familial terms obscures women's varied relationships to cars. In particular, it ignores what Sheller refers to as "automotive emotions"—the embodied dispositions of car users and the feelings associated with car use. The familiar focus on the functionality of women's car experience supposes that women's emotional needs in automotive use are met through the car's role in the safe transport of herself and family members. Yet as the participants in this project soundly demonstrate, women's relationship to the automobile is not based solely in practicality. Rather, ownership of a pony car provides them with the opportunity to remake a material object into their own image, share the driving experience with friends, engage in a popular culture moment, and fully experience the joy, excitement, and sheer pleasure associated with the automobile.

The Mercury Cougar was classified as a performance pony car until 1973. When the muscle car era ended, it evolved into a personal luxury car; it was reconfigured as a sport compact from 1999 until 2002, its last year of production. Sarai Keith doesn't mind that her 1997 Cougar XR7 no longer fits the definition of a muscle car. As she noted, "it's not high performance; it's not extremely fast. It's just pretty" (courtesy Sarai Keith).

The Retro Muscle Car: 2005 to the Present

AMERICAN MUSCLE'S RETURN TO POWER

The last Pontiac Firebird rolled off the assembly line in 2002. The Chevrolet Camaro—which shared the Firebird's F-body architecture—was discontinued the same year due to dwindling sales and an aging platform. The Challenger nameplate was revived for six years—1978 to 1983—for a version of the Mitsubishi Galant Lambda Coupe sold through Dodge dealers as a "captive import."[22] As it was never considered a respectable substitute for the original Challenger, the Japanese version eventually disappeared. The Ford Mustang, on the other hand, was not only the first pony car to enter the automotive scene in 1964, but due to the quiet departure of its longtime competitors, was also the last pony car standing.

The absence of competition, coupled with the success of the 2001 Bullitt GT and the 2003–2004 Mach I Mustang models, motivated Ford to replace the venerable Fox body with a new platform. In 2005, Ford introduced a redesigned "retro futuristic" Mustang on the SN-95 platform that married the iconic style elements of the late 1960s fast-back models with modern automotive technology.[23] As the first of what would become a growing stable of "retro" pony cars, the Mustang was a resounding success. Its popularity instituted a twenty-first century "War of the Ponies," reminiscent of the contest between the Big Three automakers some 40 years before (Newhardt 161).

Taking note of Ford's triumph, Chrysler moved forward to enter the retro muscle car field with a reimagined classic pony car of its own. The newly designed Dodge Challenger—which, like the Mustang, borrowed style elements from its various 1970s incarnations—made its entrance at the 2006 Detroit auto show. To "one up" Ford, Chrysler also added a mid-sized muscle car—the Dodge Charger—to the mix. The new Charger, Bruce Wexler writes, "was a blast from the muscle car past with a touch of modern refinement, a refined four-door sedan equipped with incredible performance" (423).

Chevrolet also got into the retro pony car game. As Newhardt asserts, "General Motors was constantly besieged by bowtie enthusiasts for a return of the marque vehicle.[24] They were tired of getting their faces rubbed in the tarmac by the Blue Oval crowd" (162).[25] Yet rather than create a new Camaro in the image of its predecessor, the retro Camaro was reimagined into a fresh design that, notes Patton, "suggests a sculpture of the original." Like its competitors the Mustang, Challenger, and Charger, the Chevy Camaro has, since its introduction, received accolades from boomers, Generation Xers, and millennials alike. While the retro muscle car represents only a small percentage of total U.S. car sales (2 percent in 2015),[26] its visibility and popularity has allowed American automakers to reclaim a little of the swagger that had been missing for so many years.

The success of the twenty-first century pony car, after decades of automotive mediocrity and near obsolescence, can be attributed to a number of factors. The production of the modern muscle car provided American automakers with the opportunity to return to what they had done best in the past. Rather than rely solely on the production of vehicles that differed only marginally from imports, Ford, Chrysler, and General Motors built the cars that foreign competitors could not. As former GM car czar Bob Lutz notes, "There's enormous good will for the glory days of American cars, when they really were American and didn't try to be Japanese or German. We all recently discovered that was a gold mine we had left fallow for a couple decades" (qtd. in "Muscles," Naughton).

In addition, baby boomers—the generation for which the original muscle car was produced—had reached a stage in life in which they were financially comfortable and often nostalgic for a romanticized automotive youth. The modern muscle car—with its technological innovations, improved handling and performance, decent fuel economy, and a bevy of safety features—provided them with the excitement behind the wheel they fondly remembered without the rough ride and unpredictability they would rather forget. As Karl Brauer, a senior director at Kelley Blue Book, asserts, "When it comes to American muscle cars they sure don't make them like they used to; they make them much better. With engines capable of producing between 400 and 650 horsepower, and zero-to-60 times approaching three seconds, the modern American performance car could chew the original 1960s versions into tiny bits of bias-ply rubber, and that's in a straight line" (qtd. in Bukszpan).

Younger car buyers, eager to stand out in a sea of automotive uniformity, viewed ownership of a retro muscle car not only as a means to give a shout-out to Detroit's past glory, but also as a way to claim individuality and identity. Much like the early Mustangs, Camaros, Challengers, and Chargers, the retro muscle car provided drivers with the opportunity to project a rebellious and outrageous self.

The twenty-first century muscle car can also attribute a good portion of its success to the woman driver. While the station wagon, minivan, and crossover have long been considered "women's cars" for their functionality and family friendliness, the retro muscle car has become popular among a growing group of female car enthusiasts for its reputation as sporty, fast, powerful, and fun. Whether single and seeking a bit of automotive independence, or as married empty nesters looking for a new lease on life, many women have found that getting behind the wheel of a modern day Mustang, Camaro, or Charger has the ability to change the way they view themselves and the world around them. Conversely, in the woman driver, automakers have discovered an enthusiastic, passionate, knowledgeable, and rapidly growing consumer base. As Edmunds.com auto expert Holly Reich notes, women's automotive buying power is higher than ever; she writes, "women purchase more than 50 percent of all new vehicles; female buyers are also the fastest growing segment of new and used car buyers today" (Reich). The women who contributed to this project represent a growing population of female motorists who seek to ditch the "mom car"—temporarily or permanently—in lieu of a vehicle that offers power, performance, pizzazz, and an exhilarating driving experience. As women who overwhelmingly embrace a conservative ideology, they turn their attention to an automotive category with a proud American legacy. As individuals who are financially secure, proud of their individual accomplishments, and confident in their driving ability, they choose autos that put those qualities unabashedly on display. For women who believe that a car is not an appliance, but rather a visible extension of one's personality, the vehicle of choice is often a retro American muscle car.

> It's control like of a big beast, you know that this thing, it's super powerful, and it's in your hands. And it's just feeling like that. It's an awesome feeling. It's a feeling of awe. And power. And it's just fun. Adrenaline.
>
> —55-year-old 2012 Dodge Challenger R/T owner

Women and the Retro Muscle Car

The women who owned retro muscle cars shared many characteristics with the participants who owned classic muscle cars. In fact, a good number of the women interviewed for this project owned both classic and retro versions. Although they skewed younger as a group—70 percent were in their 40s or 50s—than owners of classic muscle cars, all but one of the retro-owning women were white, all were married or in a long-term relationship, all but one were heterosexual, and the majority (85 percent) identified as moderate or conservative. And much like the women with classic muscle cars, they viewed ownership of a retro version as a means to display patriotism and to honor the muscle car's American past. Like the owners of pony cars, the women often modified their vehicles as a way to claim individuality and identity. However, due to the technological superiority of the modern muscle car, the women in this category were more involved in the driving experience than owners of classic and pony cars. The most notable and obvious difference between the women with retro muscle cars and those who own older models is that the women do not just put the Mustangs, Camaros, and Challengers on display, but regularly and enthusiastically drive them. While a few women in northern climates garage their cars during the winter months, the majority call upon them as daily drivers. Yet to these women, the retro muscle car not only functions as a primary means of transportation. Rather, it also serves as a symbol of success or a particular accomplishment, provides a new lease on life, represents a form of gender bending, and operates as a source of freedom and empowerment.

A New Lease on Life

In the marketing of the automobile, automakers have traditionally adhered to gendered scripts. Vehicles considered appropriate for the male driver are most often those with an emphasis on power and performance, personal luxury, or strength and toughness. As promoted in the media and popular culture, argues Judy Wajcman, the large and powerful car affords men "a means of escape from domestic responsibilities, from family commitment, into a realm of private fantasy, autonomy, and control" (134). The car most often associated with the women driver, on the other hand, possesses the qualities—reliability, functionality, spaciousness, and safety—that emphasize women's societal responsibilities as family caretakers and chauffeurs. Considered a practical necessity rather than a source of pleasure, this vehicle, writes Wajcman, is "assumed to be the family's second car for the wife and mother to meet household needs" (135). The majority of the women interviewed for this project spent much of their adult lives behind the wheel of a vehicle—hatchback, minivan, small SUV, or crossover—that fits such a description. These automobiles not only served a practical purpose, but perhaps more importantly, identified those who drove them as conscientious and caring wives and mothers.

As primarily conservative in ideology, the women in this project are respectful of gender roles and the duties that accompany them. They accept that because conservatism holds women primarily responsible for the care and well-being of children, is it honorable to drive vehicles that reflect this important status. As the 54-year-old owner of a 2014 Mustang GT remarked, "when it was my turn to buy a car we had to buy a family car so

Betty Nelson recently traded in her 2013 Jazz Blue Dodge Challenger for this 2016 Dodge Challenger Scat Pack. With a 6.4 liter V8 engine, 485 horsepower, 8-speed automatic transmission, and vibrant Go Mango color, folks can see and hear Betty coming (courtesy Betty Nelson).

that was like going to be my Windstar or something." However, now that children—and the financial responsibilities that accompanied them—are out of the house, many women seek to leave the "Windstar or something" behind for an engaging and exciting driving experience. As a 59-year-old 2005 Mustang owner explained, "I had such a long drive [to work] I thought why don't I have a fun car for a change instead of a functional car." A 54-year-old engineer remarked, "The kids are off to college; I can buy whatever I want. And drive whatever I want. And that's what I did." Whether a daily driver or second car driven on special occasions (i.e., when the snow and salt is off the ground), the retro muscle car is often regarded by women of middle age as the means to a new lease on life.

The majority of women in this group had set their sights on a muscle car at an early age. However, children and domestic responsibilities waylaid them, preventing them from acquiring the automobile they longed for. As a 58-year-old 2013 Mustang GT 5.0 convertible owner disclosed, "I have always loved Mustangs. I learned to drive on my mom's 1966 Mustang and always wanted another one, but kids came along and I had to wait until they were grown to get my dream car." A 54-year-old longtime minivan owner lamented, "I felt I didn't have a choice in what I bought, you know, in a way." These women found it necessary to put their dreams on hold until the time was right to buy a muscle car. As a 49-year-old 2010 Mustang GT owner remarked, "we had this window of opportunity. My daughter was going to be in college soon and we're like, if we're going to get this Mustang, we'd better do it before the kids start college." A 54-year-old 2014 Mustang GT owner exclaimed, "This was my first chance. It was like, I'm going to be liberated." The women viewed ownership of a practical vehicle as appropriate for a particular period in their lives. While they did not, for the most part, resent the years spent behind the wheel of a minivan or crossover, they relished the opportunity to face the future in a fast, flashy, and powerful muscle car.

As conservative women are often expected to keep a low profile, a good number of the women felt it necessary to rationalize the acquisition of a loud and colorful Mustang or Camaro. Many framed ownership of a muscle car as a reward for a lifetime of sacrifice and service to others. Others considered it a personal accomplishment based on hard work, persistence, and modest financial success. As a 54-year-old participant related, "we're at the point in life where we could afford to have a choice." Although the women were quick to mention that ownership of a muscle car was no longer cost prohibitive, they also insisted that the vehicle was not purchased as a flagrant display of their success. Of her 2014 Mustang, a 54-year-old engineer remarked, "I did not buy it to impress the neighbors or anybody else. This is for my personal life experience."

Firmly ensconced in middle age, the women expressed an understanding of their own mortality, and the importance of experiencing driving pleasure while still able to do so. As a 54-year-old 2010 Camaro owner explained, "my husband's best friend died in early 2009 and we decided we needed to start living life instead of saving, saving, saving and then retiring and dying." After years spent behind the wheel of a serviceable but often uninspiring automobile, these women eagerly anticipated the heart pumping and adrenaline rush that accompany ownership of a muscle car. As a 59-year-old advertising copywriter remarked, "everything I drove was like a pleasant sedan. I just felt that at that point in my life I wanted to do something different and exciting." Advancing age provided some of the women with the excuse to embrace an I-don't-care-what-others-think attitude. A 58-year-old semi-retired seamstress exclaimed, "You are never too old to do what you want. Even a grandma can drive a muscle car." In the acquisition of a fast, spirited, and noisy muscle car, these women threw caution, as well as stereotypes about the driving habits of older women, to the wind. They have chosen to spend the years that remain gunning the engines and taking over the streets in their modern day muscle cars, an experience that can only be described as a new and invigorating lease on life.

THE PAST IS PRESENT

Women who own muscle cars—whether classic, pony, or retro—share a reverence for the American muscle car past. Those who acquire older vehicles often do so as a way to recreate or remember a particular period of their lives. Many of the women who participated in this project had longed for a particular model as a teenager, but were denied the opportunity to own one due to the financial restrictions and cultural proscriptions of the time. Thus many older women—particularly aging baby boomers—set their sights on the 1965 Mustang or 1970 GTO they desired but were prohibited from owning when young. Gunning the engine of the classic muscle car of their dreams not only transports these women back to a nostalgic past, but through the long awaited attainment of something once forbidden, provides a sense of closure and contentment.

Like those with classic automobiles, many of the retro muscle car owners have been admirers of a certain vehicle since childhood. As a 49-year-old educator reflected, "The boys across the street; that's what they worked on. Mustangs. I would sit there and I would have my head on the quarter panel watching them work on that car." A 42-year-old 2011 Camaro SS/RS convertible owner remarked, "My first memory was of my cousin's boyfriend's 1969 Camaro when I was six. I don't remember why, but I fell in love with it when

I saw it. And that was the day I said I would have one, one day." Yet, rather than acquire a vehicle that takes them back to an automotive past that excluded them, they drive the Mustangs and Camaros that represent them as the empowered women they are today. As a 54-year-old owner of a 2014 Camaro 2SS/RS declared, "It's a real ego booster to drive around and turn heads. I feel special to be in such a beautiful machine." A longtime Dodge Challenger admirer exclaimed, "I was finally able to afford one and didn't look back." While the women acknowledge the barriers that prevented them from muscle car ownership in the past, they view ownership of a modern Camaro or Challenger today as reflective of how far they, as women, have come in the world. As women who identify primarily as conservative, they often cite autonomy, individualism, hard work, and personal accountability—characteristics championed in conservative circles—as responsible for their ability to own, drive, and appreciate the retro American muscle car.

Women who purchase retro muscle cars do so as a means to connect to the American automotive past without imagining themselves within it. They view themselves as responsible for carrying American muscle car heritage forward rather than placing too much emphasis on what came before. As the 32-year-old owner of both a 1968½ Ford Mustang Shelby GT 500 and a 2013 Mustang Boss 302 remarked, "Hopefully people would see that I have an appreciation for the classic cars but can enjoy the modern muscle car, too." While they value classic Mustangs, Road Runners, and Barracudas for their style, presence, and automotive influence, they enjoy the technological innovations that make driving the new cars a more satisfying and exciting automotive experience. A 65-year-old rancher remarked, "The main reason I chose this car was the great look Dodge gave to a retro muscle car like the Challenger." A 55-year-old 2010 Dodge Challenger owner developed her appreciation for Mopar style while a college student, and is thrilled to see it incorporated into the twenty-first century version. As she declared, "The lines of this car stayed true to the original; the heritage is evident." And as a 47-year-old IT engineered explained, "Color, performance engine, retro design to the 1971 Challenger, new interior and amenities for the 2015 year. I believe my 2015 Challenger is the modern version of a 1970s muscle car." While the women appreciate the retro muscle car for its ties to an illustrious past, they love the modern day Mustang or Camaro or Challenger for its ability to announce them as independent, strong, and ready-for-anything twenty-first century women.

Not only does a modern muscle car connect its driver to an American automotive past, but to the women from Southeastern Michigan in particular, often inspires a special sense of pride. As Eddie Alterman—former editor in chief of *Car and Driver*—argues, "What these cars mean for Detroit is heritage. They carry the value of the companies and the histories of the companies with them" (qtd. in Tolson). The significance of a car produced in her home state was not lost on a 59-year-old advertising copywriter. As she remarked, "I think that's another thing I liked about the idea of a Mustang. That it was so associated with Detroit, so it gave it this coolness that other brands would not have. I remember looking at the sticker and thinking this car was made in Michigan!" To a 49-year-old professional educator who grew up in Dearborn, Michigan—home of Ford World Headquarters—Mustang sightings were a common occurrence. As she related, "We used to go down Telegraph, my girlfriend and I. When they would cruise when we were younger. And I'd be like 'oh here comes a Mustang.'" The constant exposure to the pony car with Dearborn origins convinced her that, when the time came to purchase a vehicle, "it just had to be a Mustang." With the retro muscle car, writes Neal Boudette, American automakers not only tap into nostalgia among aging baby boomers, but "an increasing appreciation for Detroit's past glory among younger car buyers" as well. To the women who hailed from the Motor City and its environs, ownership of a modern day Mustang, Camaro, or Challenger provided them with the opportunity to drive the car of their dreams while paying tribute to their hometown's proud automotive past.

GENDER BENDING

Of the many vehicles on the market today, perhaps none is more associated with masculinity and the male driver than the American muscle car. Originally produced to appeal to a specific segment of the automotive market—young baby boomer men—and infused with qualities often conflated with male bodies and masculine behavior—power, performance, strength, and brashness—the muscle car boldly and unabashedly announced its driver as male. As Lawrence Ulrich writes, "the very words 'muscle car' conjure images of cool young toughs revving engines and menacing the streets." The modern day muscle car relies on its past associations as a tough, macho machine to appeal to individuals who took part in the muscle car experience as well as those who are familiar with muscle car heritage but never had the opportunity to gun the engine of a Camaro, Charger, or Challenger. With an emphasis on speed, style, technology, and brute power, it is not surprising that much like its classic predecessor, the modern-day muscle car is considered a vehicle for the construction and performance of masculinity.

The women who participated in this project fully acknowledge this longstanding association. As the 47-year-old owner of a 2015 Dodge Challenger remarked, "I think a lot of people believe that performance cars are a man's world." Muscle cars, noted the 49-year-old owner of a 2010 Camaro, "were typically meant for men." One of the attractions of muscle car ownership to this group of women—other than power, performance, and modern technology—is the notion they are driving an automobile specifically produced for and promoted to the male driver. They often experience a surreptitious thrill taking the wheel of a vehicle traditionally considered off limits to the female motorist. Because of the muscle car's longstanding reputation as a macho machine, ownership of a Camaro, Mustang, or Charger is often perceived as a playful form of "gender bending." As a 59-year-old 2005 Mustang owner disclosed, "I do think that it's some part of what a lot of women think, oh, I'm driving something that normally men are associated with." A 58-year-old 2014 Challenger SRT owner exclaimed, "you'll see the guys in the minivans looking at you like why is she driving that. I should be driving that." To the women in this project, the surprised reaction of others to their presence behind the wheel of a Charger or Camaro demonstrates that despite the changing role of women over the past half-century, the longstanding association between masculinity and the muscle car remains intact. Remarked a 29-year-old 2010 Camaro SS/RS owner, "There are a lot of people I see driving down the road, and they see.the car and they do a double take."

Lerman, Mohun, and Oldenziel write, "gender ideologies play a central role in human interactions with technology" (1). The division of automobile use by gender has long relied on an established conservative ideology that values and encourages traditional gender roles. As Baehr observes, conservatism holds that conventional social forms, while not perfect, "tend to be conducive to human well-being, and thus should be protected and promoted" (102). This notion suggests a dichotomy between the adherence to gender roles encouraged by conservatism and the gendered meanings attached to the muscle car. It would be expected that women who adhere to a conservative ideology—such as the majority who participated in this project—would be opposed to owning a fast and powerful machine, or at least apologetic for doing so. There were, in fact, a few women who found it necessary to rationalize their vehicle choices. Of her purchase of a 2010 Mustang GT, a 49-year-old educator qualified, "I don't want to put too much importance on it because I don't want anybody to think it's more important than my family. 'Cause it's not." A 42-year-old 2011 Camaro SS/RS convertible owner remarked, "Most who don't know me think I don't deserve this car." However, the majority of women were able to resolve this apparent contradiction through the construction of gender bending as a form of acknowledgment to the historical association between men and muscle cars.

The women understand that what men do is considered valuable in American society, particularly in conservative circles. They also acknowledge that the muscle car is indelibly linked to the male driver. Referring to muscle car ownership as a form of gender bending allows women to raise their own status in the muscle car community while at the same time conceding that muscle cars are a man's world. It awards women agency without upsetting the established gender hierarchy within muscle car culture. Gender bending, in this context, is not used to criticize gender roles, nor is it called upon to describe masculine driving behavior. It is not a means to displace or disparage male participants in the muscle car community. Rather, it is called upon to demonstrate women's automotive accomplishments by equating them to those of men. Muscle car ownership as an expression of gender bending refers to a woman's ability, and some might say right, to have what men have. As a 29-year-old 2010 Camaro SS/RS owner remarked, "this car defines me in a way that, how can I say this, girls can be car girls, too. You don't have to be big and brash and brutish to be a muscle car owner." A 54-year-old 2009 Charger R/T asserted, "I think women more and more want to be equal to a man. Women are getting more bold as to what they want to do and all; they're getting more confident about what they can accomplish." Constructing muscle car ownership as an expression of gender bending allows women to view themselves as empowered drivers without challenging gender roles. Reflecting on her 2012 Challenger R/T, a 55-year-old small business owner exclaimed, "I think it says about me that I'm a strong, powerful woman that's in control of a big car."

WOMEN POWER

There can be little argument that the most distinguishing—and memorable—characteristic of the classic American muscle car was power. Power not only separated the muscle car from its feminized 1950s predecessors, but also—through the determined efforts of auto manufacturers and marketers—marked the muscle car as altogether masculine. The brute power associated with the muscle car became an effective marketing tool, particularly when directed toward the young adult male of driving age. Through possession of a Pontiac GTO or Dodge Charger, auto advertisers claimed, young men could imagine themselves as powerful and formidable as the big-block V8 engines that fueled their macho machines. In "Men and Their Machines," Russell Belk argues that male drivers often view cars as extensions of themselves; it follows, therefore, that through identification with a Charger or Camaro, a man can take on the characteristics of the "cathected" vehicle. As Belk writes, "a powerful engine gives the owner who controls it a feeling of enhanced power [...] and high performance handling makes the man feel capable of high performance as well" (273). Dag Balkmar, writing about car modification culture, notes that vehicles such as the muscle car contribute to "the creation of a masculine 'power field' from which men may draw inspiration in constructing male identity and power" (54). A half-century after the muscle car's introduction, American auto manufacturers continue to emphasize power and performance to attract male customers as well as to construct the reinvented muscle car as a masculine talisman. As Duerringer writes in his analysis of a 2010 Dodge Super Bowl commercial, the purchase of a Charger can be best understood as "a last defense of manhood against the symbolic castration betokened by the encroaching forces of bureaucratization and empowered femininity" (137). The overabundance of power engineered into today's muscle cars suggests that the connection between powerful cars and masculinity remains much as it did in the classic muscle car era, not only as an effective way to sell cars, but to also reinforce the notion that power—automotive and otherwise—belongs in the hands of men.

However, the women who own modern day muscle cars disrupt the notion that the appreciation for automotive power is confined to the male driver. When describing what she looks for in a vehicle, a 29-year-old 2010 Camaro SS/RS owner explained, "It has to perform well in that it has to have plenty of power." A 54-year-old 2014 Mustang GT owner declared, "Oh, obviously it's got to have something under the hood. It's got to have the big block engine, right. It's got to have the performance, so. Performance obviously is first." Of her 2010 Dodge Challenger SRT, a 55-year-old engineer remarked, "I ordered this car for the power and looks hoping that the other qualifications were there. Not disappointed so far." And of her selection of 2009 Dodge Charger R/T, a 54-year-old cultural events coordinator explained, "and the power, for sure the power was a big decision, too." Power, as it turns out, draws women as well as men to the muscle car. While women who own classic muscle cars most often mention the vehicle's historical significance as reason for ownership, the improved power and performance made possible by twenty-first century technology are the primary qualities that draw women to modern American muscle. Chris Demorro, a writer for *Stang TV*, observes, "we know plenty of women who are attracted to the Mustang for the same reason as most men: its performance and its legacy." States former auto journalist Lesley Hazleton, "What women enjoy about speed is very much the same as what men enjoy about it: the excitement and the challenge of it, the test of nerves and ability, and the pure sensation of it" ("Everything" 180). As the responses of female retro muscle car owners suggest, a love of fast and powerful automobiles has no gender.

Although the auto industry continues to equate automotive power with male identity and masculinity, the women who participated in this project view the power of the muscle car in a very different light. Rather than consider power as something that is awarded to them through ownership of a muscle car, the female Camaro and Challenger owners value power for its ability to produce a more enjoyable and exhilarating driving experience.

Power in an automobile changes how women feel about getting behind the wheel. Rather than consider driving a means to an end, it is the act of driving itself that is appreciated and savored. Of her 2013 Mustang GT 5.0 convertible, a 58-year-old seamstress declared, "they are a hot car and you feel amazing driving them." A 54-year-old 2009 Dodge Charger R/T owner asserted, "I love the power of the car and what it gives me. I don't know, I just feel good driving it." And a 55-year-old owner of a pet sitting company exclaimed, "It's a pleasure, adrenaline, almost an endorphin release when I drive my Challenger."

Not satisfied with stock vehicles, many of the women add performance options or after market power modifications to make the cars faster, louder, and more responsive. As a 55-year-old 2010 Dodge Challenger owner noted, "I added bolt on power adders—high flow mid-pipes and exhaust, CAT, 180 t-stat, and a custom tune." The result, she added, is a "big blue sexy beast" she describes as "badass." A 55-year-old 2012 Dodge Challenger R/T owner disclosed, "I have added a lot to the car over the years. All kinds of performance mods, engine mods to make it go faster, suspension, tires, wheels, brakes. It's a serious car." A 41-year-old 2006 Dodge Charger owner spoke with pride when describing the modification process. As she exclaimed, "It was the first time I modded a car, having the mid muffler and resonators removed and twin Borlas put in their place to give the whisper-quiet V6 the roar of a muscle car. It was an empowering feeling." As the responses of these women suggest, the power built into a muscle car elevates the driving experience from passive and predictable to exhilarating, invigorating, and empowering. As a 29-year-old 2010 Camaro SS/RS owner remarked, "women like power, too. And muscle cars allow us to demonstrate that we like it."

While the women appreciate automotive power in the same degree as men, they do not view muscle car ownership as a cure for powerlessness or as a means to assert power over others. And although they understand that historically, powerful automobiles have been considered a male province, they do not consider driving a muscle car as a radical feminist act. As Kersten notes, the conservative feminist views equality in universal terms; she believes that as long as women have equal access, and are governed by the same rules and judged by the same standards, gender equality exists. The ways in which these women frame equal access to automotive power often reflects a conservative feminist viewpoint. They consider the ability to appreciate and handle the power of a muscle car not as an affront to men or a symbolic victory for women, but rather, as indicative of gender equality. As a 59-year-old 2005 Mustang convertible owner declared, "Women can drive cars like this, too. I don't have to drive some safe soccer mom car. I can drive something beautiful and powerful."

FREEDOM BEHIND THE WHEEL

Women who own muscle cars—whether classic, pony, or retro—share a number of important qualities. They are passionate about their cars. They recognize the significance of the muscle car to American automotive history. They actively and enthusiastically break down woman driver stereotypes. They take pleasure in sharing their muscle car knowledge with others. And they view muscle car ownership as a means to something greater—stronger relationships, service to the community, and the formation of new social networks and friendships. However, the women who drive twenty-first century muscle cars experience a sensation that owners of classic muscle cars do not. Advances in automotive technology over the past fifty years have resulted in modern day Camaros, Mustangs, and Challengers that are not only loud, vibrant, and powerful, but are environmentally friendly, safe, and reliable as well. Thus to the women who drive them, one of the most important attributes attached to the retro muscle car is freedom.

The freedom that accompanies retro muscle car ownership takes many forms. Perhaps the most basic is freedom from worry. Due to decades of use or neglect, aging components, and outdated technology, classic muscle and pony cars are not altogether dependable. When driving a classic Mustang, Camaro, or Firebird, it is not uncommon for motors to stall, engines to overheat, brakes to fail, or the electrical system to suddenly burn out. Thus owners of classic muscle or older pony cars must continually worry about the possibility of a vehicle breakdown. Of her 1966 Mustang, a 22-year-old college student remarked, "when I started to drive it again we found out it had an overheating issue at speed which we were never able to track down." Warranties on classic cars do not exist; therefore, when automotive problems occur, repairs costs are a major issue. Parts for older vehicles are not easy to find and are often expensive. Classic muscle and pony cars often require extensive restoration and fixes to make them drivable and legal under today's road regulations and conditions. As the 56-year-owner of both a 1965 Mustang and 2008 Bullitt Mustang explained, "the 1965 spent the first four springs at Vinsetta's Garage in Royal Oak, Michigan. We were ready to put Jack (the owner) as a co-signer on our checkbook." Due to the likelihood of some sort of vehicle failure at any given moment, ownership of a classic muscle or pony car is accompanied by the very real possibility of unexpected and unavoidable repair bills.

Although there are certainly women who are perfectly capable of caring for classic cars themselves, the majority of those interviewed rely on mechanically inclined husbands or male companions for vehicle maintenance and repair. Those without familial resources are often at the mercy of untrustworthy service personnel who are not only disrespectful to female customers, but who often attempt to take advantage of a women's perceived lack of automotive knowledge. A 43-year-old veterinarian, who often relies on her father for mechanical advice, frequently has her auto knowledge questioned when taking her 1966 Charger in for service. As she exclaimed, "Every time I go in for the oil change they're always hitting me up for something and I'm like no, you're not going to do that today. I will go home and ask my father and if my father says it needs to be done then so be it." However modern day muscle cars, often under extended warranty, receive regularly scheduled maintenance; consequently, the associated costs are manageable if not expected. While women's experience at dealerships has traditionally been less than solicitous, improvements in auto service, and the growth of "woman friendly" rating systems for service establishments, has resulted in better experiences for female owners of modern cars. Thus owners of retro Challengers, Camaros, and Mustangs experience a freedom from worry over excessive car repair costs and disreputable service personnel often unavailable to owners of classic muscle and pony cars.[27]

Owners of retro muscle cars also experience freedom from apprehensive driving. Although women enjoy driving their classic muscle and pony cars, they do so with a fair amount of caution. Because of the historical status and value of a classic Barracuda, GTO, or Superbird, as well as the lack of power steering and brakes in most older cars, classic muscle and pony cars are driven respectfully rather than unreservedly. Of her 1966 Charger, a 43-year-old veterinarian remarked, "if somebody pulls out in front of you or a light changes, I mean you just can't stop." As the 47-year-old owner of a 1972 Barracuda explained, "You could not drive the muscle car and talk on the cell phone. You have to kind of keep off your phone, and then worry about it being out in traffic, and rock chips, and that sort of thing, or an accident and people not paying attention." Certainly modern muscle owners also worry about damage to their cars. As the 54-year-old owner of a 2009 Dodge Charger R/T asserted, "I would really hate if somebody, you know, would smack, scratch it, whatever." A 49-year-old 2010 Camaro owner exclaimed, "I love to drive them and how free you feel when you drive them. But also, I hate to drive them because I'm always cautious about stone chips and such on the paint, tar on the paint." However, whereas the fear of damage to a classic car tempers how women drive them, the sense of freedom women experience when behind the wheel of a modern day muscle car overrules such apprehension. Asked to compare the experience of driving her 2013 versus 1984 Mustangs, a 58-year-old self-employed seamstress explained, "It's a lot more fun. It's empowering."

Finally, the modern day muscle provides its drivers with freedom from everyday challenges and daily obligations. As married and often conservative, the majority of women in this project willingly and unapologetically take responsibility for gendered duties at home. Thus owning a retro Mustang, Camaro, or Challenger allows women to experience the freedom—albeit temporarily—often missing in their lives. When asked how she felt when driving her 2013 Boss Mustang, a 32-year-old nurse practitioner replied, "Free. No matter what is going on, there is nothing like just being able to drive." A 49-year-old 2010 Mustang GT owner responded, "It kind of means freedom. If you call me you've got to wait; I'm not answering the phone while I'm driving." A 59-year-old copywriter purchased her 2005 Mustang convertible for the freedom it promised. As she noted, "As a kid I always thought that Mustangs were like, they seemed like freedom to me." Although classic muscle and pony car owners also framed driving their vehicles as an escape from domesticity, the constant worry over breakdowns, repair costs, and the actions of other drivers prevented them from experiencing the freedom enjoyed by the women who own modern day muscle cars. As a 29-year-old auto industry product manager exclaimed, when driving her 2010 Camaro SS/RS, "I feel happy; I feel empowered; it makes me feel confident. It puts me in a good mood. It makes me feel invincible."

The freedom the retro muscle car provides—from worry over the possibility of unexpected breakdowns and repair costs, from overly cautious driving behavior, and from the grind of daily obligations—offers the woman driver a driving experience that differs considerably from that which accompanies a classic muscle or pony car. As a 49-year-old educator exclaimed when describing her 2010 Mustang GT, "The ah factor, you know. When I sit in her and I'm driving her you just feel different." While owners of all generations of muscle cars share a unique automotive experience, the increased horsepower, up-to-date technology, and advanced accoutrements of modern day muscle delivers a sense of freedom unique to this generation of cars. As a 58-year-old grandmother asserted, when behind the wheel of her 2013 Mustang GT 5.0 convertible, "I feel wonderful, young, and free."

The American muscle car started its engine in 1964, stuttered through the last quarter of the twentieth century, and made a powerful comeback in the new millennium. Each generation of muscle car produced over the past 50 plus years is characterized not only by its style, stance, and performance (or lack of), but also by the population of individuals who have and continue to embrace it. The women in this project—while all muscle car enthusiasts—have each gravitated toward a specific generation and model of car for reasons that are rarely practical but always personal.

Yet while the generation of muscle car—classic, pony, and retro—serves to distinguish one group of female car enthusiast from another, the women who participated in this project share a number of important qualities. The next chapter will examine those similarities by focusing on the roles women assume and the strategies women employ as a means to gain acceptance and legitimacy within the historically masculine fraternity of muscle car culture.

2

Women's Roles in American Muscle Car Culture

The association of powerful cars with masculinity is an underlying current in American automotive history. It is not surprising, therefore, that surges in the American muscle car's popularity can be linked to two distinct eras in which manhood was believed to be under siege. The rise of the original muscle car during the late 1960s and early 1970s is often framed as a response to the erosion of individual male autonomy caused by the "coddling suffocating culture of 'Momism'" of the Cold War era (Seiler 78). As Margaret Walsh writes, "In the 1950s anxieties about the feminization of American culture, the decline of rugged masculine traits, and the perceived transformation of American society into a matriarchy suggested that men could and should continue to claim authority and self-expression through their motor vehicles" ("Review"). Ownership of a noisy, rowdy, raucous, and powerful Charger, 'Cuda or GTO was promoted by automakers as the antidote to the crisis of masculinity instigated by women's growing self-governance and political agency.

The rise of the retro muscle car—vehicles produced after 2005—coincides with a perceived threat of emasculation among the American male population as well. In his analysis of a 2010 Dodge Charger commercial, Christopher Duerringer argues that the professional, economical, personal, and political rise of American women in the late twentieth century resulted in an escalation of male insecurity in the public and private spheres. The acquisition of a new performance-driven American muscle car—of which the Charger is an example—is presented as an appropriate and effective response to "the trials facing contemporary hegemonic masculinity" (147). In this scenario, Duerringer notes, women are identified as the source of the crisis whereas manhood—"articulated as fiercely independent, spontaneous, strong, and instrumental"—is considered its victim (145). The flagrant power and performance of the muscle car, asserts Duerringer, offers the possibility of transference of those qualities to the male driver. In times of crisis, Seiler writes, "automobility seemed to provide the means to resuscitate masculinity and individuality in a climate that, according to a myriad of voices, threatened to extinguish both" (89).

The eras that witnessed a rise in the link between powerful cars and masculinity

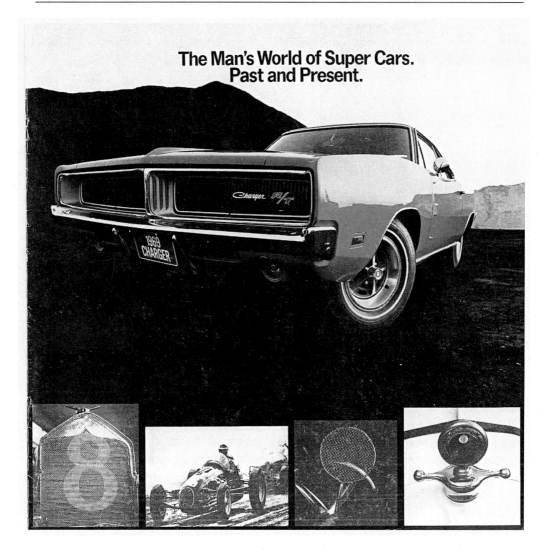

The Man's World of Super Cars.
Past and Present.

Dodge Performance Brochure: "Man's World of Super Cars. Past and Present" (1969). Labeling the contents of an automotive brochure as a "man's world" is reminiscent of the "no girls allowed" signs posted on the childhood forts and secret hiding places of young boys.

were invariably hostile to the woman driver. If manhood was the precursor to mastery over a fast and powerful car, it became necessary to construct women's driving as something less. The postwar era witnessed a rise in early twentieth-century stereotypes that presented the woman driver as an inept and careless "clown or problem" (Seiler 85). Young women were deemed ill equipped—emotionally and physically—to handle a muscle car and were thus relegated to the sidelines. Although women have demonstrated an affinity for the twenty-first century muscle car, women's interest is viewed as a detriment, as the association of the female motorist with a particular vehicle is believed to devalue the car in the eyes of male consumers. Therefore, female muscle car enthusiasts—in advertising and marketing at least—are kept out of sight. As Seiler suggests, during historical moments in which manhood appears threatened, "automobility performed a restorative role by giving that selfhood a vital form conducive to the existing arrangement of power" (3). And that arrangement delegitimized women's attachment to the muscle car.

The women who participated in this project recognize the association between masculinity and the muscle car, and understand that their participation in muscle car culture has not always been welcomed. Consequently, they have developed inventive strategies to ease the integration of the female car enthusiast into what has long existed as a testosterone-laden fraternity. As primarily conservative in ideology, the women who contributed to this project were reluctant to directly challenge their male peers. However, they were able to make an important place for themselves within the culture through the creation of roles that integrated and promoted conservative values. Through these inventive and inspired tactics, the women not only created a women's space within what has long existed as a masculine confine, but have—in the process—irrevocably changed the nature and the face of American muscle car culture.

While the previous section elaborated on the qualities that distinguish one category of female muscle car owner from another, the roles women assume within muscle car culture are most often shared across all generations of women and cars. What follows are those roles that were especially notable among the 88 women who participated in this project.

Caretaker

One of the earliest critiques of women's car use was that it would encourage wives and mothers to forsake their caretaking responsibilities. With automobility, writes Michael Berger, "it was feared that women would fall prey to the lure of the outside world and would neglect their husbands, children and homes" ("Impact" 70). The construction of women as natural caretakers had its origin in the separate spheres ideology of the Industrial Age in which the roles of men and women were narrowly and unequivocally defined. The ideology dictated that men's role existed in the public realm as provider, whereas women's was that of caretaker in the home. Despite the passage of one hundred years and the growing influx of women into the paid workforce, the notion that women's primary and most important role is that of caretaker continues to be promoted, reinforced, and celebrated in contemporary American society. As a popular lifestyle commenter asserts, "Women are the caretakers of society: We provide for basic needs, remedy injuries, make peace, and in general play the unique and essential dual roles of (superstar) supporter and (underrated) leader" (Oz).

Although the focus on women's domestic responsibilities was originally called upon to discourage women from driving, the auto industry soon recognized the importance of the female consumer base and adjusted its marketing strategy accordingly. Rather than suggest the automobile would cause women to abandon their caretaking role, auto manufacturers developed a product and an advertising plan that both confirmed and celebrated it. The station wagon grew out of this philosophy, as did its successors the minivan, hatchback, small SUV, and crossover. Functional, reliable, sturdy, and safe, these vehicles not only addressed the needs of wives and mothers, but firmly reinforced women's role

Eric and Nicole Mott began accompanying mom Annie to cars shows at a young age. Now in their twenties and out on their own, they remain active in the muscle car hobby and try to make it home every August for the Woodward Dream Cruise. And while they no longer have daily access to a fast, loud, and powerful muscle car, as pilots in control of their own aircrafts, Eric and Nicole are able to recreate the excitement and exhilaration they experienced as young car enthusiasts in the front seat of mom's 1970 Dodge Challenger Hemi R/T (courtesy Annie Mott).

as the family caretaker. Rather than remove women from domesticity, the "family car" assured she was firmly ensconced within it.

While the family vehicle—and its association with caretaking—became an acceptable mode of transportation for the woman behind the wheel, the muscle car morphed into its opposite. The objection to women as muscle car drivers gained traction not only due to the perception that women were biologically incapable of handling such a powerful machine, but also because it removed women from the quiet, safe, and proper confines of domesticity and placed them into the noisy, rebellious, and masculine seat of a muscle car. The contradiction of these two locations dictated that the woman who identifies as caretaker has neither a reasonable nor legitimate place in this hyper masculine space.

Yet the women who own muscle cars today have, in fact, integrated themselves into muscle car culture. They have achieved this not through rebellion against gender mandates, but rather, through the assumption and reinvention of the caretaker role. The women understand that in the conservative car culture community, women will be more easily integrated through acceptance of traditional gender roles rather than rejection of them. As women who identify primarily as moderate to conservative, they understand the importance of the caretaker role to family and community. As Baehr notes, conservative feminism "seeks to reconcile women to conventional social forms" (118). Taking on the caretaker role within muscle car culture allows women to position themselves as valuable in a number of ways. The women establish themselves as caretakers of husbands, family, and relationships. They view their involvement in muscle car culture as a means to strengthen marital relationships through a shared interest in cars, to promote family values, and to encourage automotive interest in future generations. The women also promote themselves as caretakers of community. They take on leadership roles within muscle car organizations, organize events that benefit local charities, and arrange social gatherings that bring members of the community together. And lastly, the women assume the role as caretaker of cars. This is exemplified through historical caretaking, i.e., using their own cars to promote the history of the muscle car, as well as the physical care of the automobile.

Fifty years ago, women who attempted to enter muscle car culture were dismissed as unessential and problematic and relegated to the sidelines. Today's female muscle car enthusiasts have made an important and acceptable place for themselves in muscle car culture as caretakers of family, community, and cars. By assuming a caretaker role in multiple ways, these women are able to contribute to muscle car culture in a manner consistent with conservative values while proving themselves invaluable to the culture itself.

> *At first the guys were leery of women; it really was a "boys'" club when I first joined but as more women have joined, they realize we love our cars and take care of them and work on them, and once they realized that we loved the cars for the cars they are and not to be "sexy," more women were accepted.*
> —63-year-old 1966 Ford Mustang owner

CARETAKER OF FAMILY

The majority of women interviewed for this project—no matter what generation of car owned or driven—take part in events or activities associated with the muscle car. While the women enjoy the social aspect of participation, what is considered of primary importance is how their involvement in the muscle car hobby has the potential to strengthen spousal relationships and promote family unity. Married women view participation as a way to get to know their spouses better through a joint interest in cars. Mothers often encourage up-and-coming car enthusiasts to accompany them to automotive events, or seek automotive advice from their car savvy adult offspring. These women engage their children in auto-related activities not only to instill automotive interest in future generations, but to also construct muscle car activity as a family activity. Through attendance at muscle car events—alongside husbands or with children in tow— these women demonstrate support of spousal endeavors as well as the importance of family to their lives. As they insert themselves into muscle car culture as caretakers of relationships and families, the women gain legitimacy as muscle car owners while remaining true to conservative values.

Many of the women cited a young man's car as the catalyst for a relationship. The 48-year-old owner of a 2003 Mustang met her husband-to-be on an online Mustang forum. As she explained, "He had a '68 and we got to talking and one thing led to another. And pretty soon he's selling his car for my engagement ring." As teenagers, many found young men with hot cars to be irresistible. As a 55-year-old 2010 Challenger owner remarked, "My college boyfriend was into cars, specifically Mopars. He had a 1973 Duster with a 340 4-barrel. His friends were car guys and we all hung out together or would go cruising together." To others, interest in a young man's car became a way to attract his attention and keep it after tying the knot. Noted the 58-year-old owner of a 1972 Mustang, "my husband, who I met in high school, was always into cars; so I became interested over 39 years of marriage." A 62-year-old 1970 Plymouth 'Cuda owner confessed that she wasn't interested in muscle cars "until I started dating my now husband in 1966." While many of the women developed an appreciation for cars under encouragement from car-crazy spouses, other cited an interest in Camaros or Mustangs as a qualification for marriage. A love of muscle cars was a priority for a 49-year-old 1969 Charger owner, divorced from her first husband, upon contemplation of the dating pool. As she remarked, "I had really hoped that I'd meet a guy that liked to work on cars. And I'm thankful [to have met my fiancé] because [cars are] such a part of my life."

Yet no matter how the muscle car served to link couples past or present, the married women in this project cultivated an interest in the muscle car as a means to nurture and maintain relationships. As a 58-year-old 2014 Dodge Challenger SRT owner confessed, "That's possibly what kept [my husband] and I together all these years, was the fact that we always had an interest in the cars." Although most had to put their own automotive desires aside for domestic responsibilities after marriage, they kept their love of cars on hold until the circumstances were right to join their husbands in the hobby. They view joint muscle car ownership as an indication of how much they care for their husbands and value their marriage vows. Participation alongside spouses in car clubs or driving events demonstrates how they honor and respect the caretaking role. As Baehr notes, the conservative feminist subscribes to the notion that "social relationships are constitutive of, not mrerely potentially instrumental to, well-being" (106). The women in this project believe they are responsible not only for their own well-being, but that of family members as well. The assumption of the caretaking role within car culture allows women to express their love not only for the American muscle car, but also for the men in their lives.

Female muscle car owners also take on the caretaker role to construct muscle car culture as a family activity. Rather than consider involvement with fast and powerful cars as an adult-only pursuit, the women encourage children to take an interest in cars as a form of family sharing and bonding. Many of the women pass on their love of muscle cars as a way to keep families intact. As the owner of a 1970 Dodge Challenger explained, "My husband, you know he kind of shares those same thoughts, and [our daughter] certainly enjoys it, so it's become kind of a family affair. If any one of us didn't enjoy it, I don't think it would have blossomed like it did." The 27-year-old owner of a 1971 Pontiac GT-37 grew up in a car household and although now on her own, takes part in a local car show each year to catch up with family. As she noted, "this event has become tradition and the four of us get to spend time together." A 53-year-old store manager has passed on the love of Pontiac Trans Am to her two sons. The Trans Am is recognized for the iconic Firebird decal—commonly referred to as the "bird"—on its hood. As she noted, "we do carry the tattoos; we have the bird tattoos on us. It's truly a family thing. When you can carry the tattoo of a Firebird, that's a pretty big commitment." Creating a space in muscle car culture for family provides women with the opportunity to demonstrate that ownership of a muscle car does not result in abandonment of the caretaking role. Rather, it offers the potential to expand and celebrate it.

Many of the women developed an interest in muscle cars through male offspring. After her husband's death, a 62-year-old widow was encouraged to get involved in muscle cars by her son as a means to "get out of the house" and "meet new people." As she noted, "He was the only one; he was the one I started going [to car shows] with." A 66-year-old 1966 Dodge Charger owner would often come home to find that her son had scattered car parts all over the house. Yet rather than admonish him, she took an interest in his hobby. Now she, her husband, and son attend car events together. As she explained, "usually the son takes his '69 and we take our two '66 Chargers and we all park together; it's just a fun time." The women in this project viewed sharing the automotive interests of husbands and sons as an important component of the caretaking role. As Kersten notes, a woman's focus on caretaking duties does not require that she "deny her own needs and interests to please others, as women have been forced to do in the past." Rather, as Kersten argues, the conservative feminist understands that it is the web of connections with others that produces a sense of purpose, "by creating a meaningful role in an enterprise larger than her own finite existence." To the women who own muscle cars, the role is often that of family caretaker.

Constructing muscle car culture as a family affair not only provides women with the opportunity to strengthen family relationships, but to pass on automotive knowledge to the next generation as well. Often the auto education starts early; it is not uncommon at local car events to see a baby carrier in the back seat of a powerful, throaty Mustang or Camaro. The 41-year-old owner of a 1970 Dodge Charger R/T has been taking her son to car shows since he was three months old. As she related with a fair amount of pride, while attending a local car show at the age of two, her son "was pointing out the Challengers and the 'Cudas. The guy in front of us stopped and said, 'boy, he really knows his cars.'" A 65-year-old owner of a 1970 Plymouth Superbird was delighted to mention that her son's first words were "beep beep." Many of the women have passed on or purchased muscle cars for children and grandchildren as a means to sustain and encourage family automotive involvement. As the 62-year-old owner of a 1970 Plymouth 'Cuda remarked, "We gave our grandson a 1972 Duster for graduation. He and his dad both drag race their Dusters." To the women in this project, the passing on of automotive knowledge from one generation to the next was considered integral to women's caretaking role. Not only does it demonstrate women's care and devotion to family, but also insures the future care of the American muscle car.

Caretaker of Cars

The reluctance to accept women as muscle car drivers stems from the longstanding belief that women are neither interested in, nor are they capable of, attending to the mechanics of cars. In the first few decades of motoring, knowledge of auto mechanics was often considered a prerequisite to driving. The complexity of the machinery, and the filth associated with car care suggested that only male drivers were properly qualified to attend to the mysterious machinations of the gasoline automobile. Commenting on the representation of a female automotive consumer in a 1932 Fisher Body ad, Laura Behling writes, "her overtly accentuated characteristics of attractive feminine womanhood, a long-legged blonde beauty and comically inept mechanical nuisance, epitomizes her disinterest in the male-dominated realm of technical knowledge" (28). However, automotive history suggests that rather than an innate incapacity to understand automotive mechanics, it was gender prescriptions of the time regarding proper female behavior that discouraged all but the most determined women from learning about the inner workings of cars.

Although women's automotive interest and experience has increased significantly since the early motor age, the woman driver remains technologically suspect. Gender stereotypes continue to portray the woman behind the wheel as an individual who—exasperated and confused by auto mechanics—leaves car care to those more qualified. Facing the longstanding perception of women drivers as technologically incompetent, the women in this project often gained legitimacy in muscle car culture as caretakers of cars. This was accomplished in various ways: through display of mechanical expertise, acquisition of automotive knowledge, and demonstration of proficient and meticulous car care.

A few of the women have always had an interest in how cars operate and use the opportunity of muscle car ownership to hone and display their expertise. A 51-year-old non-profit director performed most of the restoration work on her 1966 Chevrolet Impala. As she related, "I have done everything except detailed body work, welding, and specific upholstery work." Growing up in a car family provided the opportunity for many of the women to learn about basic car maintenance and repair. To these muscle car owners, family projects often included tearing a car apart and putting it back together again. As a 22-year-old 1966 Mustang owner remarked, "my father and I built this car with some occasional help from my mother and sister." A 37-year-old 1974 Chevy Nova owner learned about cars as a young girl working alongside her father. As she explained, "he'd have us out there, helping him with brake jobs, when we were little kids."

Some of the women pursued auto shop classes in order to become familiar with the inner workings of automobiles and to become more self-sufficient. The owner of a 1978 Camaro LT attended night classes in order to learn basic maintenance skills. A 42-year-old receptionist, who acquired her 1982 Mustang when she was 17, enrolled in auto body-work and painting courses at a local community college. As she noted, "then I got involved into making it go quicker and painting the car and just kept it all those years." Others worked on their own cars under the tutelage of husbands. As the 56-year-old owner of a 1973 Dodge Challenger explained, "I've helped [my husband] when he stripped the motor out of it and stripped the engine compartment. I learned to sandblast; I learned to paint; I did lots of things."

Women with retro muscle cars—which are more complicated to work on than older cars due to the computerization of auto technology—mastered automotive basics to keep the cars running smoothly. As the 41-year-old owner of a 2006 Dodge Charger Daytona remarked, "I empty the catch can, top up the fluids, and wipe out the throttle body. I help my husband change the tires and change the oil." Working on one's own car—whether alone or with a family member—not only provides women with a sense of accomplishment, but also suggests they are to be taken seriously as muscle car owners. Recognition as a caretaker of cars provides them with important access into muscle car culture.

Those without the experience in auto maintenance seek out individuals who are skilled, trustworthy, and competent for car care. Often the women look no farther than their own garages. Of her 1993 and 2012 Mustangs, a 50-year-old automotive project coordinator remarked, "my husband has a hoist in our pole barn. We don't let anybody touch them." And as a 63-year-old 1970 Dodge Challenger owner asserted, "no one touches this but my husband." However, those without technologically inclined family members are likely to ask for recommendations from other muscle car fanciers and interview prospective mechanics extensively. When it comes to caring for a woman's muscle car, only the best and most honest will do. Noted a 54-year-old 1967 Pontiac LeMans owner, "I have a great and trustworthy mechanic who has taken very good care of the car for me." A 39-year-old 1967 Dodge Dart owner stated, "I do the cleaning and minor stuff but leave the majority of work to the local shop professionals. I've been going there for years and have a comfort level with some of the mechanics." Although those with newer cars under warranty take them to the dealership for service, older cars that require special care are handed over to trusted muscle car experts.

Whether women work on their own cars, share in maintenance with husbands, turn the cars over to mechanically inclined sons, or put them in the hands of trustworthy professionals, there is one aspect of car care nearly all women share. And that is detailing. Detailing in the car hobby refers to the practice of thoroughly cleaning, restoring, and finishing an automobile to a quality level of detail. Although mechanical issues are often relegated to male family members, the women consider muscle car detailing as their responsibility. As a 62-year-old 1970 Plymouth 'Cuda owner remarked, "I clean and shine the car. My husband does the mechanical repairs." A 65-year-old 2013 Dodge Challenger R/T owner has an extensive maintenance routine. As she noted, "probably the best thing I do is the detailing. I learned how to use a Porter Cable D/A polisher, and I don't know anyone else around here that even knows what they are. I love to keep my paint scratch free and wash the car at least once a week!" And as a 54-year-old 2014 Chevy Camaro 2SS/RS owner explained, "I detail the engine myself, clay and clean the entire car."

Claiming detailing for themselves, the women in this project call upon a traditional gendered task to gain acceptance as muscle car owners. Despite women's entry into the workplace, women are still considered responsible for household cleanliness.[1] As Cindy Donatelli writes, although men have taken on a greater share of household duties in the twenty-first century, "women continue to bear primary responsibility for housework" (90). Various industries and products have been developed, marketed, and sustained on the premise that a woman's worth is linked to how well her home is maintained. As Ruth Schwartz Cowan argues, during the twentieth century "inventors and entrepreneurs and advertising copywriters and consumers simply assumed that the separation of spheres was a normal arrangement" ("More" 69). However, due to the automobile's association with masculinity, detailing has long been considered an acceptable form of "cleaning" among male car aficionados. As Dag Balkmar notes, although cleaning is commonly associated with femininity and something that women do, taking care of cars by washing and polishing them is a "male-defined expert position" (194). Thus women who engage in detailing are using their own gendered prescribed position as "cleaners" to take over what has traditionally been considered a male practice. Reconfiguring detailing into women's work provides female motorists with access into muscle car culture. Through the practice of detailing, women provide evidence of both their dedication to car care and their legitimacy as muscle car owners.

CARETAKER OF COMMUNITY

There can be little argument that the muscle car offers women an automotive experience that is invigorating, empowering, and exhilarating. Yet while the women who contributed to this project were quick to cite the physical pleasures of muscle car ownership, the benefit cited repeatedly was access to an extended car community. Not only does muscle car culture offer the possibility of new social networks, but provides women with the opportunity to serve, enrich, and advance the community through the role of caretaker. In its original incarnation, muscle car culture served as a site for the production and performance of masculinity. However, the integration of women into its ranks has transformed the culture from that of a male-centric automotive space into a community focused on the sharing of information, charitable works, and attending to others. As they assume the role of caretaker, the women in this project honor the muscle car not only for its power and technology, but also as a means to serve the car community and the region at large.

When participating in car events, the women's priorities often differ from those of husbands. While the men like to compete for awards, the women's intentions tend toward the altruistic. As a 59-year-old 1965 Mustang owner remarked, "I participate in events that are charity involved. I know I'm no competition for a lot of the cars there. I go because I want to go." Although not all women seek membership in car clubs, many of those who do take an active part as officers and organizers of fundraising events. Stated the 49-year-old secretary-treasurer of the Wayne County Misfits—a Detroit area club—"we do car shows and fundraisers here locally, and then we donate the money to various charities throughout the year." A 58-year-old 1970 GTO owner and Runaways of Michigan Car Club officer remarked, "We host a car show to raise funds in our community for the food shelter." A 43-year-old veterinarian noted that one of her first acts as a 1966 Dodge Charger owner was to hold a car show to benefit the local humane society. As she noted, "We organized it, got food, got the music, you know packed up the flyers, got games for the kids, and everything." The women in this project were especially active in fundraisers for organizations associated with women and children. They worked tirelessly to organize, promote, and put on car shows that benefited causes such as breast cancer, local women's shelters, special education, and juvenile diabetes.

While the women were active in fundraising endeavors, they also called upon the muscle car to bring joy to inhabitants of local institutions and organizations. A 47-year-old accounting manager parked her 1972 Plymouth Barracuda under the DAR Veterans tent at the Woodward Dream Cruise—an annual Detroit celebration of the muscle car. As she reflected on the men who came to admire the cars, "It was nostalgia for them, because that was right after Viet Nam, so it helps bring back a lot of memories, good kinds." A 62-year-old 1971 Ford Gran Torino owner organizes car shows at local senior communities. As she remarked, "I've been to several nursing homes with the car. And the older people get such a kick out of seeing the cars they grew up with." Car shows are also held at children's wards at local hospitals as a way for kids and their parents to spend a few hours together out of the hospital room. Female muscle car owners organize and participate in these events so that those who can't physically transport themselves to car shows can experience the joy and exhilaration of a noisy and powerful Mustang or GTO.

The women who contributed to this project also work to make the muscle car community more open and welcoming for those new to the hobby. They mentioned the sharing of information, sources, and advice with car enthusiasts as an important component of participation. Women with older cars—classic and pony—use the opportunity of car shows and local automotive events to exchange information and share resources. As a 39-year-old 1969 Plymouth GTX owner related, "I've learned about some good service companies in the area and taken advantage of the references to these businesses." Women with past car experience believe an important part of car community participation is the passing of automotive knowledge to others. A 56-year-old 1971 Pontiac Firebird owner remarked, "It gives me a sense of satisfaction to help people working on their cars. That they can benefit from what I've gone through." Women with retro muscle cars often seek advice on online automotive forums. As a 58-year-old 2014 Dodge Challenger SRT owner explained, "The information, the data base that you can get from one of these forums now is just incredible." Many of the women—who have experienced sexism from male car enthusiasts—have taken on leadership roles within the online community to make the car forum experience more welcoming to female muscle car enthusiasts. A 55-year-old 2012 Dodge Challenger owner—and administrator on a national Challenger forum—has developed close online friendships with other female participants. As she confessed, "the Challenger forum is a home away from home for me." Through taking part in physical and virtual car communities as administrators, leaders, and organizers, these women work to make the muscle car community a more caring and inviting place.

In her philosophical reconstruction of Elizabeth Fox-Genovese's treatise on conservative feminism, Amy Baehr notes, "when Fox Genovese writes 'women's lives are important to themselves but also to society,' [...] she means that women play a crucial role in the kinds of relationships that are constitutive of well-being [...] She means it is important for women to live a certain way because their well-being and the well-being of others depends on it" (106). While the women who contributed to this project do not self-identify as feminists, their actions are indicative of a conservative feminist sensibility. As they assume the role of caretaker within the car community, female muscle car owners quietly yet effectively alter the culture's ethos. As women incorporate themselves into muscle car culture through the role of caregiver, they have the opportunity to transform it into a community that not only celebrates the automobile, but also calls upon a material object they share—the muscle car—to benefit the lives, needs, well-being, and experiences of others in meaningful and important ways.

Sentimentalist

The male driver's interest in the classic muscle car is often attributed to nostalgia. While men still in their peak earning years are likely to view an older muscle car as an investment, the majority of aging auto aficionados consider the classic GTO or Charger as a means to relive or reimagine an illusory past. Nostalgia, write Michael Pickering and Emily Keightley, "is centrally concerned with the concept of loss" (923). It is expressed through a longing for a lost time or for something that is no longer attainable. Thus men

Jenny Brinker-Wagstrom grew up in a family of 10 children and shared cars with her brothers and sisters. She purchased her 1970 Plum Crazy Dodge Challenger brand new (top) with the money saved from her first job right out of high school. Jenny has kept the now restored Challenger (bottom) all of these years because, as she noted, "it's the only thing I've ever owned that I paid for. And just the fact that I fell in love with her" (courtesy Jenny Brinker-Wagstrom).

often purchase cars that replicate those they had as teenagers, or acquire the cars they desired but couldn't afford when they were young. When behind the wheel of a loud, powerful, raucous classic muscle car, balding seniors are temporarily transported to a time of their lives when they were young, handsome, virile, and carefree. While as teenagers they congregated on street corners and urban thoroughfares, these aging car buffs and their classic machines can now be found at car shows and cruises talking about engines, speed, performance, and the good old days. As a 52-year-old 1969 Super Bee owner asserted, to men of a certain age, owning a classic muscle car "is all about nostalgia."

Nostalgia plays a role in men's attraction to the modern day muscle car as well. In recapturing the style, performance, and brazenness of their automotive ancestors, the twenty-first-century Mustang, Camaro, Charger, and Challenger harken to an automotive past in which American power—and masculinity—were celebrated. In the production of modern day muscle, notes former Chrysler design chief Trevor Creed, "our job is to make the dream come true and give [men] back the reality they remember" (qtd. in "Muscles," Naughton). Not only is the modern muscle car appealing to those who came of driving age during the 1960s and 1970s, but is also attractive to younger car buyers who possess an "appreciation for Detroit's past glory" (Boudette). The ability of the modern day muscle to evoke a powerful automotive past makes it a nostalgic choice for male consumers no matter what the generation.[2]

However, while nostalgia in the traditional sense—i.e., longing for a past time—may be considered the motivation for men's present day muscle car interest, it is expressed and experienced differently by the female muscle car owner. Women's past muscle car experience is unlike that of their male peers, particularly to members of the baby boomer generation. While there were some young women who participated in classic muscle car culture as drivers, the majority took part vicariously through boyfriends or brothers or not at all. Even in the present day it is not uncommon for young women with an interest in American muscle to be directed toward more practical, gender appropriate cars. Thus rather than frame participation in muscle car culture as a nostalgic reliving of the past, the women in this project often consider the muscle car as a sentimental—and significant—connection to an individual or experience from their personal history. To many female car enthusiasts, possession of a Camaro or Mustang allows them to pay tribute to a cherished family member, acknowledge past automotive desires, move on after a loss, or celebrate the muscle car as a longtime companion. Pickering and Keightley argue that rather than consider nostalgia only as a desire to return to an idealized past, nostalgia can also be called upon "to recognize the past as the basis for renewal and satisfaction in the future" (921). While women's expression of nostalgia differs from that of men, the shared affection for the muscle car as a connection to something or someone from an earlier time or experience serves as common ground with male enthusiasts and provides women with an entryway into muscle car culture.

> *Oh, it was my husband's dream car. [Before he passed] he made me promise him I would take it out. So I do it, and I do it grumbling. It can put a smile to my face or it can bring a tear to my eye. You know it's just, it's that bittersweet. I would love to have him back in the driver's seat of it.*
>
> —58-year-old 1970 Mustang owner

In Memoriam

The inscription on the front license plate of a 1974 Chevy Nova reads, "In memory of my Dad, I'll race you in heaven." Like many of the women who participated in this project, the Nova's 37-year-old owner developed an interest in automobiles through her father. As she remarked, "I started going to car shows while I was in a stroller with him." She purchased the Nova because her dad "fell in love with it." They worked on it together until his sudden death of a brain aneurism. As she noted, "I don't think I could ever get rid of it now, with my dad and everything. There's a lot of my dad in that car." A 47-year-old 1965 Mustang owner often accompanied her father to his job as a mechanic when she was a girl. As she remarked, "I remember going into the garage where he worked, and I just loved the smell." After his passing, she decided to honor him and his love for cars by using his childhood nickname for her on the classic Mustang's personalized license plate.

A 43-year-old veterinarian developed an interest in cars as a child in order to become closer to her father. As she remarked, "So he was always in the garage, and as he said, he had two girls, but he treated us just like if we were his sons, and we were always out there helping him in the garage and handing him tools." When she had the means to acquire a classic muscle car of her own, her choice was a 1966 Dodge Charger, which while growing up was the family car. She and her dad drove down to an auction in North Carolina together to make the purchase. As she noted, she could never give the car up "because this is something I share with my dad." A 32-year-old nurse practitioner spent many years of her childhood in the garage alongside her father as he worked on various cars. They spent much of that time working on the 1968½ Ford Shelby Mustang now parked in her garage. As she exclaimed, "the Shelby means a lot because my father entrusted it to me; I am so blessed that we still get to enjoy it together, too!" To many of the women interviewed for this project, growing up around car-crazy dads not only created an affinity for automobiles, but also provided them with the opportunity to develop a close relationship with the first man in their lives. As a 2011 Camaro SS/RS owner explained, helping her "car guy" dad and accompanying him to automotive events "was a way to bond with him." To these women, a muscle car often serves as a means to remember, honor, or connect to a much-loved father.

Women who develop a passion for cars through car-loving husbands are often unable to let go of the vehicle after a spouse's passing. Stated a 61-year-old 1970 Monte Carlo owner, "My cars mean a whole heck of a lot. My cars, my husband, there's so much of him in there." When asked how she feels when driving the 1994 Camaro that belonged to her late husband, a 71-year-old widow remarked, "I think about him a lot when I'm driving it just because he was so proud of that car." A 1970 Mustang was a project a 58-year-old nurse and her late husband worked on together. During his time in hospice, she pledged to him she would continue to take it out on occasion. As she noted, "I want to keep the promise to him; he would have done this, oh my gosh he would have been in it day and night. He loved it." Before the husband of a 56-year-old Michigan factory worker passed away from cancer, he presented her with her dream car, a 1968 Camaro. She and her son rebuilt the car together as part of the healing process after her husband's death. As she remarked, "[the Camaro] is a part of me and a loving gift from him that I will always treasure."

While these women may not have been the primary driver of the car when the original owner was alive, retaining ownership of the automobile is a means of keeping a deceased loved one close. Of her 1972 Mustang, a 58-year-old secretary remarked, "My mother bought it new and it was her daily driver until her stroke until 1992." A 58-year-old retired special education teacher enjoys driving her grandchildren in the 1970 Pontiac GTO once owned by her late husband. A 65-year-old educator has four classic muscle cars accumulated over her 37-year marriage. Although her husband passed away a number of years ago, she maintains and drives the cars as a way to keep active in the classic muscle car community, convey the historical significance of the classic muscle car to future generations, and to keep the memory of her husband alive. As she stated, "I'm really glad that I kept them after my husband passed because we had so much fun with them." While these women had the option to sell the cars upon the death of a loved one, each chose to keep, maintain, and drive the vehicle as a means to honor that individual's love of automobiles. In the process, each of these women developed a special and sentimental relationship to the muscle car.

As Kathleen Franz notes, corporations, engineers, and consumers aided in the construction of the automobile, determining its cultural importance as a machine, consumer product, and form of mobility" ("Automobiles" 53). However, as this group of women demonstrates, the meanings women attribute to the automobile often have little to do with popular conceptions of its "cultural importance." Rather, the women who inherited an interest in cars through fathers, as well as the women who shared in the classic muscle car hobby with husbands, view those vehicles as a means to keep a loved one close by celebrating that individual's life and passion for automobiles.

LONGTIME ADMIRER

Young boys are often introduced to cars at an early age through interaction with toys, books, films, and video games. Exposure to these car-themed materials while an impressionable youngster often leads to a lifelong interest in and familiarity with automobiles. As Wendy Varney suggests, automotive playthings and other "toys that move" have traditionally been designated as "boys' toys" as a way to enforce gender roles and encourage interest in masculine activities (154). These auto influences often follow a young boy through his teenage years and into adulthood. It should not be surprising, therefore, that the majority of participants in various car cultures are male.

However, as the interviews with the women in this project suggest, enthusiasm for cars is not a male-only proposition. Many of the women developed automotive interests at an early age through their relationships with fathers, brothers, and male friends. As they witnessed the joy, confidence, and freedom cars brought to the men in their lives, they longed to acquire these automotive experiences themselves. A 65-year-old 1969 Camaro Z/28 owner—who grew up with eight brothers—coveted one of her siblings' Camaros. As she confessed, "I would steal that car at age 14. And I would go out riding through the neighborhood." A 54-year-old 2009 Dodge Charger R/T owner spent her teenage years among car-crazy young men. Her brother and the boyfriend who was to become her husband would routinely take motors apart, reconstruct them, and enter the souped-up vehicles in local demolition derbies. As she reminisced, "they were always into the cars so I always followed them and I never had one of my own." A 49-year-old office manager grew up in a family with an affinity for Chargers. As she noted, "my brother got one when he was a junior in high school and I was like five years old. And my dad got him a new one. And by the time I was twelve I realized I wanted one." A 50-year-old 2012 Mustang GT owner attributes her interest in cars to her father, who worked for Ford Motor Company. As she exclaimed, "I grew up in Dearborn, Michigan, so we were always exposed and right in the heart of seeing all the new models and prototypes. I don't know anything different."

As the responses suggest, women who have frequent contact with male car enthusiasts at a young age are likely to develop an enthusiasm for cars similar in intensity to that of male peers. In their study of masculine and feminine automotive behaviors, Smart, Campbell, Soper and Buboltz, Jr., conclude, "Traditionally, men have been more exposed to automotive technology and have been educated about such functions. Women's liberation and emancipation have contributed to increased female interest in activities previously considered largely within the male domain." In addition, the women in this project were often influenced to favor a particular make or model based on the automotive loyalties of fathers, brothers, and boyfriends and kept that preference for a lifetime. Because most young women were unable to act upon their own automotive desires, their passion for a Mustang or Camaro grew exponentially over time. As longtime admirers of a special car, these women experienced both satisfaction and joy when the circumstances were right to procure the long admired dream cars for themselves.

Some of the women's lifelong admiration for a particular car began as what can only be described as a "car crush." As teenagers, they often collected car photos and other auto related paraphernalia in the same manner as their girlfriends accumulated pictures of teen idols. A 65-year-old 2013 Dodge Challenger R/T owner added, "As a young child growing up in the late '50s, I must have been drawn to cars! I have pictures of cars pasted in an old scrapbook that I cut out of magazines when I was maybe 10 years old." A 55-year-old 2012 Dodge Challenger R/T owner asserted, "I still have every single Matchbox that I played with when I was five years old. I never owned a Barbie doll. It's always been cars." While the majority of their female peers spent free time perusing popular teen publications, these women were more likely to borrow car magazines from brothers and boyfriends. As a 41-year-old 2006 Dodge Charger owner remarked, "growing up I always liked Corvettes and read *Car Craft* magazine." And although, as a teenager, most of her peers developed crushes on rock stars, a 47-year-old elementary teacher shared her love of Camaros with her best friend. As she recollected, "we used to pick out sports cars sitting at her house looking at I95, staring at cars going by." As an adult, she placated her muscle car craving with not one but two Camaros: a 1989 Camaro RS and a 2001 Berger Camaro SS. As the testimonies of these women suggest, a love affair with the muscle car often begins when a teenage girl comes of driving age. Yet those dreams are often required to be put on hold until the women's financial, professional, and personal circumstances make it possible to acquire a muscle car.

Because the majority of women who participated in this project hailed from Southeastern Michigan, many had ties to the auto industry in some capacity. To these women, the admiration for a particular car developed from exposure, proximity, and brand loyalty. A 50-year-old 1993 Mustang GT owner grew up in a Ford family; as she exclaimed, "I have Ford Blue blood!"[3] She now works as a Decommissioning Project Coordinator for Ford Motor Company. Her family background in the auto industry, as well as her experience at the prototype plant, has made her a longtime admirer of Ford in general and the Mustang in particular. As she declared, "I was born and raised to be a car chick." A 54-year-old engineer's longtime interest in cars led her to a career in the auto industry and a 2014 Mustang GT in her driveway. As she remarked, once her daughter left for college "it was the time to have a Mustang." A 56-year-old project manager worked on the Camaro program in Australia. When the opportunity came to work for General Motors in the U.S., her affinity for the Camaro intensified. It was at this time, she exclaimed, "I just really, really had to have one."

While young women today have fewer financial and cultural obstacles to obtaining a muscle car, the majority of women in this project—particularly those of the baby boomer generation—often had to put their dreams of a Mustang or Camaro aside until they had the means and opportunity to become muscle car owners. Often the barriers were financial. As a 64-year-old Pontiac GTO owner remarked, "I always wanted one when I was in school. I wanted one but I couldn't afford it." Family responsibilities were also a factor. A 60-year-old 1971 Dodge Charger Super Bee owner explained, "I always wanted one but like I said, it just wasn't in our budget at the time we were raising our kids. Just couldn't afford 'em." And gender proscriptions of the time—i.e., what women should and shouldn't spend money on—also influenced a woman's auto purchase decisions. Although a 47-year-old accounting manager took part in the muscle car scene with friends as a teenager, it was always as a passenger, never as a driver. As the 1972 Plymouth Barracuda owner declared, "they told us that you're not supposed to be in it, that kind of thing."

The endless wait from dream to reality made the possession of a muscle car all the sweeter for this group of women drivers. Whether attributed to financial success, encouragement from children or spouses, or serendipitous circumstances, the opportunity to finally own a Charger or Challenger was revered, appreciated, and celebrated by women of all ages and with all generations of cars. As a 1965 Mustang convertible owner declared, "I never thought my dream would come true."

LONGTIME OWNER

The original muscle car was produced, marketed, and used as a daily driver. As Mark Yost writes, muscle cars "weren't the specialty vehicles that Detroit made for car shows and drag races. These were the cars that Detroit mass-produced." And although many modern day muscle cars are garaged in the winter, the majority of new Mustangs and Camaros are called upon for everyday use. As a daily driver, it would be expected that the muscle car would have a road life comparable to that of other automobiles of its respective era. The automotive archives bear this out. During the 1960s and early 1970s, men's muscle car ownership was often cut short due to a heightened incidence of speeding tickets and the high insurance rates that inevitably followed. In today's automotive marketplace, the average length of time drivers keep a new vehicle is estimated at 6 years.[4] As a vehicle subject to rising repair costs, technological obsolescence, and changing driver preferences, the daily driver is rarely a long-term investment.

Although automotive habits and history would indicate that the muscle car was a relatively short-term acquisition, the responses from the women in this project suggest otherwise. To many of these women, ownership of a muscle car—whether classic, pony, or retro—is a lifelong commitment. While it may have been originally purchased as a daily driver, the muscle car has, in many cases, become an important part of a woman's personal and automotive history. Because of this unique auto-human connection, a good number of the female contributors held onto their muscle cars for decades, if not a lifetime.

While the majority who contributed to this project did not own muscle cars as young adults, there were a few who were able to save up for a new Mustang or Firebird. As single young women, they often lived with parents and worked part-time jobs in order to accumulate the down payment for a muscle car of their own. However, many of the women faced considerable resistance to muscle car ownership, particularly after marriage. There was an expectation that once wed they would give up their fast and powerful vehicles for something more practical and family friendly. Some women found it necessary to acquiesce to the pressure they experienced as young wives. A 53-year-old auto industry engineer used wages from her first job to purchase a new Trans Am. As she noted, "I worked hard to pay cash for this car and everything." Yet upon marriage to her childhood sweetheart, she reluctantly gave up the car she worked so hard for. As she remarked, "[my husband] made me get rid of it, not long after we were married, buried it in a snow bank in front of our house." Although she was able to purchase the Mustang of her dreams as a single woman working at Ford Motor Company, the young administrative assistant had to give it up for a more gender appropriate vehicle after marriage. As the now 73-year-old 1964½ Mustang owner proclaimed, "And so I just fell in love with it, and owned one in 1965, and had to sell it three years later because it just was not a family car, 'cause there were two children. And an Irish Setter."

However, there were others who held onto their muscle cars despite opposition from spouses and family members. A 53-year-old store manager purchased her 1977 Pontiac Trans Am right out of high school. As she asserted, "This car has been a part of my life. I've been through my husband badgering me to sell it because we needed to pay bills. I'm so fortunate that I still have this car." The special attachment women have for the muscle car can often be attributed to their ability to acquire and hold on to a Camaro or Challenger over a persistent chorus of dissenting voices.

Many of the women who contributed to this project—particularly those of the baby boomer generation—spent very little time as single independent women before marriage. Some went directly from their childhood residence to one shared with a husband. Most did not work outside the home while raising children. As primarily conservative women, they embraced the ideals of traditional marriage and subordinated their own desires to those of husbands and families. Thus the muscle car is often the only possession in their household of which they can claim sole ownership. A 63-year-old retired retail manager fell in love with her Plum Crazy 1970 Dodge Challenger when she saw it pictured in an automotive catalog. As she told me, "I was not quite 21 when I ordered her and she was in the center of the brochure. I saw it and that was it. I just knew it was my car and I ordered it right there." She kept the Challenger for over 40 years, for as she explained, "I worked hard for her and no one helped me out." A 47-year-old 1989 Camaro RS owner exclaimed, "I bought that car when I was 21. It was brand new. It was my first Camaro. She's my baby." Of her 1993 Mustang GT, a 50-year-old Ford project manager remarked, "It was my first baby. That was my first toy that I bought myself." While many automotive consumers consider their first vehicle as a starter car, these women—who worked hard to obtain the most substantive material possession of their young lives—kept their muscle cars as a reminder and symbol not of their youth, but of the fortitude and determination of a younger self.

While some of the women's first cars were purchased new, others were inherited or acquired from family members. A 56-year-old business analyst's 1971 Pontiac Firebird was originally purchased in 1977 as an extra car for the family. As she explained, "I bought it from my dad in about 1982. And I've had it ever since. Pretty much one of my absolute favorite cars." The car has been with her through two marriages and multiple across-the-country moves. As she remarked, "I've basically owned this car almost forever. And so it's just a part of me." When she needed a car for college in 1988, a 47-year-old x-ray technician purchased her brother's 1969 Mustang. It eventually became her school car, her work car, her bike-racing car, and her dog transport car. As she noted, "there were times when my whole life was in the car." A 39-year-old engineer learned to drive in the 1967 Dodge Dart that was given to her by her father as a graduation gift. As she noted, "the Dart is not only my first car but also the one I had in college, at the wedding, and every important event in my life." While the women were not the original owners of these muscle cars, as carriers of their personal histories the aging Mustangs, Camaros, and Firebirds have become irreplaceable.

Auto journalist Nanette Byrnes suggests that in the purchase of a muscle car, the male consumer is likely to consider qualities such as resale value and return for investment. For the majority of women who contributed to this project, the muscle car has significance beyond its monetary appreciation or iconic status. As a 49-year-old 1969 Dodge Charger owner asserted, "If it came down to me only being able to afford to have one car I would try to hold on to this one 'til the end. You know, I would hope that I have this car to the day I die."

REVENGE, RENEWAL, REINVENTION

The muscle car has long been associated with power, performance, risky behavior, and a little bit of outrageousness. While these qualities are attractive to individuals seeking a seat-of-your-pants driving experience, they also have special appeal to women recovering from personal loss. To women who have experienced the end of a relationship through death or divorce, getting behind the wheel of a Mustang or Challenger can be an empowering act. Whether seeking revenge, renewal, or reinvention, these women embodied the qualities ascribed to the muscle car as they entered a new phase of their lives.

Some of the women in this category indicated they were either forbidden to own a muscle car while married or had been forced to give up a Camaro or Firebird by a controlling spouse. The acquisition of a muscle car not only served these women as a less-than-subtle means of revenge, but also allowed them to establish themselves as tough, strong, and in control of their destinies. Of her 2003 Mustang, a 48-year-old massage therapist exclaimed, "I bought it as a divorce present to me because my ex-husband told me that I could never ever have a Mustang. So of course six months later I have a Mustang, and yes I did send him pictures." A 31-year-old color analyst lost her 1986 Firebird in a divorce. Yet rather than lament her loss, she worked hard to save for another. As she remarked, "When I was married I had a rough time. And when I got to pick the Firebird and drive a Firebird, that was the start of a new chapter in my life. Where I wasn't going to be a doormat anymore." After a 51-year-old graphic designer divorced, she set her sights on a 2014 Dodge Challenger SRT. As she declared, "I traded my wedding rings from my first marriage for it, too. It was kind of a symbol of my independence. And my freedom. And it was mine, and it wasn't going to mess around on me." The automotive choices these women made were as deliberate as they were symbolic. They chose muscle cars to demonstrate strength, determination, and courage. As a 31-year-old 1991 Firebird owner asserted, muscle car ownership became a declaration of, "being in charge of my own life and not letting anyone push me around ever again."

While some of the women viewed muscle car ownership as a form of revenge after a troubling relationship, others framed it as a way to restore happiness to their lives. A 73-year-old retired storeowner was unable to keep her original Mustang after her divorce. As she remarked, "I sold it and there was a big hole in my heart." Once she was on her feet financially and emotionally, her friends helped her find a 1973 Mustang convertible that she now describes as "the joy of my life." A 55-year-old CPA wanted to go into another automotive direction after the breakup of her marriage caused her to give up her Jaguar XJS. While she had not been a classic car enthusiast, as she noted, "my interest developed probably after I got divorced." She soon became the owner of a 1973 Mercury Cougar convertible and is now a regular participant at local muscle car events. A 46-year-old divorced special education teacher traded in her small economy car for a 1996 Mustang convertible. As she remarked, "At the time I was looking for a car that was more fun. More young. That didn't pigeonhole me as a certain kind of a person. Something that was out of my, out of the box, for me." A 59-year-old x-ray technician had an interest in muscle cars as a teenager, but was often left behind while her future husband cruised Woodward with his friends. She renewed her muscle car passion after her divorce through the acquisition of a 1965 Mustang. As she exclaimed, participation in muscle car culture "has made me branch out in different directions from what I've been used to all my life." As the responses from these women suggest, muscle car ownership has the potential to not only renew an infatuation with automobiles, but also offers the opportunity to set one's life journey on a new and exciting path.

Muscle car ownership also provides the possibility of reinventing oneself after a spouse's passing. A 62-year-old retired Ford employee was encouraged by her son to get involved in the muscle car hobby. Now the owner of a 1973 Mustang convertible and a 1971 Ford Gran Torino, she can often be found exhibiting her cars on weekends and cruising on Detroit thoroughfares on summer nights. As she remarked, "I was very depressed when my husband passed. And this has helped me get out and meet new people." Although she treasures the 1966 Mustang she shared with her late husband, a 63-year-old registered nurse found new hope with a new spouse and a 2006 Mustang convertible they purchased together. As she reflected, "[my husband] and I thought it might be fun to get a newer Mustang to be able to go in more comfort on longer cruises when our club gets together."

A 42-year-old manufacturing analyst lost her husband at a young age. She used the insurance money received after his passing to purchase a 2011 Camaro SS/RS convertible. She has subsequently found companionship and camaraderie through membership in a local 5th Gen Camaro Club and participation in Camaro themed events. As the inscription on the engine cover of her Silvermist-themed Camaro reads, "Dreams do come true."

Mimi Sheller asserts that when cars move beyond transportation to become something other that what they were intended—i.e., members of families, repositories for treasured offspring, and devices for demonstrating love—"they bring into being nonconscious forms of cognition and embodied dispositions which link human and machine in a deeply emotive bond" (232). As the responses from project participants suggest, women often develop an emotional connection to the muscle car after a personal loss. They call upon the muscle car's reputation as tough, strong, and outrageous to begin new lives as resilient and empowered women.

Pioneer

Although the relationship between women and cars is a subject that has not received a great deal of attention in academic and automotive literature, there is one category of woman driver that appears with some regularity in both locations. The "exceptional" woman driver—as represented in scholarship and popular culture—is most often an individual who has overcome significant hurdles to gain recognition in an automotive pursuit

As a Decommissioning Project Coordinator for Ford, Cindy Gillespie-Lena had the unique opportunity to follow the build of "Red Hot Ember"—her 1993 Mustang GT. As she explained, on the day production of the car was to be started, "I went over to Dearborn Assembly with my husband and our camera. We went into the plant with my coworker, and tracked down my car on the line as it was coming through the trim shop." She stopped driving the car to work for fear of debris and fallout from the plant. As Cindy exclaimed, "I kind of cherish my baby" (courtesy Cindy Gillespie-Lena).

commonly associated with the male driver. Those who populate this classification are most often female motorists of the early automotive age who traveled long distances in unreliable automobiles in unpredictable circumstances, or contemporary women who have achieved success in male dominated auto sports. Road trip chronicles such as *The Road North*; *Eight Women, Two Model Ts, and the American West*; and *A Reliable Car and a Woman Who Knows It* construct the woman driver during particular moments in American automotive history as courageous, audacious, adventurous, autonomous, independent, and inspirational.[5] The popular literature on women in the field of auto racing—with titles that include *Fast Women, Mad for Speed, Fearless, The Bugatti Queen*, and *Icons of Women's Sports*—frames the exceptional woman driver as "trailblazing women who broke through the gender barrier" (McCarthy).[6] In each of these literary locations, the woman driver is praised and admired for her tenacity, courage, and ability to drive through obstacles—gendered and otherwise—to achieve success or notoriety in what is most often considered a masculine endeavor.

Many of the participants in this project identify with the trailblazing women drivers who came before them by taking on the role of pioneer. Because of women's late entry into muscle car culture, those who have gained acceptance as muscle car owners remain somewhat of an anomaly. As a 56-year-old 1973 Dodge Challenger owner remarked, "It takes a special breed." A 65-year-old 1970 Chevelle owner referred to herself, and to all female muscle car owners, as "more daring." As she exclaimed, "Because a lot of women wouldn't even think of getting in one and driving it." Because their gender places them in the muscle car minority, many of the women feel a responsibility to serve as role models for other female muscle car enthusiasts in order to increase women's participation in what has historically existed as an exclusive masculine activity. They assume the role of pioneer in an effort to make the muscle-car–owning woman more visible, to serve as an example to women hesitant to participate, to change men's opinions of the female muscle car enthusiast, to make muscle car culture more welcoming to women, and through their example, change the perception of the woman driver.

> It makes me feel good. That I might be the one that breaks through; you know, it's not just men that can have muscle cars; women can do it, too. I mean we're very able. So I'm hoping I break a mold.
>
> —53-year-old 1977 Pontiac Trans Am owner

LEGENDARY FEMALE RACERS

Female racing personalities often serve as inspiration for the women who own muscle cars. Many of the project participants consider themselves successors to female driving legends such as Shirley Muldowney, Janet Guthrie, Lyn St. James, Sarah Fisher, and Denise McCluggage, as well as recent racing stars Ashley Force and Danica Patrick. The participants appreciate these competitive women not only for their considerable accomplishments in what has long existed as a male-dominated arena, but for the awareness their collective success has brought to all women who compete in motorsports and other car related activities.

The participants in this project recognize the difficulties racing legends such as Muldowney and Patrick experienced as they entered the masculine world of auto racing. In his analysis of women in motorsport, Ehren Pflugfelder writes, "Women drivers in motorsports face a number of astounding obstacles to their success—continual skepticism over their ability to drive in a field of men, embodied experiences of being 'othered' in a homogenous sport, limited and limiting representations of femininity, positive and negative consequences of 'feminine' presentation, and status as symbolic ruptures of the driver-car assemblage" (424). Identifying with female racing icons allowed the women in this project to acknowledge the existence of gender bias not only in auto racing but in other male dominated automotive arenas—such as muscle car culture—as well. As a 60-year-old 1971 Dodge Charger Super Bee owner noted, "I think that the men wanted to keep the women out of the muscle car. You know they don't think women can drive anyway." When a 50-year-old 1969 Mustang owner started drag racing, she was often the only woman at the track. As she recalled, "when a guy beat me his friends go, 'you're supposed to let her win cause she's a woman.' And I just looked at him and he looked at me and says, 'it's a man's sport.'" Pflugfelder argues that in professional sports such as auto racing, "women must often confront assumptions about their inferiorities that are designed into the rules of the game and ingrained into the material conditions of the playing arena" (411). By aligning themselves with female racing icons, the women in this project acknowledge the presence of gender bias in muscle car culture without having to provide personal testimonies of its existence.

Identifying with racing figures such as Force and McCluggage also allowed the project participants to suggest that, like the female icons they emulate, the ability to enter a historical masculine community was made possible by their own hard work, talent, persistence, and strong temperament. In their analysis of advertising images of women in motorsports, Ross, Ridinger, and Cuneen assert that, when allowed input into how they are to be represented, female race car drivers choose to focus on expertise, athleticism, and "a strong connotation of competence" rather than femininity (211). While some of the participants attributed their status as pioneers to conditions made possible by equal rights, the majority cited personal qualities—modest financial success, fortitude, and the accumulation of automotive knowledge—as responsible for their inclusion. As women who practice what Kersten would define as a conservative feminism, the women in this project often presented themselves as the embodiment of the conservative up-by-your-bootstraps model of self-sufficiency and self-reliance. In accordance with the general conservative worldview, conservative feminists believe that individuals are only accountable for themselves. They uphold what Klatch describes as the laissez-faire conservative belief that men and women are "self-directed actors, capable and responsible for autonomous action." Thus, to many of the women in this project, it was the relentless pursuit of individual goals, rather than the eradication of societal obstacles, that made their roles as pioneers possible.

Much like the women in auto racing, the women in this project call upon their own participation in muscle car culture to bring attention to women's growing acceptance in various automotive pursuits. When a 50-year-old homemaker began drag racing her 1969 Mustang 429 Cobra Jet over 20 years ago, there were very few women on the track. But as she noted, "Now women are just starting to come into it, like John Force's daughter and all that. Kind of opening the eyes that women can do this sport as well; it's not just strictly for men." A 54-year-old 2009 Dodge Charger R/T owner referred to the influence of NASCAR racer Danica Patrick on the growth of women's automotive participation. As she remarked, "[Patrick] has probably helped women to say 'hey, why not, go for it.'" The racing hero of a 53-year-old 1977 Pontiac Trans Am owner is the legendary drag racer Shirley "Cha Cha" Muldowney. As the nonprofit store manager exclaimed, "Shirley had to pave the way for the women today to get into the racing aspect of it, with NASCAR and everything. And so maybe I can pave the way. For women to be more comfortable, to be able to take these cars and to show." The women in this project insert themselves into the company of Patrick, Force, and Muldowney not to imply they possess similar accomplishments and skills, but rather to suggest that, like the legendary racing women before them, they have the ability to inspire and encourage women with a passion for speed and cars to enter the male-dominated world of American muscle car culture.

Paving the Way

The participants who identified as automotive pioneers understand that women's entry into muscle car culture is best accomplished through male approval. Thus one of the goals of these self-anointed trailblazers is to subtly yet convincingly demonstrate women's worthiness for inclusion. These women are not pioneers in the traditional feminist sense; as primarily conservative in ideology, they do not seek to dismantle the hierarchy within muscle car culture nor do they intend to challenge male leadership and replace it with their own. As Kersten writes, "unlike most contemporary feminists, [the conservative feminist] does not leap to the conclusion that equality demands that the results of every social process be identical for men and women." Rather, these female auto enthusiasts hope to demonstrate through enthusiasm, automotive knowledge, and attention to the automotive community that women's participation will embellish rather than diminish what has long existed as a masculine enclave. The female automotive pioneer—through her own example—suggests there is a place for women within muscle car culture that doesn't threaten the status quo. By her presence and performance she seeks to convince the male majority that women are not only knowledgeable about cars, but have a lot to offer the muscle car community. As a 43-year-old 1966 Dodge Charger owner remarked, "I think it shows them what we can do and that cars aren't just for men. I mean women appreciate cars; women know things about cars; women can drive them. Because most people don't think that." A 62-year-old 1964½ Mustang owner added, "I think they respect and understand that [muscle cars] are not just for the men anymore."

The women who identify as pioneers often take on roles within automotive organizations to demonstrate women's importance to the muscle car community. They serve as club officers, organize events, edit newsletters, manage websites, and act as online forum administrators. Women's eagerness to take charge of particular club functions often makes them invaluable to car organizations. As a 54-year-old 2014 Camaro 2SS/RS owner declared, "there are more women officers in our club than men at the present time and I am so honored to be one of them." A 63-year-old 2006 Mustang owner is now in her second term as secretary of a regional Mustang organization. As she noted, "When I became active in the club in 2004 I volunteered so I would be sure to be involved in activities." A 60-year-old 1995 Mustang GT owner proudly displays the plaque she received for her contributions to her local car club. As she remarked, "It's called the Generator

Award and I was the first woman to ever receive it." Kersten argues that an important component of conservative feminism is dedication to community. As she writes, "the conservative feminist strives to make time for voluntary organizations […] which provide her community's social glue and enhance its quality of life." The women who work tirelessly within automotive clubs—as officers and organizers of charitable events—not only incorporate good work with a love of cars, but by proving themselves invaluable to the muscle car community, also pave the way for other female motorists to follow suit. As a 60-year-old member of a local Ford restorers organization exclaimed, "Since I've joined and started working for the club, other women have stepped up and started doing things, too."

The participants who identified as pioneers are dedicated to laying the groundwork so that other female auto enthusiasts have an easy and uneventful entry into the muscle car community. Many of the women, particularly those with classic vehicles, work toward this goal on the ground at car shows, cruises, and in car organizations. Those with pony cars and modern muscle are likely to direct their efforts toward making online car environments more welcome to the woman driver. They participate on multiple sites in order to point out those that are female friendly, and to change the atmosphere of those that are not. A 41-year-old 2006 Dodge Charger owner who has evolved from forum lurker to avid contributor exclaimed, "it was an empowering feeling to have credibility to hang with the boys and some experience to talk about on the Charger forum I belong to." While the primary reason women participate on online forums is to obtain information and advice about their cars, many female muscle car owners serve as administrators or in other leadership capacities. In these roles they not only police the forums for flaming and sexist banter, but through providing advice and information to participants regardless of gender, demonstrate that women have the capacity to know and understand cars. As a 49-year-old Mustang forum administrator remarked, "some of the positives [of car forums] are that I learn things, too. Some of the negatives are like people who don't know how to behave themselves and bash people and they just need to keep their mouths shut."

As their work in clubs and online forums suggests, female muscle car enthusiasts are interested in attracting women to the world of the American muscle car and are eager to welcome them into various automotive venues. One of the women interviewed for this project works as a photographer for an automotive publication, a role that, she admits, changed how she looks at the events she photographs. As she explained, "[I ask myself] how can I portray what I'm seeing so someone else sees it like through my eyes? How can I tell them how much fun we've had, or things like that?" The women who identify as pioneers call upon their own accomplishments within the muscle car community to make muscle car ownership more attractive to female car enthusiasts and to encourage others with an interest in Camaros, Mustangs, and Firebirds to become more active in the muscle car community.

CHANGING THE PERCEPTION OF THE WOMAN DRIVER

John Sloop writes, "in the case of automobiles, not only do most of us have some vague idea of what colloquially constitutes a 'male' and a 'female' car, but we know that cars, like all new technologies, enter a culture with gendered meanings that in turn shape its meaning" (195). While female ownership of a muscle car is no longer as incongruous as it was during the vehicle's golden years, the muscle car's longstanding association with masculinity—and the stereotypes that remain attached to the woman driver—still affect how individuals react to women's presence behind the wheel of a loud, powerful, and outrageous machine. The female pioneers who contributed to this project understand that reclaiming the muscle car as genderless is not a realistic goal. They acknowledge that in order for women to be accepted into muscle car culture it is necessary to alter the current and common perception of the female muscle car driver.

Through their enthusiasm, automotive knowledge, and work within the muscle car community, these women have slowly but effectively normalized and legitimized women's inclusion into what has long existed as an exclusive male province.[7] As they exhibit their cars at local car events, take on leadership roles within the muscle car community, serve as administrators on various automotive forums, and display a knowledge of cars in online and real life locations, these women are not only securing their own place in muscle car culture, but are effectively paving the way for others to follow. As a 49-year-old 1969 Dodge Charger owner remarked, "I think sometimes when people meet me and they realize how passionate I am about my car or cars and even guys, even guys that are skeptical of woman and a car, I think they, most of them get a little bit of a different image about women and cars by the time they talk to you." Through identification with the "exceptional" women who came before them, these women consider themselves pioneers of change within the masculine muscle car community. As a 53-year-old 1977 Trans Am owner declared, "it's just one of those things that I might just turn it around so women came come forward where the men have always been superior, you know?"

Storyteller

Car stories have always been an integral and important component of automobile culture. While car shows, cruises, car clubs, and other auto-related pursuits are most often organized as a means of exhibition and competition among dedicated car enthusiasts, the unofficial but primary activity that takes place at these events is the sharing of car stories. Muscle car admirers of every persuasion—old car guys, young hot-rodders, middle-aged couples, and 30-something professionals—gather at these locations not only to discuss design, power trains, performance, and provenance, but also to share personal narratives from their own automotive experiences.

As scholars from a variety of disciplines suggest, stories serve an important function in American culture. Storytelling is universal; as Daniel Cantor reflects, "it is a pillar of the human experience, ubiquitous across time and culture." Storytelling, writes N. Bowles, has been used for centuries as "a powerful vehicle for communication, education, recreation, and the preservation of cultural identity" (365). Stories provide a context through which people, communities, and society can transmit messages, experiences, and knowledge to others. Human development scholar Robert Atkinson notes that stories create bonds, foster a sense of community, and help us to understand the established order around us. As he explains, "stories clarify and maintain our place in the order of things" (10). Stories are powerful; they have the capability to convey values and emotions, and

Susan Bess's 1965 Ford Mustang convertible has a unique history. Susan won the car in a radio sweepstakes and picked it up on her birthday. Searching for the perfect wedding vehicle, Calvin Ford, a descendant of Henry Ford, "borrowed" Susan's Mustang for the momentous occasion. The car was subsequently featured in an article about the wedding in the *New York Times*. As Susan remarked, "It was very exciting. It was very exciting to own the car" (courtesy Susan Bess).

can uncover differences and similarities between the experiences of individuals and groups (East et al.). Clinical psychologist Elizabeth Reichert suggests that storytelling has the potential to make hidden experiences visible; Joanne Banks-Wallace considers storytelling as a vehicle for the formation of new relationships and support systems. As East, Jackson, O'Brien, and Peters write, "elucidating personal stories involves sharing which can help form bonds and supportive networks" (17). Theatre and drama scholar Daniel Cantor adds, "all cultures need to tell stories, and our stories themselves are connected—iterative variations of one another." Storytelling provides a number of important functions among car enthusiasts. It encourages a common bond through shared interests, brings folks together through a collective and nostalgic automotive past, provides a social network among like-minded individuals, and perhaps most importantly, humanizes automotive history and makes it accessible to future generations.

In locations where car folks congregate, classic automobiles are perhaps the greatest initiator of such storytelling, as nothing spurs conversation among a group of auto aficionados than a vehicle with a connection to an individual's past. Cars from another era can spark memories of newfound independence, teenage romance, childhood friendships, and drag racing on hot summer nights. A 39-year-old 1967 Dodge Dart owner remarked that classic muscle cars "represent a time in history when people wanted to be free to do things their way, to not be tied down with all the rules and regulations of the structured everyday life. People were able to afford a vehicle that wasn't just for necessity and the kids (young adults) took to the cars as a way to get out and have fun." Vehicles of more recent vintage are also significant conversation starters. Twenty-first-century muscle cars, for example, provide the opportunity to connect one's own car history and automotive experiences to those of past generations. As Caperello and Kurani suggest, in their encounters with cars, individuals create narratives "to integrate their past, present, and future " (504). Traditionally, storytellers in these locations have been male; in fact, since the early years of automotive history, men's car stories have been a popular subject of books, film, and magazines.[8] In the twenty-first century, men's automotive narratives are often found in locations such as car TV, podcasts, online blogs and forums, automotive websites, and digital newsletters. However, the recent entry of the female car enthusiast into the muscle car community has changed the dynamics of storytelling as well as the stories being told. Women's car stories have made their way out of the shadows and into popular culture and onto library shelves.[9] In the muscle car community, women have not only added their own car stories to the historical and cultural narrative, but have remade and reimagined storytelling as an inclusive rather than exclusive activity.

Studies in disciplines as varied as nursing, sociology, management, and communication have suggested that storytelling offers women a way to explain pivotal life events, find meaning in experiences, educate the uninformed, and bond with others (Grassley 2447). As East et al. argue, stories are influenced "by environments, social situations, changing perspectives, the audience, and purpose of relating the story" (19). Because women's automotive experiences differ from those of men, their stories complement as well as add a new dimension to muscle car history, as recorded and remembered. Acting as storytellers—i.e., providing new narratives as well as encouraging the recounting of car stories by others—has not only allowed women access into muscle car culture, but has also given them the opportunity to contribute to the muscle car community in new and important ways. In the role of storyteller, the participants in this project act as conduits of automotive history, educate and inspire the next generation of car buffs, promote and strengthen the muscle car community, and—as female car enthusiasts—add a missing and significant chapter to the automotive archives. As storytellers, women have the opportunity to construct an important place for themselves within muscle car culture.

> *Three thousand six hundred pounds of American steel, as I glide my hands over your soft, hard metal, I remember how you feel, how you smell even with new parts. Some things, never change.... I remember rural roads, South/North Dakota, eastern Montana, "cousins" drive through liquor stores, reservations and the roaming hands of curious boys ... sheet metal, and new paint defy age, thankfully, you will rise again, and there will be the second coming of my sweet 66, this I promise.*
> —Car story as told by 51-year-old 1966 Chevrolet Impala owner

CONDUITS OF AUTOMOTIVE HISTORY

In the muscle car community, automotive history is recalled and reformed through the sharing and overlapping of car stories. Car stories combine individual car experiences with the cultural and historical relevance of a class of automobiles at a particular moment in time. Many of the women in this project spoke of the joy they experienced when their muscle cars inspired others to reflect upon personal auto histories. At a neighborhood gas station, a 53-year-old 1977 Trans Am owner was approached by a police officer whose intention was not, as she initially feared, to give her a citation, but rather to ask about her car. As she exclaimed, "all he kept saying was I had one of these when I was in school. I hear that at every show I go to. I had one of those. There's so many stories and so many payoffs that this car brings to me." A 62-year-old 1964½ Mustang owner noted, "we get a lot of stories from different people who used to own this same type of car. And they're very tickled to see it." Of her 1966 Dodge Charger, a 43-year-old veterinarian declared, "And when people see it, like I said it wasn't everybody's favorite at the time, it wasn't the most popular at the time, but they definitely remember it. They definitely remember it and a lot of people have a lot of memories about riding around in a '66 Charger with a friend or somebody down the street had one, or they can remember when they first came out and they thought they were pretty." Although gender restrictions—cultural and financial—of the 1960s and early 1970s prevented most women from actively participating in muscle car culture, the women in this project have a personal attachment to the cars they own and drive through a connection to family, friends, or a young woman's dreams. As they call upon this association to create, share, and exchange car stories with fellow muscle car enthusiasts, the women contribute to the muscle car's cultural and historical chronology.

Car stories not only provide a connection to the events of a personal past, but link folks together through a common automotive memory and love of cars. And when folks with multiple generations of Camaros, Mustangs, and Chargers gather together at car shows, car forums, and other auto-related activities and events, car stories intersect and converge, providing a trajectory of automotive history as well as intertwining narratives of how the muscle car affected individual lives. As a 58-year-old 2014 Dodge Challenger SRT owner explained, "I chose the Challenger because of my prior ownership with the '72 and '73." Referring to her modern day 2012 Dodge Challenger R/T, a 55-year-old small business owner remarked, "I had an original Challenger; I had a 1970 Challenger TA back in the day. I can relate to this car in that way." In their examination of the hybrid electric vehicle, Caperello and Kurani suggest that individuals often use automobiles in the creation and expression of self-identity narratives. As they note, "telling car stories" provides men and women with the opportunity to talk about the practical, emotional, and symbolic attachments to an automobile (495). While car stories are often dismissed as nostalgia, the women in this project understand the importance of the muscle car as both a historical phenomenon and an object with special and unique meanings. As East et al. write, "although the stories we tell are individual and subjective, stories of personal experience are original and hold meaning and value to the storyteller and the listener" (19).

While the women in this project have their own stories to tell, they believe they are part of a grander automotive narrative. The storyteller role allows them to share their own automotive experiences; however, it also provides them with the opportunity to elicit narratives from others as a means to generate camaraderie, community building, automotive knowledge, and historical preservation. As East et al. note, "stories convey values and emotions, and can reveal the differences and similarities in people's experience" (17). As they encourage fellow exhibitors, spectators, and other assorted car enthusiasts to share car stories, these women not only create an important role for themselves within the muscle car community, but in the process, also facilitate a living history of the American muscle car.

INSPIRATION TO FUTURE GENERATIONS

Women with all generations of vehicles call upon their Mustangs, GTOs, and Firebirds to spark automotive curiosity in folks unfamiliar with American muscle. Some of the women in this project expressed discouragement in young folks' disinterest in the muscle car's illustrious history. As a 62-year-old 1971 Gran Torino owner lamented, "people, the younger generation, a lot of them will say 'well why do you do that?' They have no concept of what these cars mean." Many of the participants emphasized the importance of engaging and inspiring young people to take an interest in the muscle car as both a modern machine and historical icon. They call upon the role of storyteller to eagerly and patiently answer questions about their automobiles, foster car club participation from younger fanciers, and encourage their own children and other family members to become active in the muscle car hobby. As a 47-year-old accounting manager remarked, the major reason her 1972 Plymouth Barracuda is exhibited at community events is so "future generations know what was out there at the time, back in the early '70s and what we were doing." A 47-year-old elementary school teacher drives her 1989 and 2001 Camaros to school and uses them as learning tools in order to engage her students in automotive history. As she remarked, "I don't do it to impress them. I do it to show them how much fun it's been and how much it's given my life." The 17-year-old daughter of two car buffs participates in automotive events with a 1987 Pontiac Trans AM GTA she calls "Kitt." Referring to the older car folks she encounters at car shows and cruises, the high school senior remarked, "some of the guys have actually told me that they're just happy that a younger group is getting into it." A 50-year-old decommissioning project coordinator at Ford Motor Company and 1993 Mustang GT owner encourages the budding automotive interest of her teenage daughter. As she noted, "I took my daughter, she's 14, and her boyfriend, with me and they rode back with me, so it was kind of a little special deal for them. So, yeah, I think I've given my daughter the bug, too. She fights it sometimes but I think she's gotten the bug for the cars."

Stories, argues Jane Grassley, can be effective and valuable educational tools. Personal narratives provide an effective and accessible means to integrate anecdotes, events, and experiences into a historical and cultural timeframe. The muscle car has a rich and often contradictory history. It marked what was perhaps the most exciting period in American automobile culture as well as the definitive end of an era in U.S. automotive production and use. Young auto aficionados—often unfamiliar with the history of the Charger or Mustang they may be coveting—can gain important knowledge simply by asking questions and listening to the stories of past and present muscle car owners. The women in this project—many of them parents of budding muscle car enthusiasts—have taken on the responsibility of creating an environment in which young people—and their car questions and experiences—will be welcome. As Kersten notes, the conservative feminist "finds happiness in striving to fulfill her responsibilities, to cultivate wisdom, [...] and to pursue excellence in all her endeavors." The women in this project welcome the opportunity to cultivate and share automotive knowledge with young car enthusiasts through the facilitation of car stories.

While some of the women in this project were disheartened by the lack of automotive interest and participation in younger generations, others cited evidence that attempts to engage and inspire young car enthusiasts were showing positive results. As a 43-year-old 1966 Dodge Charger owner declared, "And I have noticed that, within last year and this year that there are a lot of young kids that are back into it again. Which is really, really nice to see them pick up that hobby and want to know things about cars, and appreciate the older things. And to see that happening again because I think we kind of lost that. I'm happy about that when I do see a younger person; I really want to take the time to talk to them and encourage them and thank them for their appreciation of this interest and a good hobby for them." In the role of storyteller, the women in this project call upon their own car narratives and experiences to impart the historical importance of the muscle car and promote active participation in muscle car culture to future generations.

WOMEN'S CAR STORIES

The embedded masculinity of the muscle car has influenced how men and women experience automobiles. In an article focused on the car hobby as an avocation, Dale Dannefer describes the "late bloomer enthusiast" as an individual who had a passionate interest in cars in youth, "but it dissipated or was suppressed from about age 20 until middle life when it was resumed" (398). As the narratives from Dannefer's research suggest, men's car stories emanate from their early automotive experiences and participation in American car culture. While some women spent their teenage years behind the wheel of a Mustang or Camaro, most took part in muscle car culture vicariously. Consequently, the car stories the women tell evolve from a place distinct from that of male enthusiasts, and offer a fresh and often unfamiliar perspective to the automotive archives. As Barbara Johnstone writes, "men and women live in different worlds, be these affective and/or cognitive psychological worlds; social worlds involving relationships of prestige, power, and status; or worlds of belief and knowledge created by culture; and that the world in which a person lives helps to shape the person's talk" (68). The early muscle car experiences of women of the baby boomer generation most often originate from a location of absence and longing; i.e., without vehicles of their own, they were most often cast in the role of observer, cheerleader, or admirer. As a 49-year-old 2010 Camaro owner recalled, "One of my boyfriends had a 1970 Camaro and my first husband had a 1972 Grand Prix. I always wanted to drive them." And a 54-year-old 1967 Pontiac LeMans owner noted, "I remember what it was like when I could only look at the nice rides going by." Young female drivers of modern day muscle—while not subjected to many of the inequalities experienced by members of the baby boomer generation—are likely to offer stories that disrupt the common assessment that women have little interest in powerful and performance driven machines. They share tales of car vacations, road trips, and various automotive adventures that put the woman in the driver seat of both the car and the story. Of her 2010 Camaro SS/RS, a 29-year-old auto industry product manager noted, "I have taken her to Houston on an eight-day-round-trip road trip, with another friend who has a Camaro. That event was Camaro5 Fest, which was a gathering of about a thousand Camaros from all over the country. It's held every year in a different location. We're going to this year's event [...] And I'm driving down; it'll be a one day nine hour road trip. And I'll be traveling with a few other Camaros. That's just examples of the types of, kind of on the extreme end of it, the kind of road trips I like to do in her." By eliciting and contributing stories of the female automotive experience, these women change the perception of the woman driver and in doing so, become part of the evolving history of muscle cars. As a 55-year-old 2012 Challenger owner and forum administrator noted, "I always ask some of the new women that come on the forum, we just got a brand new woman, I think she's 31 or something. So I asked her, 'why did you pick this car?' She obviously never grew up with them, like I did. It intrigues me."

Linguistic scholar Barbara Johnstone argues that men's and women's stories differ in significant ways. Men's stories, Johnstone asserts, tend to be about contest, whereas women's are about community. As Johnstone writes, "the community is the source of women's power and this social power is tapped through discourse " (76). The emphasis the women in this project placed on drawing out automotive experiences from fellow car enthusiasts rather than dwelling exclusively on personal stories lends credence to Johnstone's analysis. While they have their own narratives to add to the automotive archives, the participants understand on some level that the acceptance of women as storytellers within muscle car culture relies on the ability to generate, value, propagate, and nurture the car stories of others within the muscle car community. As Kersten suggests, conservative feminism incorporates a view of human nature, and of justice and equality, that relies on connections to others through community building. As women who identify primarily as conservative, female storytellers seek to strengthen the muscle car community and contribute to the automotive archives through the sharing, collection and distribution of car stories. In the storyteller role, the women in this project have gained access to muscle car culture and in the process, are making important contributions to the historical and cultural legacy of the American muscle car.

Anne Kelly acquired her 1966 Chevrolet Impala from the original owner in 1993. She has spent the past 20 plus years driving it, restoring it, loving it, and learning from it. The car has been one of the constants in Anne's life; her two sons grew up with this car, and she has no plans of ever giving it up. As Anne explained, "I just work on making it better and better so that I can keep driving it" (courtesy Anne Kelly).

One of the Guys

Muscle car culture originated as a uniquely masculine space. Not only were the qualities associated with the muscle car—power, performance, and bad behavior—conflated with its young male drivers, but acceptance into 1960s muscle car culture was often dependent on the possession of particular masculine attributes. While any young man with modest means could purchase a Charger, GTO, or Chevelle, recognition and respect within the muscle car community was granted to those who demonstrated three crucial attributes: mechanical ability, driving skill, and automotive knowledge. Certainly young women were present where teenage boys in cars congregated. However, women's lack of the three requisite automotive credentials excluded them from legitimate membership in the male-centric muscle car culture.

In the twenty-first century, there are certainly men who purchase Mustangs and Camaros without any real understanding of the automobile's mechanics or history. Rather, they view muscle car ownership as a source of identity, status, and masculine performance. However, recognition as a true muscle car enthusiast remains dependent on the demonstration of automotive prowess. Automotive locations such as car clubs, car shows, cruises, and online forums often serve as gathering places for men to display mechanical ability, driving skill, and automotive knowledge and in the process, reaffirm muscle car culture as a masculine space.

While the roles women take on in modern day muscle car culture are often adapted from those they assume in their everyday lives, a few female motorists choose to take a different route. Rather than depend on a reconfiguration of traditional gender roles, these women enter muscle car culture through identification as "one of the guys." This claim is not a reference to sexual orientation. As primarily conservative heterosexual Christians, most do not openly accept homosexuality as a lifestyle, nor are they generally welcoming to the LGBTQ car enthusiast.[10] While they may refer to themselves as "not girly," "tomboy," or "sporty," they do not take on male personas nor do they behave in any way that could be considered butch or masculine. Their self-classification as "one of the guys" refers to the possession and display of the mechanic ability, driving skills, and automotive knowledge traditionally associated with the male car aficionado. Through recognition as skillful and knowledgeable, these women have constructed a place for themselves within the masculine confines of American muscle car culture.

> *I have a passion for driving. I enjoy cars because I know how they are made and how they work. I probably should have been a mechanic. I love seeing and hearing those engines working right.*
> —63-year-old 2006 Mustang owner

MECHANICAL ABILITY

The association of masculinity and mechanical ability has two origins. The first was a reaction to the loss of many traditional sources of male identity brought on by industrialization. During this unsettling time, mechanical skill emerged as a means to restore masculinity to factory employees reduced from individual workers to units of production. As Clay McShane notes, "increasingly, males were defining their gender in terms of mechanical

RAMBLER AMERICAN ROGUE

343 CUBES

THE 1967 AMERICAN MOTORS

THE NOW CARS

We don't build them the way we used to. For American Motors to stuff a 343 cube Typhoon V-8 into an innocent-looking Rambler American is guaranteed to cause news. But 1967 looks to be a *driver's* year like no other, and the 1967 American Motors has risen to the occasion. Witness this Rogue hardtop. Its 343 cubes are fed by a 4-barrel Carter to develop 280 horses, and this mill winds up to higher rpm's faster and pays off in quicker shifts. The 4-speed stick is mandatory (as you'd expect in a machine of this caliber), and you can opt for a fat pile of goodies including a special handling package, power disc brakes, Twin-Grip rear axle, electric tach, shoulder belts, and extra-wide-profile red line nylons mounted on 5.5" rims.

So you see, we *don't* build them the way we used to. That's our message. With this added plus: American Motors believes any driver's year must be a safe driver's year. So you get an energy-absorbing steering column, deep-dish wheel, Double-Safety brake system, shoulder belt anchors, and many other built-in safety features. See what a 343-CID Typhoon looks like in any of 7 Rambler Americans, at your American Motors/ Rambler Dealer. It just might end up *you* don't build them the way you used to, either!

AMBASSADOR · MARLIN · REBEL · RAMBLER AMERICAN

Rambler American Rogue Advertisement: "343 Cubes." In order to be part of muscle car culture during the 1960s and early 1970s, young women hung around young men with hot cars. While a teenager, a 61-year-old 1970 Monte Carlo owner didn't have a "cool" muscle car of her own. As she remarked, "I suppose some of the boys I knew in high school did. Of course you were always interested there" (*Motor Trend*, July 1967).

skill" (1995). The second was the introduction of the gasoline-powered automobile. As Michael Berger writes, "everything about the car seemed masculine, from the coordination and strength required to operate it, to the dirt and grease connected with its maintenance" ("Drivers" 257). When, during the early auto age, women expressed their preference for the gasoline-powered automobile over the electric, possession of mechanical skills became a way to claim male automotive aptitude as superior to that of the female motorist. As Julie Wosk writes, "men had long been portrayed as strong and technically able, women as frail and technically incompetent, or at least unsuited to engaging in complex technical operations" (9). Although women appreciated the gasoline-powered cars for their power and range, they were discouraged from working on them. As Berger asserts, it was believed that women who engaged in mechanical tasks "were likely to diminish their femininity" ("Drivers" 259)

During the Second World War, women displayed technological ability while working as truck drivers, mechanics, or in the mechanical and civil engineering jobs soldiers left behind. However, the cultural climate of the postwar era—and the reestablishment of traditional gender roles that accompanied it—effectively took the wrenches out of women's hands. In the decades that followed, technological expertise was reestablished as the sole province of the male driver, reaffirming the association between mechanical ability and masculinity. Membership in the youth car cultures of the 1950s and '60s was most often dependent on mechanical ability. Brenda Bright writes, "Men's interest in cars often begins as a predominantly—but not exclusively—male adolescent concern with style, personal identity, and mechanical skills" (594). Many young male "motor heads" formed car clubs to further automotive expertise, and to bond with other auto aficionados. The ability to take a car and put it back together again became a badge of honor among "car crazy" young men. As Foster writes, "nobody gained full acceptance into [the car] fraternity until they could remove, rebuild, and reinstall an engine in their vehicles" (66). In the context of formal and informal auto clubs and organizations, cars functioned as representatives of masculinity and male relationships (Bright 594). The focus on mechanical skill as a requirement for membership excluded most young women from full participation in muscle car culture.

However, despite efforts to maintain the status of women as technologically ignorant, women drivers of the twenty-first century have become more car savvy. Many were tutored as young girls alongside fathers and other male family members; they grew up with a familiarity with how cars work and continue to be very involved with maintaining their own vehicles. Some had brothers or boyfriends who were racing enthusiasts, and spent much of their formative years accompanying them to the track. Others took it upon themselves to learn about cars on their own initiative. Whether enrolled in automotive courses, or calling on car savvy friends for information and advice, these women considered the attainment of mechanic skills as a source of empowerment. Many of the female participants feel very comfortable around cars and often identified themselves as former tomboys, not girly, or "one of the guys" to claim legitimacy as car enthusiasts. They indicated that while there are a few male holdouts that don't believe women can possibly know anything about cars, most men they encounter are both surprised and supportive when women display automotive skills and expertise.

Many of the mechanically inclined women in this project had male family members who fostered their automotive interests. These dads, brothers, and husbands encouraged their wives, sisters, and daughters to become knowledgeable about the automobile. They took them to car events, answered their automotive questions, and taught them to work on their own vehicles. To a 37-year-old 1974 Chevy Nova owner, the best times of her young life were spent around her dad and cars. She worked alongside him in the garage, accompanied him to auto junkyards, and asked his advice before acquiring a muscle car as a race vehicle. As she explained, "[my dad] came to Norwalk, Ohio, and watched me race it there for Super Chevy which was pretty cool. And he'd come to the track and stuff so it was fun." A 39-year-old 2010 Dodge Challenger owner received an auto education while assisting her father. As she remarked, "[My dad] loves to work on the cars in the garage and I was there to help get tools. I learned a bit by watching." While some dads encouraged automotive education through a hands-on approach, others provided learning environments that nurtured technological interests in their daughters. As a 47-year-old IT engineer—who performs most of the maintenance on her 2015 Dodge Challenger—explained, "While my father is not a performance car enthusiast, he appreciates performance cars. I was an Army brat and learned more about airplanes, tanks, and military equipment, and that led into appreciating cars." The automotive skills these women acquired through "apprenticeships" with fathers, brothers, boyfriends, and husbands provided them with the ability and confidence to enter muscle car culture on their own terms.

However, not all women with mechanical ability acquired skills alongside car savvy fathers. Many had to seek out other sources of automotive education. When restoring her 1967 Pontiac GTO, a retired mother of five did much of the work herself. As she explained, "I pulled the dash and rewired it. I had to teach myself. My brothers helped a little bit." Those who belong to car organizations find that male members are often willing to help out those who demonstrate a willingness to learn. As the 63-year-old owner of a 1966 Mustang coupe remarked, "the guys in the club are always ready to help and they like that I have done so much work myself." A 31-year-old 1991 Firebird owner added, "I change my own oil and I can do some general maintenance. And, with the help of some of my guy friends who are more, you know, automotive savvy, I have them supervise and help me do things and stuff like that. Cause it helps them realize that girls can be into cars, too." As the responses of these women suggest, women's entry into muscle car culture is often facilitated by the inclusion of male teachers in one's automotive education. While the possession of mechanical skills allows women to construct themselves as "one of the guys," an admission that women occasionally require male automotive "help" maintains the conservative gender hierarchy [and assuages male egos] within the masculine muscle car fraternity.

Social historian Kathleen Franz dispels the notion of the woman driver as mechanically inept by drawing on accounts of early female motorists involved in the practice of "tinkering." During the early days of automobility, car owners of both genders actively reinvented and repurposed automobiles for their own use. Women, who recognized their credibility as drivers was often based on mechanical ability, became capable and enthusiastic "tinkerers" as a means to dispel notions of female automotive ineptitude. Mechanical skill, unlike physical strength, offered a level playing field on which women could claim equality with men. While the notion of women as technologically capable was eventually displaced by the reassertion of female domesticity, the women who participated in this project demonstrate that, like their tinkering predecessors, they have the desire, intelligence, and capability to work on their own automobiles. As a 58-year-old 2014 Dodge Challenger SRT owner offered, "I pride myself on the fact that I know how to take care of that stuff. I know what a torque wrench is; I know what a box wrench is; I know what a ratchet is. I'm not afraid to get in there." Through the demonstration of mechanical ability, these women are able to insert themselves into muscle car culture as one of the guys.

Driving Skill

The original woman driver stereotype—which depicted women as easily distracted, careless, emotional, inept, overly cautious, unpredictable, and accident prone—was promoted in the years following World War I as a means to discourage women from driving. As Scharff notes, in the early years of automobile history, women drivers were repeatedly characterized as "incompetent and flighty behind the wheel, helplessly ignorant in the face of mechanical problems, terrified of the rigors of motoring over mud holes or in storms, and timid (though dangerous) on crowded city streets" (167). The early stereotype constructed women as less capable drivers than men; the male driver, on the other hand, was most often portrayed as knowledgeable, skilled, mechanically gifted, confident, and in possession of natural automotive intelligence. The woman driver stereotype that emerged after the Second World War focused on the qualities that were admired in wives and mothers but assumed to compromise women's driving ability. The woman driver as careful, practical, and concerned with safety, comfort, and reliability was continually positioned at odds with the man behind the wheel whose "natural" confidence, driving ability, and daring constructed him as a more proficient and therefore, more legitimate driver.

During the 1960s and early 1970s, the skills deemed necessary for the woman driver—passivity, conscientiousness, and a heightened concern for safety—were in direct conflict with those considered essential for managing a muscle car. The American muscle car was originally conceived as a legal street racer. It was meant to appeal to the young male driver through its power, performance, speed, and its not-so-subtle encouragement of risk-taking behavior. To the young man behind the wheel of a Charger or Mustang, taking on a powerful, rough handling, fast-in-a-straight-line, and potentially dangerous vehicle was not considered indicative of poor driving habits; rather, it was framed as evidence of exceptional driving skill. Balkmar and Joelsson argue that driving recklessly and speeding generates positive reinforcement to young men. As they note, the need to speed "is built into the conception of the young driver (the practices are normalised and perceived as necessary and evident) thus making it crucial to stress the importance of driving skills instead of refraining from the dangerous practices" (46). Consequently, the attention to caution and safety associated with women's automobile use in the late twentieth century suggested the woman driver had neither the skills nor temperament to adequately handle a muscle car. Although in the twenty-first century, female racing personalities such as Danica Patrick have brought attention to women as exceptionally skilled drivers, old stereotypes regarding women's driving ability steadfastly remain. Thus one of the ways in which women gain access into muscle car culture is to display driving skills on par with "one of the guys."

Because of the muscle car's early association with illegal street competitions, many of the women called out their experience in various racing venues as evidence of driving skill. Some of the racing was done informally [and often unlawfully]. The 64-year-old owner of a Pontiac GTO spent her teenage years drag racing on a marked off neighborhood road. As she recalled, "We'd take our car down there sometimes and run the quarter mile." A 65-year-old 1969 Camaro Z/28 owner, who grew up in the rural South, used to accompany her brothers to gravel back roads for the purpose of drag racing. As she recalled, "So I would make the dust; it would be so many rocks flying until they couldn't see me. And when the dust settled I was so far ahead it was unbelievable." Other women's racing experiences took place on commercial tracks or drag ways. Of her 1969 Mustang 429 Cobra Jet, a 50-year-old homemaker remarked, "I've run the ladies clock with it. That was fun. It was like an acceleration and adrenaline rush. It made you feel like 'wow.'" A 55-year-old 2009 Charger R/T owner exclaimed, "I've been on the track; I did the quarter mile. But because it's my daily driver I didn't want to make a habit of it. It's so easy to get addicted to the track." The 55-year-old owner of a 2012 Dodge Challenger R/T asserted, "I like to take it to the track every now and then which is fun. I'm not looking to beat anybody; it's just fun to go fast." As the late Charles Sanford once observed, "women have acquired a reputation for not enjoying speed in transport or caring about cars as passionately as men" (140). The testimonies of those who participated in this project suggest otherwise. These muscle-car-owning women race on neighborhood streets, country roads, and formal tracks not only as a means to display exceptional driving skills, but to also experience the exhilaration of speed and control traditionally denied to the woman behind the wheel.

Although many of the women developed driving skills through time at the track, others acquired advanced driving techniques through auto education. They attended driving schools, took courses offered at local racetracks, and honed their skills at track days and other racing events. As a 29-year-old 2010 Camaro SS/RS owner explained, "I'm a good driver; I have done driver training; I've done race school driving; I've done track work in my car." The 49-year-old owner of a 2010 Camaro—which she has nicknamed "Poseidon"—remarked, "We had a Ladies Track Day last year at Gingerman Race Way with about five of us girls who own cars. It was rather fun. I was not super comfortable in Poseidon, but by the end of the day I was very comfortable in the car." As a 54-year-old engineer noted, she chose a 2014 Mustang because, "I wanted a fun performance car. I am considering taking a course, like a driving course you know. Like you have to buy a helmet and all that. Not that I'm going to race this car; I'm not going to drag race it; I'm not going to go to like motocross it or anything. I just want to be a better driver." These women understand that owning a fast and powerful muscle car comes with a certain amount of responsibility. They take on the task of self-improvement to improve their driving skills, as well as to fully experience all the muscle car has to offer.

While the women in this project enjoy the experience of muscle car ownership for the excitement and exhilaration it offers them, they also get joy out of surprising and impressing male peers with their considerable driving skills. A 42-year-old health center receptionist, who regularly competes with her 1982 Mustang at the local dragway, remarked, "Most guys are intimidated because most of them, you know, they'll get down there at the line and they'll look over and oh it's a girl, easy win. And then when you do win and you watch their demeanor and they're so mad about it." A 42-year-old owner of a 2011 Camaro reflected on an early racing experience. As she recalled, "When I was 16, I bought a 1979 Z/28. Back then, guys had long hair, so I was constantly having other guys try to race me until they realized it was a girl driving. And I would egg them on to race anyway. Little did they know that I actually knew how to race." A 56-year-old 1971 Pontiac Firebird owner mentioned the fun she has when challenging men at a street light. As she declared, "guys don't expect to get beaten by girls driving a car like that." Because driving skill has traditionally been framed as a male expertise, the women in this project compared their automotive acumen to those of male peers to claim legitimacy as muscle car enthusiasts. By performing like "one of the guys" behind the wheel, these women not only have the time of their lives, but prove themselves worthy of entrance into the muscle car community.

AUTOMOTIVE KNOWLEDGE

Muscle car culture originated as an exclusive male fraternity in which automotive knowledge was created, shared, and put into practice. Whether in informal groups or organized car clubs, young male auto aficionados congregated at every opportunity to share automotive tips, work on each other's cars, and test their automotive acumen through activities such as drag racing and cruising. The exclusion of women from these groups not only intensified the association of the muscle car with masculinity, but also contributed to the construction of automotive knowledge as a masculine province. Conversely, women's presumed lack of automotive knowledge became an effective means to limit if not prohibit the female motorist from full participation in muscle car culture.

It is not surprising, therefore, that one of the ways in which women claim legitimacy as muscle car drivers is through the acquisition and display of automotive knowledge. An understanding of automotive history, awareness of advances in automotive technology, familiarity with automotive terms and categories, and a basic grasp of the inner workings of automobiles provides women with an unofficial standing in the muscle car community as "one of the guys." While some of the women in this project obtained such knowledge with the help of fathers and brothers, others took it upon themselves to learn everything possible about muscle cars in general and about their own Chargers, Mustangs, and 'Cudas in particular.

The women who contributed to this research received their automotive education in a number of ways. Some sought knowledge at car shows, cruises, and other car related events. Within these automotive "classrooms" the women were able to ask questions, seek advice, attend auto vendor demonstrations, and eavesdrop on or engage in conversations with experienced car buffs. As the 64-year-old owner of a 1967 Pontiac GTO remarked, "I like going to shows and I enjoy talking to the people. You learn so much; you'd be amazed at the stuff that you learn if you listen." A 58-year-old 1965 Mustang owner has traveled as far as 500 miles to attend automotive events. As she noted, "I see and learn more every time I am a participant. I view it as an enlightening time where I learn as much as I share with others about my car." Of her 1969 Mustang, the 50-year-old owner remarked, "I didn't know a whole lot when I first got it, but as we've gone to different car shows and stuff, I hear my husband talking about it and I just kind of pick up on stuff."

While many women gain automotive knowledge through in-person interaction in public spaces, others have looked to online sources for information. Women with retro cars in particular call upon online car forums and blogs as an effective and accessible means to learn more about their Mustang, Camaro, or Challenger. As I discovered in a previous project, online forums are especially conducive to women's participation for a number of reasons.[11] The Internet, often referred to as the "great equalizer," is considered non-hierarchical (Ebo 8). Online communication encourages a vocal community rather than a voice of domination. Women in public spaces are often silenced or disparaged, especially in environments where they are not expected to have experience or expertise. The online car group offers women the possibility of a non-threatening environment to talk and learn about cars. A 54-year-old 2014 Dodge Charger R/T owner often logs onto an automotive forum for answers to her car questions. As she noted, "you can exchange ideas, you can exchange advice. And you can exchange also where you get your parts. If you have a problem on your car then you can get some information. Or somebody will figure it out for you; somebody will help you out." A 58-year-old 2014 Dodge Challenger SRT remarked, "If there's something going on with your car you want to know about it, you can find out through one of these forums. And people are usually more than willing. [The forum] is made for people to learn, to help others." Much like online learning environments, car forums and blogs provide women with easy and convenient access to an automotive education. The women look to these forums not only for automotive information, but to disseminate what they have learned to others as well as share their love of cars. As a frequent 65-year-old Challenger Forum Z contributor exclaimed, "[The forum] has given me some people with a common interest in Challengers to exchange ideas, learn more about my car, and make friendships with people who love Challengers as much as I do."

Not only do women gain automotive knowledge through online and in person participation, but many conduct their own research on their own cars in order to document the vehicle's authenticity and to be better able to answer questions of interested spectators and exhibitors at car events. As a 73-year-old retired Ford administrative assistant explained, once she acquired her 1964½ Mustang, "I went out and got books, and I have like a scrapbook [of the vehicle's history] that I carry in my car." Some of the women have taken a more hands on approach; they acquired automotive knowledge on their own through the restoration, repair, and maintenance process. A 42-year-old 1982 Mustang owner enrolled in classes in auto body and painting to further her automotive education. As a 49-year-old office manager noted, the 1969 Dodge Charger that she and her husband restored was "a very educational car. I know how to do things now that I never did before."

Many of the women who participated in this project enjoy the challenge of acquiring knowledge and experience in an area that was once off limits to them. Although, as a teenager, a 47-year-old accounting manager was interested in learning about the inner workings of cars, the gender prescriptions of the time prevented her from doing so. As the 1972 Plymouth Barracuda owner explained, getting involved in muscle cars became a "try to do something you're not allowed to do kind of thing." Once they acquire automotive knowledge, women enjoy displaying what they've learned, particularly in front of doubting male spectators and exhibitors. As the 54-year-old owner of a 1967 Pontiac LeMans noted, "Men who find out about my car generally seem to be impressed. All of a sudden they seem to credit me with a little more intelligence, and feel I know more of what I'm talking about." The 51-year-old owner of a 1969 Mustang Mach I remarked, "Men when they look at me and I know what I'm talking about, it blows them away."

Because of the longstanding association between the American muscle car and masculinity, male acknowledgment of women's automotive knowledge often serves as source of validation to women's muscle car culture participation. Reflecting on gender differences in the production and use of technologies, Lerman, Mohun, and Oldenziel note that dominant gender ideologies often determine who has access to technological knowledge or control over a particular form of technology. The women who contributed to this project recognize that historically, men have been ordained as the keepers of automotive knowledge. They also acknowledge that admission into the historically masculine culture of muscle cars is dependent on male support and approval. The women understand that through the accumulation of automotive knowledge, they can claim legitimacy as "one of the guys" and in the process, gain access into the masculine brotherhood of American muscle car culture.

Outlier

The muscle car community is a fairly homogeneous group. The majority of folks in Southeastern Michigan who gather together on a regular basis to celebrate Chargers, Mustangs, and Firebirds are white, Christian, middle-class, married, heterosexual, and moderate to conservative in ideology. It should not be surprising, therefore, that the women most successful in making a place for themselves within muscle car culture most closely resemble the men who have traditionally inhabited it. Non-white and non-heterosexual men have addressed their exclusion from mainstream car communities through the establishment of separate car cultures. Latino, African-American, Asian, and gay auto enthusiasts have formed distinct automotive networks that link members through social identity rather than an automotive category. However, attempts to establish separate female car communities have been—for the most part—unsuccessful. While this could easily be attributed to the lack of a significant female enthusiast base, it is more likely due to the notion that a male presence is necessary to add legitimacy to an automotive community. Thus while white-straight-Christian-middle-class-conservative women have developed effective strategies to gain entry into muscle car culture, the integration of "outlier" women—i.e., women of color, members of the LGBTQ community, and younger female car fanciers—has been much more difficult to achieve. Although the responses of women within the dominant demographic did not reveal any conscious discrimination toward those unlike themselves, the hesitancy of "outliers" to seek membership in muscle car organizations suggests they often feel uncomfortable among mainstream muscle car enthusiasts.

I have never been a fan of car clubs because they usually have a lot of drama.
                                                 —22-year-old 1966 Mustang owner

RACE

The racial composition of women in this project supported my own observations at car events in Southeastern Michigan—the majority of folks active in the muscle car community are white. As the original muscle car was developed in 1964 to appeal to a very specific demographic—the young, moderately affluent, white, baby-boomer male— there remains a notable scarcity of minority car enthusiasts in muscle car organizations. Muscle car culture's link to conservatism—mirrored in the ideological makeup of the participants [85 percent of those who indicated an ideology identified as moderate or conservative]—and conservatism's association with whiteness—also contributes to the lack of diversity in the muscle car community.[12] Eighty-three out of 88 participants identified as Caucasian; the remaining five were African American, Hispanic, Asian, and of mixed race (white/Native American, white/Asian, white/Hispanic). The race of the participant was often mitigated by marital status. Non-white women married to white men had an easier time assimilating into the muscle car community. A 56-year-old former auto industry engineer of mixed race—born in Japan but raised in Naperville, Illinois—does not drive her own car but attends muscle car events alongside her husband in a 1969 Dodge Dart. While her parentage is mixed, her twenty years of employment in the auto industry, her thirty-five-year marriage to a white male car enthusiast, and her role as "passenger" rather than driver contributes to her acceptance within muscle car culture. The sole African American woman in this project—a 65-year-old 1969 Camaro Z/28 owner—attributes her failure to integrate into the muscle car community to gender rather than race. As she remarked, "I inquired about two Camaro clubs and they wouldn't let me in." However, since Camaro clubs in Southeastern Michigan have a fair amount of female members, it could be argued that her exclusion is due to the fact that she doesn't look like anyone else.

SEXUAL ORIENTATION

There is an old stereotype that links the lesbian identified woman with the muscle car. The muscle car's longstanding association with masculinity led to the assumption that powerful, fast, and loud Chargers, 'Cudas, and GTOs would naturally attract women who embraced what Judith Halberstam defines as a form of "female masculinity."[13] However, as a writer for *Lesbian News* argues, the familiar stereotype is "a throwback to the time when only butch dykes were brave enough to be out" (lesbiannews.com). As she notes, while lesbians as a group tend to gravitate toward particular models (the Subaru Forester, Jeep Wrangler, and Ford Ranger top the list), sexual identification has little bearing on whether or not the automobile in the driveway is a muscle car. Although only three of the 85 women who provided information regarding sexual orientation identified as lesbian, they owned and drove muscle cars for many of the same reasons as their straight sisters. As a 54-year-old professional gardener explained, she enjoys her 1967 Pontiac LeMans for its "good looks, power, sound, and [connection to] happy memories from the past."

In "Out on the Highway"—a project focused on the automotive experiences of gay men—many of the individuals interviewed reflected on the difficulties they faced as homosexuals in a pastime dominated by heterosexual men. Although many have attempted to integrate into mainstream automotive culture, when attending car shows, cruises, or other auto-related events they often feel awkward and out of place. As a 43-year-old 1978 Lincoln Mark V owner remarked, "I usually get the vibe that many don't really care for our 'kind'" (Lezotte "Highway" 129). The rebuffing and rejection of gay men from mainstream car culture resulted in the formation of an automotive organization—Lambda Car Club International—dedicated to the LGBTQ car enthusiast. While LCCI membership is open to women, the overwhelming majority of participants in club activities are male. As a female 51-year-old 1966 Chevy Impala owner and participant in this project noted, "I belong to a gay car club, although I hardly ever attend events." The presence of lesbian women in Southeastern Michigan muscle car culture suggests that, gay car clubs notwithstanding, the women prefer to take part in mainstream automotive activities. However, their small numbers within the muscle car community would imply there is not a significant population of lesbian muscle car enthusiasts overall, or—much like gay male enthusiasts who attempt to infiltrate mainstream automotive culture—as individuals on the margins they do not always feel entirely at ease.

While the women who identified as lesbian in this project attend automotive events, they are reluctant to join mainstream automotive organizations. A 54-year-old 1967 Pontiac LeMans owner attributed her lack of club membership to gender and marital status rather than sexual orientation. As she remarked, "I have not felt very comfortable doing so as a single female, as members are overwhelmingly either guys or couples." Although these women did not specifically mention discrimination due to sexual orientation within the muscle car community, the conservative base of muscle car culture would suggest an underlying uneasiness with homosexuality as a lifestyle or practice. As Shackelford and Besser argue, "heterosexuals' negative attitudes toward homosexuality are reasoned to stem, in part, from their conformity to traditional gender belief systems" (108).[14] Much of women's acceptance as muscle car drivers is a result of their willingness to adhere to cultural gender roles within the muscle car community. As lesbian lifestyles do not comply to conservative norms, the assimilation of lesbian women into muscle car culture could be considered problematic.

While acceptance of gays and lesbians has risen dramatically among the general population—particularly among millennials—many conservatives—especially those of the boomer generation—do not recognize, approve, or consider alternative sexual identities or practices.[15] This became evident when a number of participants were unable to provide an answer when questioned about their own sexual orientation as they had no understanding of what was being asked. The relationship between Christianity, conservatism, and uneasiness with the homosexual lifestyle within the muscle car community no doubt creates an uncomfortable environment for those whose sexual orientation places them outside the mainstream.

AGE

As an American automotive icon, the muscle car—of any and all generations—is culturally and emotionally tied to a particular era in automotive history. It should not be surprising, therefore, that the majority of individuals who contributed this project—i.e., women who belong to car organizations and participate on forums, in car shows, and other automotive events—identify as middle aged or as senior citizens. Of the 88 women interviewed, 55 (63 percent) were between 40 and 59 years of age and 24 (27 percent) were over the age of 60. While those interviewed often mentioned the importance of creating interest in the muscle car among millennials, the muscle car hobby remains dominated by members of the boomer and post-boomer (Generation X) generations. Consequently, younger muscle car enthusiasts often feel out of place or invisible at automotive events. This sentiment was particularly prevalent among young women with older cars. As a 22-year-old 1966 Mustang owner declared, "It is actually pretty difficult to participate at my age. First, it takes a lot of money to go to shows and work on cars. Secondly, most car people do not take young people seriously." Finances also affect the participation of young women with retro muscle cars. Although modern-day Chargers, Challengers, and Mustangs are not categorized as expensive automobiles, they are not as affordable to young buyers as they were during the classic muscle car era. As Mueller notes, "this financial reality serves as a cold slap in the face, an often painful reminder that cars aren't playthings anymore; they're major investments" (190).

Cultural mores also play a role; although women's salaries have risen significantly relative to those of men over the past 50 years, women are often admonished for spending money on what is considered an impractical automobile. While at a car show, a 42-year-old 2011 Camaro SS/RS owner was approached by two much older gentlemen, one of whom blatantly asked how she could afford the car. As the young widow noted, "I was shocked. So I spit out the first thing that came to mind: 'my husband passed away and I used his insurance money.' That shut them up and they walked away with their tails between their legs." Millennial women, considered too young and inexperienced to fully understand or appreciate the muscle car by older car guys, often have their automotive "creds" challenged or questioned. Those who participate on online muscle car forums and communities are especially prone to age and gender related attacks on their credibility. Of her experiences online, a 37-year-old Mustang GT owner remarked, "some discredit me and think I have [the car] just for attention but don't understand me and don't take the time. They are dismissive, especially when I ask questions, even though they were better and more technical than most of the guys. They also didn't give my answers to questions much credit. Mostly, I just got hit on." A 47-year-old 2015 Dodge Challenger owner attributed the negative treatment she receives online to her age and her gender. As she noted, "I joined to learn more about my car, its problems and to share experiences. Sometimes I have experienced that because I am a woman that I get treated differently. I feel less than welcome because I am playing in the 'men's sandbox.'"

Despite their outlier status, the women in this project who do not fit the white, Christian, middle-class, middle-aged, heterosexual model of the muscle car community share a passion for cars more powerful than the ostracism and disregard they sometimes experience in muscle car organizations and events. They participate in the muscle car community not as a means to challenge cultural norms, but to acquire and share automotive knowledge, gain access to automotive resources and networks, and to celebrate the American muscle car.

3

Making Meaning
Out of the Muscle Car

As a fast, powerful, noisy, colorful, and unpredictable vehicle originally conceived, produced, and marketed to a young male audience, the dominant meanings ascribed to the American muscle car have traditionally been considered from a male perspective. To the young man who drove it, the original muscle car served as a symbol of rebellion, power, virility, masculinity, individuality, proficiency, sexual prowess, and audacity. As Mark Foster explains, "For teenagers and many young men in their early twenties, racing powerful, noisy cars at maximum speed was a symbol of self-expression and perhaps, a rebellion against the cautious, conservative values of their Depression-era parents" (78). The loud, powerful, and attention-getting muscle car was the ultimate expression of freedom and self. As Naughton et al. write, "On the road the Me Generation became the Look at Me generation" (64). It served as a source of identity for the young male auto enthusiast who embraced the popular mantra "you are what you drive." The young men who came of age during the muscle car era are now approaching retirement age or are full-fledged senior citizens. While they still appreciate the classic muscle car, the meanings assigned to them have changed over time. Aging boomers still in their peak earning years often view the classic muscle car as an investment. However, the majority of greying muscle car aficionados considers the classic GTO and Camaro as a way to relive their youth, obtain something they longed for in the past, or celebrate the era in which the American auto industry had presence and power.

While many aging boomers remain attached to the cars of their teenage years, others have turned their attention to modern day muscle. The twenty-first century Mustangs, Camaros, Chargers, and Challengers allow boomers to connect to their automotive past while taking advantage of the latest advances in automotive technology. As they crank up '60s tunes on their Sirius radios and synced audio technology, these graying AARP members enjoy improvements in automotive comfort, fuel economy, safety, handling, and most importantly, power. As *Carfax* blogger Aaron Turpen writes, "for this automotive segment, there is no 'grown up' as there is always a way to get bigger, faster, better, and prettier. Today's American muscle car is as grown up as they get." Modern-day muscle can serve as an antidote for the loss of power men often experience as they grow older.

Thus the retro muscle car creates meaning not only as a historical link to the past, but also for the way it makes this aging male population feel in the present.

Although greying boomers compose a significant percentage of new muscle car owners, the average age of retro Mustang, Charger, Challenger, and Camaro drivers hovers just under the 50-year mark.[1] For this group of GenXers—the demographic sandwiched between boomers and millennials—modern muscle cars provide the means to stand out from the crowd. As Mike Tolson writes, "a muscle car is attitude. It has a stance that reeks of testosterone and challenge, a presence and a sound that demands to be noticed, like the loudest guy at the party." Due to the similarity in factory conditions and building protocols among automakers, the automobile, asserts Christopher Finch, has evolved into an "agent of conformity." Modern muscle—with its speed, power, loud colors, and even louder engines—not only draws attention to itself, but announces the driver as someone who is neither unassuming nor conventional. To the 40-something male auto enthusiast, the meanings associated with the modern muscle car center on individuality, personality, power, and once again and always, masculinity.

The study of objects, writes Daniel Miller, not only contributes to an understanding of artifacts, but "is also an effective instrument for the study of social values and contradictions" ("Back cover"). The majority of women who contributed to this project came late to muscle cars. Thus, although it is now common to see female participants in various muscle car communities alongside men, the meanings women ascribe to all generations of Mustangs, Camaros, and Challengers differ considerably—and are often contradictory—to those of male car enthusiasts. While the women in this project appreciate the power and performance of the muscle car as much as their male counterparts, the value they place on these vehicles is more celebratory than nostalgic. Because financial and cultural limitations restricted women's participation in muscle car culture during the 1960s and early 1970s, the women have constructed new ways of revering the muscle car that do not dwell too heavily on the historical past but rather, reflect women's status in the world today. Christopher Tilley argues that a material object—such as the automobile—can be a powerful medium through which individuals reflect on their world. He writes, "through the artifact, layered and often contradictory sets of meanings can be conveyed simultaneously" ("Objectification" 62). While the women in this project ascribe a multitude of meanings to the muscle car, those shared by most include the muscle car as a symbol of achievement, a source of new identities, a means to respect, a display of gender equality, and perhaps most importantly, a vehicle of escape and empowerment.

The Muscle Car as a Symbol of Individual Achievement

At the turn of the twentieth century, the first automobiles made available to the American public were individually handcrafted and assembled by experienced artisans. Expensive to build and costly to maintain, the early cars were accessible only to those with considerable financial means. Primarily powered by electricity or steam with limited range and power, they were considered expensive fashion accessories rather than practical driving machines. As Cotten Seiler remarks, American culture in the late nineteenth century perceived the automobile as "an expensive whirligig produced for the

The throaty, rumbling, and roaring sound of a muscle car is often what attracts woman to it. Of her 1965 Mustang, Judy McEwan remarks, "I could just get a nice little coupe that's quiet and doesn't make any noise and it would still look good, but I don't know; I like the sound of it. When you drive into a car show, and you've got this car that's making some noise and it's rumbling when you're standing still, you know, people look" (courtesy Judy McEwan).

amusement of the effete rich" (52). While impractical for anything than short pleasure drives, the early automobile's primary function was to impart status and social standing to the individual behind the wheel. Writes Warren Brodsky, "during this era large specialist crafted luxury cars functioned as upper class status symbols [...]" (4). However, the introduction of Henry Ford's mass-produced, gasoline-powered Model T in 1908 resulted in affordable and available automobile ownership for "Everyman" (Scharff 53). And as automobility spread to lower socio-economic classes, mere automobile ownership was not sufficient to express one's status. In order to distinguish themselves from other car owners, individuals looked to particular car brands and models as emblems of power, prestige, elegance, financial achievement, and professional success (Brodsky 8).

The original American muscle car was produced and promoted as an affordable, hard-driving, no frills vehicle for the young male driver. As the first vehicle category developed specifically for the youth market, the status the muscle car awarded its driver differed significantly from that of automobiles that preceded it. As rough, loud, powerful, and dangerous, the muscle car announced its owner as undeniably masculine. Although over 50 years have passed since the muscle car made its rumbling and roaring entrance, its association with masculinity remains intact. Aging boomers often acquire classic muscle cars as a means to reassert themselves as masculine in a youth oriented, technology centered automotive culture. And 40-somethings purchase modern-day Mustangs and Camaros to stand out as powerful and exceptional men in an auto climate dominated by indistinguishable sedans, hybrids, and SUVs.

Brodsky suggests that the status derived from a particular car type is often linked to social affiliation, subcultures, gender roles, and sexual orientation (2). The male driver has many opportunities to announce his status in this manner; the sports car, luxury car, convertible, sedan, coupe, hatchback, pickup truck, van, hybrid, full-sized SUV, and muscle car each define him as a particular masculine type. Certainly many driving women call upon family vehicles such as the minivan and crossover to announce their status as mothers and caregivers. However, when women venture into automotive categories typically reserved for men, there is not an existing status to accompany them. Thus, rather than rely on established historical and cultural links between car and driver, female muscle car drivers must create their own associations. While married women often call upon the classic muscle car to announce their status as caring and car-loving partners, single women—unmarried, divorced, and widowed—are more likely to view the Charger and Mustang as reflective of their status as accomplished individuals. To the single women who own them, the muscle car holds meaning as representative of the attainment of a lifelong dream, a personal or professional achievement, or as a source of awards and rewards.

> Single women are getting the muscle cars that say, ["we can do it, too."] It's probably the wage-earning women that say, "I can have the car that I want."
> —72-year-old 1973 Mustang owner

ATTAINMENT OF A LIFELONG DREAM

Like many of those interviewed for this project, single women often held a fascination for muscle cars during their teenage years. However, financial limitations, cultural expectations, and the construction of muscle car culture as a masculine space often restricted women's participation. As a 59-year-old x-ray technician remarked, "My [ex-husband] and his boyfriends used to go up to Woodward all the time. [But] I wasn't ever taken." Young women sometimes compensated by driving less powerful—and less expensive—versions of "pony cars" and imagined what it would be like to drag race down Woodward in a loud and fast Dodge Charger or Plymouth 'Cuda. As a teenager in the late 1960s, a motor city journalist would sometimes drive the family Pontiac Tempest to her part-time job in suburban Detroit. As she remarked, "I'd gun it down Woodward and hope people would think it was a GTO" (qtd. in Genat 44). Other young women would set their sights on a favorite car—Mustangs and Camaros were particularly popular—and dream of the day they could have one of their own. As a 59-year-old 1965 Mustang owner replied, "I was pretty focused on getting an education, getting married, having a family, having a house. I never fathomed that at my age I would have one." While young men were encouraged to purchase fast and powerful cars as a way to demonstrate masculinity, young women understood the societal repercussions of using their limited financial resources for something as impractical and unfeminine as an American muscle car. A 65-year-old 1969 Camaro Z/28 owner grew up in a family of car crazy boys. Although her brothers allowed her to "borrow" their vehicles on occasion, as the retired beautician reflected, "I said one of these days I'm going to own my own fast car." A 42-year-old manufacturing analyst had her heart set on a Camaro, but as a widow with young children, opted to use her savings to honor her children's wishes rather than her own. As she noted, "In 2008 I found my exact dream car in North Carolina. I was so close to buying it, but chose to invest into Disney vacations for me and my kids for the next 50 years." A young woman's fancy of a fast and attention-getting car was often put on hold until personal and financial circumstances were more accommodating.

Now on their own, with kids grown and no one to answer to, these single women have the resources and opportunity to purchase the cars they have long admired. As a 59-year-old 1965 Mustang owner remarked, "I had the means, because I'm working and I had some extra cash that I saved. I wanted something that kind of brought back memories to me about that Mustang back in my younger days." A 54-year-old 1967 Pontiac LeMans owner explained, "I purchased the vehicle from a classic car dealer I used to drive by on a regular basis. I would always eye what was on the lot and wish I could have one. So when I was finally able to afford to indulge myself, that was the first place I went." A 58-year-old retired occupational therapist, while driving with her younger son, spotted a red 1965 Mustang convertible at a classic car dealership. As she reflected, "[My son] told me that here was my dream of a lifetime and if I did not follow through it would be a great loss." To many single women, the acquisition of a classic muscle car not only serves as an act of independence, but also represents the attainment of a lifelong dream.

PERSONAL ACHIEVEMENT

The single women interviewed for this project acknowledged that the gendered expectations and domestic responsibilities of the 1960s and 1970s deterred if not prohibited women's participation in muscle car culture. As a 55-year-old CPA remarked, "I was busy working, and career, then kids, so I kind of missed that in my life." Stated a 64-year-old 1967 Pontiac GTO owner, "I had five kids so I had to raise them first." Yet rather than reflect on the past as an era in which women had fewer opportunities and privileges—including driving and owning a muscle car—these single women focus on the present. They consider the ability to purchase a classic muscle car as not only the fulfillment of a lifelong dream but also a personal achievement based on hard work, persistence, and modest professional and financial success. As a 46-year-old 1996 Mustang convertible owner noted, "I had raised a family; I had the minivan, the family car. I had been divorced and was [at] the point in my life where I was making a little more money and I could afford a better car." Of her 1997 Mercury Cougar, a 50-year-old USPS worker remarked, "I think it says I'm a little bit older, because I have the money that I can put this car aside and not use it." The muscle car often represents power in an individual's personal life; however, to many of the single women in the project, it reflects financial power made possible through work or career.

While it is not uncommon for successful men to purchase an additional sporty or impractical automobile for recreational use, women—whose driving preferences are assumed to lean toward the functional—are presumed to be satisfied with the reliable and roomy family car. In addition, if women do have discretionary income, it is expected they will spend it on personal items or their family rather than something as extraneous or frivolous as a loud, attention-getting, high performance vehicle. The purchase of a Challenger, Charger, or Barracuda, therefore, not only signifies a certain amount of financial freedom, but the empowerment that accompanies it. As a 72-year-old 1973 Mustang owner remarked, "women are high wage earners today, and they can go out and buy their own, they don't have to ask and grovel." A 73-year-old 1964½ Mustang owner—who in 1994 had to "fight with the lady at the bank" in order to finance an automobile on her own—declared, "[Women] have their own jobs, they have their own money and they can go out and get these cars. They can afford them. They can get loans on them."

The women in this project who consider the acquisition of a muscle car as a personal accomplishment echo what Kersten describes as a conservative feminist philosophy. As noted by a reporter covering the 2017 Conservative Political Action Conference, "conservatism generally holds that people should have equal opportunity but aren't entitled to equal outcomes [...]—that it's a matter of hard work" (Blake). Special assistant to the president Kellyanne Conway, interviewed at the aforementioned conference, referred to this ideology as a way to frame her own accomplishments and success. As Conway stated, "I look at myself as a product of my choices, not a victim of my circumstances. That's really to me what conservative feminism, if you will, is all about" (qtd. in Blake). The women who contributed to this project offered similar sentiments. Rather than ascribe the ability to own and drive a muscle car to the influence of the women's liberation movement, they were more likely to cite their own hard work and determination as responsible for the attainment of such goals. To many of the single muscle car owners, it was effort and ambition, rather than the eradication of societal obstacles, that made the realization of the lifelong dream of owning an American muscle car a reality. Noted a 64-year-old retiree, ownership of a 1967 Pontiac GTO signifies that "I am proud of what I've accomplished."

AWARDS AND REWARDS

While single women are more likely to frame ownership of a muscle car as a personal accomplishment than those in a marriage or longtime relationship, both single and partnered women may seek recognition of their hard work through competition at automotive events. Prizes received at these events are a point of pride among fellow car buffs and award the vehicle owner a certain amount of bragging rights. As a display at the Petersen Automotive Museum reads, "participation in car shows [...] provides the means for owners of unique and interesting automobiles to display their vehicles and earn recognition from aficionados and the general public alike. Trophies from these events are a tangible way to showcase a vehicle's merit and can help establish what makes it praiseworthy."[2] Car shows offer a myriad of awards; plaques and/or trophies are given out in a number of designated show categories determined by the show-giving organization. Awards are determined by the public, by fellow exhibitors, or—particularly in larger and more prestigious shows—outside auto experts. Many of the women were quick to claim that prizes didn't matter to them; they stressed that winning was, in fact, more important to the men. As a 64-year-old 1966 Dodge Charger owner explained, "it's not about winning; it's just really about the fun of taking [the cars out] out and driving them, and just letting people see them." A 59-year-old 1965 Mustang owner remarked, "I don't go to win awards because I know I'm not in that kind of classification. I just go to have fun."

However, while some women downplayed their competitive streaks, most exhibited a fair amount of pride when commenting on the awards the cars have received. A 50-year-old 1968 Plymouth Barracuda owner remarked, "it is gratifying to get acknowledgement of, that other people appreciate your vehicle by getting awards and trophies and acknowledgement of it. I won't lie about that; it does give you the warm fuzzies when you do get one." Although she had attended car shows for years, a 73-year-old 1973 Mustang owner won her first "real" trophy in 2013. Because she was proud to finally beat the "good ole boys," as she revealed, "at night my trophy is on the pillow next to me." Of her 1972 Barracuda, a 47-year-old accounting manager exclaimed, "I'm proud of it, I like to take it to shows. And I just won, this year, the best of class at the Packard Proving Grounds show. That was exciting." Competition at car shows and other automotive events not only provides women with bragging rights, but also serves as a source of validation from other muscle car enthusiasts. Winning automotive awards, noted a 37-year-old 2006 Mustang GT owner, "[means] I get more respect, especially from males."

Whether framing muscle car ownership as the attainment of a lifelong dream, a demonstration of professional or personal success, or the means to awards and rewards, the women in the project often cited the power of women's work—whether in reference to a good-paying job or hands-on automotive skills—to making the dream of a Mustang or Challenger possible. As a 31-year-old 1991 Firebird owner exclaimed, "I like going to the shows 'cause I like winning trophies; I like feeling like I'm doing something right. [I like] getting rewards for my hard work and all the money and time and energy that I put into my car." A 22-year-old 1965 Mustang owner remarked, "Those people outside the car world that I know seem to respect me a little bit more for my accomplishments." Having the financial means to purchase a 1967 Pontiac GTO, as well as the motivation and skills to restore it, was, in the words of a 64-year-old retiree, "A big accomplishment. It felt good. To be able to do it." The muscle car—classic, pony, and retro—holds meaning for this group of women not only because of its history, reputation, and unique driving experience. Rather, to the ladies who own them, the importance of the American muscle car lies in its status as a symbol of women's achievement.

The Muscle Car as an Expression of Identity

The American muscle car—in its original form as well as its twenty-first century reboot—was produced as a daily driver. However, as a vehicle that incorporated excessive power, impressive performance, and imposing presence, the muscle car soon established itself as a source of status and identity for the man behind the wheel. As British psychologists Peter Marsh and Peter Collett argue in the seminal work *The Psychology of the Car*, "the automobile satisfies not only our practical needs, but the need to declare ourselves socially and individually" (5). During the 1960s and early 1970s, young men drove Chargers and Challengers to present themselves as aggressive, brash, and formidable. Although the modern day muscle car is not as crude, rude, or dangerous as its predecessor, its reputation as distinctive, spirited, and just a little bit brazen is often appropriated by the

Marsh and Collett note how American drivers often use specialized license plates to draw attention to themselves. As they write, for some drivers the vanity plate "serves the role of a personal testimonial, displaying the owner's sense of humor or his ability to challenge the wits of other drivers" (75). Susan Glass calls upon a vanity plate to express the identity she claims when behind the wheel of her 2014 Chevy Camaro 2SS/RS (courtesy Susan Glass).

40-something-year-old man who drives it. As auto writer David Newhardt notes, "today's cars are environmentally friendly, safe, and fun and—unlike most of the rolling dreck clogging the roads—they make a personal statement" (165).

Traditionally, women's identification with the automobile has been limited to character traits associated with motherhood. Over the past half century, purchase of a family vehicle—e.g., station wagon, hatchback, minivan, crossover, or small SUV—has acknowledged and underscored the woman driver as a conscientious, practical, economical, and dutiful wife and mother. Ownership of a muscle car—whether classic, pony, or retro—not only suggests that women's car choices are more varied than characterized in automotive advertising campaigns and popular culture, but also that women's identities are more complex—and often more surprising—than common representations of the woman driver might have us believe. Much like the men who drive them, women view ownership of the muscle car as an expression of who they are. However, due to women's longtime exclusion from the muscle car community, the identities they assume when behind the wheel of a Charger or Camaro differ considerably from those of men. Rather than rely on historical archetypes—i.e., associations between the muscle car and masculinity embedded in the past—women call upon the muscle car to assume, create, and display identities that announce who they are in the present. More than a means of transportation, the muscle car allows female motorists to present themselves as certain types of individuals, to project an unexpected part of their personality, or to create entirely new personas. The new subjectivities made possible by muscle car ownership not only serve as a form of empowerment, but also effectively trouble the common perception of the woman driver.

At the 2017 Detroit Autorama, participants were asked to include "something of themselves" alongside their vehicles. Women of Michigan Mopar Muscle exhibitor and 1973 Plymouth Road Runner owner Rose Mrosewske combined her name and her love of muscle cars in this unique display (courtesy Rose Mrosewske).

I think that people that own faster cars or muscle cars, I think they exhibit adventure. And danger. So, anybody that I know that owns a muscle car is, I consider, a person who likes to take chances.

—47-year-old 1965 Mustang owner

MY CAR IS ME

The women in this project view the American muscle car not only as an enjoyable and exciting method of transportation, but also as a means to expose, enhance, or complement characteristics they most value in themselves. While the women often assume conventional personas in their daily lives, driving a muscle car provides them with the opportunity to reveal their true personalities. Of her 1995 GT Mustang, a 60-year-old professional dog handler declared, "it says I'm wild. I'm crazy. I'm fun." Owning a 2010 Camaro SS/RS, stated a 29-year-old automotive project manager, "says that I'm passionate. That I have a strong character. And I like yellow." Of her 1982 Mustang, a 42-year-old health clinic receptionist remarked, "It just shows off my personality. And it's fun, so I guess it shows I'm a fun person." John Wolkonowicz, an automotive historian and former Ford Motor product planner, reflects on how many individuals—particularly those of the boomer and post-boomer generations—rely on automobiles to define them. As he asserts, "for people who grew up and lived in the twentieth century, the car was a visible expression of you and your personality" (qtd. in "Boomers," Naughton). The framing of the automobile as a reflection of an individual's personal attributes was a common theme among this population of muscle car owning women.

Sex has often been used to market muscle cars to men. Whether featuring a scantily clad female draped over the hood, or promoting a particular vehicle as a certifiable "chick magnet," automotive advertising has traditionally implied that ownership of a muscle car carries the promise of enhanced sex appeal to the man behind the wheel. While the women in this project recognize the association between the muscle car and sexual attractiveness, they call upon this relationship in a different way than their male peers. To a few of the women, the sexiness associated with the muscle car carries over to how they feel while driving it. As a 59-year-old advertising copywriter exclaimed, when behind the wheel of her red 2006 Mustang convertible "I felt brave and I felt sexy and I felt alive." As a 23-year-old certified pharmacy technician noted, driving her 2002 Mustang GT convertible makes her feel just a little bit more "sexy."

Yet while some of the women attributed a feeling of sexiness with muscle car ownership, others relied on Chargers or Camaros to display their masculine side. As a 49-year-old 2010 Mustang GT owner exclaimed, "[this car] says I'm a tomboy. Because you're really made to feel, not an oddball, but just more like a guy." A 58-year-old graphic designer identifies with her 2014 Challenger SRT because, as she exclaimed, "I've always been a little bit of a tomboy. I guess you could say I was never the normal; I was never a girly girl." A 63-year-old nurse enjoys how her 2006 Mustang brings out her "wild, renegade, rebel, tomboy side." As she declared, "being a tomboy has always been part of my life and I love to be able to 'go with that' when I'm in the car!" As Christopher O'Connor and Katharine Kelly note in their work on youth car culture, young women often describe themselves as "tomboys" as a means of remaining feminine while justifying participation in a predominately male activity (262). Participants who claimed membership in the LGBTQ community were perhaps more forthright in identifying with the masculinity of the muscle car. Of her 1966 Chevy Impala, a 51-year-old nonprofit director remarked, "my car is a butchy femme. Kind of like me." However, the straight women in this project called on terms such as "tomboy" and "not girly" not as a reference to sexual orientation, but rather to equate their participation, knowledge, and level of interest to that of male car enthusiasts. As men—by virtue of their sex—are assumed to have a "natural" affinity and understanding of cars, aligning themselves with male participants in this manner awards female muscle car owners legitimacy.

Dodge Challenger...
The sports car that knows how to treat a lady.

If you didn't know better, you'd almost think Challenger had been designed by a woman. Who else would have made it low and sporty-looking, but still big enough so you don't get that squashed feeling when you're inside? Aren't things like the sports-type steering wheel and color-coordinated carpeting women's touches? Who but a member of the female sex would be smart enough to combine looks with practicality? Take those flush door handles. They aren't just for looks, you know. They're safer, too. And those thrifty standard six- and eight-cylinder engines. Both use regular gas. Speaking of thrift, Challenger's price is pretty nice, too. If Challenger was designed by a man, I bet he talked to his wife first.

If you think all this was worth waiting for . . .

you could be **DODGE MATERIAL.**

Dodge Challenger advertisement (1970): "Dodge Challenger. The sports car that knows how to treat a lady." While the headline seems to suggest that the young bikini-clad woman standing next to the car is the driver, the model's absence of shoes (as well as clothing) and her position on the passenger side of the vehicle would indicate that the car's female friendly features serve as a means to lure a woman into the car, rather than get behind the wheel of it.

Auto journalist Lesley Hazleton writes, "for most of us, a car's identity is a mix of both the car itself and the driver" ("Everything" 16). The female muscle car owners who contributed to this project were quick to make this connection. A 51-year-old automotive test driver describes herself and her 1969 Mustang Mach I as "rough and tough." The 51-year-old executive director of a nonprofit likes to think of herself as a "badass" when behind the wheel of her 1966 Chevrolet Impala. As she exclaimed, "I identify my car as female; she has a name and she is a badass, too." When a 50-year-old school bus driver pulls into a car show in her Frost Blue 1968 Plymouth Barracuda with a personalized "princess" vanity plate on the front, attired in an ensemble color-coordinated with her car, she is not only announcing herself as the owner of the vehicle, but is suggesting she is as "flashy and out there" as the car she drives. Many of the participants attributed a certain degree of "coolness" to the muscle car and by extension, to themselves. As a 54-year-old 2014 Chevy Camaro 2SS/RS owner exclaimed, "I'm cool, the car is cool, and I'm really proud." To a 45-year-old pharmacist, driving 1969 Mustang Mach 1 reveals "that I am more self-assured and also more approachable and maybe a bit more 'cool.'" To a 53-year-old automotive engineer, driving a hot Panther Pink 1971 Dodge Challenger convertible demonstrates that "I'm a cool old lady." Humanizing a car in this fashion, note Marsh and Collett, denotes the special significance a car has for its owner. As they write, "we give [cars] personalities which reflect the nature of our relationship with them" (13). As was oft repeated by the female Mustang, Camaro, and Charger owners, "my car is me."

Expect the Unexpected

While many of the women view the muscle car as an extension of themselves, others choose to drive cars with characteristics diametrically opposed to their own. Women who are normally passive and unassuming, for example, often enjoy taking on the bold personas of their Mustangs and Chargers, even if only temporarily. As a 27-year-old 1971 Pontiac GT-37 owner remarked, "at first impression I'm young, feminine and quiet spoken. Owning this car goes against all of the stereotypes for those three qualities." A 49-year-old prospect researcher is commonly thought of as "very straight-laced, prim, and proper." As she asserted, "When people see that I drive a Camaro, they look at me in a different light—their faces change." Although she turns heads when behind the wheel of her rumbling Plum Crazy 1970 Dodge Challenger, as the 63-year-old retired support manager explained, "I'm naturally [a] very quiet lady who just enjoys her car." Acquaintances of a 56-year-old business analyst are surprised to discover she owns a 1971 Pontiac Firebird. As she noted, "and when you take into consideration that my other hobbies are sewing and that type of thing, that's a contradiction."

More than half of the women (60 percent) who participated in this project are mothers. While they acknowledge and respect this crucial part of their personhood, they call upon ownership of a muscle car to display and affirm other—and often unexpected—facets of their identity. A 55-year-old registered nurse observed that folks are very surprised to learn she drives a 1973 Plymouth Road Runner. For as she explained, "I've always been more of a typical female, as a nurse, mother, and wife." A 46-year-old special education teacher noted that ownership of a 1996 Mustang convertible "took me out of the traditional mom-woman kind of role." While advertising, the automotive industry, and popular culture most often place women in the practical and passive driver category, this group of Charger, Challenger, and Mustang owners challenge such representations and have a great deal of fun while doing so. As the owner of a Panther Pink 1971 Dodge Challenger convertible with a "six-pack" under the hood remarked, "I don't think I fit into the soccer mom minivan mold."

As feminist scholars Dafna Lemish and Varda Muhlbauer argue, women—particularly those over the age of 50—are often rendered invisible in the media and in public life. The ubiquity of the typical "woman's" car—i.e., minivan or crossover—assures that women's invisibility carries over into American car culture. Consequently, when women in their 50s, 60s, and 70s get behind the wheel of a noisy, colorful, and powerful muscle car, they not only make themselves visible, but suggest they are not the quiet, passive, and conventional moms others make them out to be. Of her 1978 Trans Am Bandit, a 53-year-old automotive engineer remarked, "I don't think it's hurt my image. A lot of the moms are like wow!" As a 54-year-old 2009 Dodge Charger R/T owner explained, "Well, you know, I'm in my 50s, and I'm very short, so [people] don't expect a little lady coming out in her 50s driving a muscle car like that. And then I've had young kids pull up beside me and think they can take me, and I lose 'em!"

The sound, style, and undeniable presence of an American muscle car guarantee it will receive a fair amount of notice no matter who is driving it. However, when a woman is behind the wheel, attention shifts from the car to the driver. The women in this project enjoy the element of surprise that accompanies ownership of a muscle car. As the responses in this project suggest, women drive Chargers and Camaros not only for the way the cars makes them feel, but for the way it compels family, friends, and all they encounter to think differently about them as women and as drivers.

Name That Car

Due to the muscle car's longstanding association with masculinity, many of the women name or mark their cars in some way to claim ownership and display a personal identity. As Marsh and Collett note, "naming is a particularly strong way in which to announce our attachment to something which is much more than just an object" (13). In order to assure that ownership of a 1965 red Mustang convertible was attributed to her rather than her husband, a 47-year-old analyst attached a personalized license plate inscribed with her childhood nickname on the back bumper. A 47-year-old teacher had "She Devil" airbrushed prominently on both her 1989 RS and 2001 Berger SS Camaros. As she noted, "I get the funniest comments about that. 'So is that the car or the woman?'" A 54-year-old cultural events coordinator, who hails from Montreal, personalized the engine cover of her 2009 Dodge Charger R/T with an airbrushed Quebec flag. To feminize the car and make it her own, she hand painted the engine and fuse box covers and added a few engine items "that make the engine bay look a little bit more pretty." A 29-year-old New Zealand native, whose 2010 Camaro SS/RS is adorned with bumble bee imagery and carries the license plate "Kiwi Bee," has taken identification with the car to a whole new level. As the automotive product manager explained, "I'm constantly accessorizing myself to match the car. My computer laptop bag is yellow; I have a yellow purse; my fingernails I paint yellow and put black bowties on them."[3]

A display at the Petersen Automotive Museum reads, "Many people consider automobiles to be their outermost layer of clothing. Those seeking the ultimate in individuality can tailor their rides to match their personalities in a near infinite number of ways."[4] Marsh and Collett note that the original muscle car served as a "standard form of uniform" for young men; a little bit of embellishment provided the opportunity to transform the vehicle into a "social statement" (93). The women in this project call upon naming and marking to identify with a category of automobile historically associated with the man behind the wheel. By doing so they make the car their own, and project a revised and reimagined image of the woman driver.

The most oft mentioned identity claimed by the female muscle car owners was "unique." Although women represent a growing number of muscle car owners, they are still rare enough to be considered an anomaly in an automotive community historically dominated by men. Yet rather than feel intimidated by their underrepresentation in the muscle car community, the women claim uniqueness as an important component of their personhood. As a 22-year-old 1966 Mustang owner exclaimed, "I like having a muscle car because it is a piece of who I am. It makes me unique." Getting behind the wheel of her Vitamin C orange 1970 Plymouth Superbird Road Runner, asserted a 51-year-old auto industry manager, makes her feel "powerful and unique." As a 54-year-old professional gardener exclaimed, driving a 1967 Pontiac LeMans means "that I am not afraid to go against traditional stereotypes for women. I can participate in a male-dominated activity and gain respect." Of her 2014 Dodge Challenger SRT, a 58-year-old graphic designer remarked, "I'd like to believe it says I'm a little different than your normal female. I'm not boring. There's more to me than meets the eye." Vannini writes, the "identity and subjectivity of women have been shaped by technological choices that reinforced existing binary gender oppositions and dominant sexist hierarchies" (19). Many of the women in this project—particularly those of the boomer generation—have lived traditional lives in which a woman's identity was considered primarily in relationship to others. The cars they drove often reflected this status. Ownership of a muscle car, therefore, disrupts the notion of a woman driver as conforming, conventional, and ordinary. Rather, zooming down the street in a throaty Mustang or rumbling Camaro announces her as distinctive, interesting, and unique.

To the women in this project, muscle car ownership often rendered a shift in how they viewed themselves. Although, as Rebecca Klatch suggests, the conservative feminist does not view women as "bound to traditional roles" (151), the majority of the participants spent a good portion of their lives driving vehicles that announced and reinforced their identities as wives and mothers. The muscle car—in which "mom" features such as back-seat cameras, seven-passenger seating, hands-free liftgate and sliding doors, in-vehicle vacuums, and accommodation for multiple child-safety seats have been replaced with V8 hemi engines, high horsepower, launch control function, impressive torque, and rapid acceleration—encourages women to confront, appreciate, and enjoy other facets of their identities. Of her gold 1998 Pontiac Trans Am, a 43-year-old optician remarked, "I just know that four years ago it changed the way I looked at things. And it changed who I was." Of her 1965 Mustang, a 59-year-old x-ray technician remarked, "it says I've got a little bit of spunk still." When gunning the engine of her 1966 Dodge Charger, remarked a 64-year-old grandmother, "I guess you could say that I'm sassy." As the participant responses suggest, women who own and drive muscle cars often feel different about themselves when behind the wheel. Reflecting on her white 1973 Mustang convertible, a 73-year-old retired store owner exclaimed, "It just gives me a zest for living."

Cotten Seiler introduces the concept of expressive individualism to describe how consumer culture can provide resources for the "construction and performance of a distinctive individual identity" (34). The comments collected for this project suggest that muscle cars offer women the possibility of alternative and unexpected identities outside of the traditional roles of wife and mother. To those who own them, the muscle car is a place where a woman can be her own person. She can be loud, powerful, daring, adventurous, unique, fun, sexy, spunky, or sassy, just like the car she drives.

The Muscle Car as a Display of Gender Equality

The muscle car culture of the 1960s and early 1970s was developed around the automotive needs, desires, and habits of the teenage male. As Holloway writes, "muscle cars were designed to appeal to young men who wanted big engine performance at a blue-collar price" (73). It was a culture in which ear splitting engines, reckless driving, excessive speed, and illegal street racing were promoted as symbols of a youthful and rebellious masculinity. It has been argued by automotive scholars and students of popular culture that the role of the teenage girl in muscle car culture was that of passenger, observer, or enthusiastic cheerleader. Advertising and other imagery from the classic muscle car era rarely feature young women as drivers. Rather, if women are included at all, it is in the passenger seat or on the sidelines casting admiring glances. While a few of the women interviewed for this project took part in cruising culture with borrowed cars from brothers or boyfriends, the majority acknowledged that gender excluded them from participation in muscle car culture as drivers. As a 59-year-old 1965 Mustang owner noted, "For some reason I got left out of that scene."

Over 50 years have passed since muscle cars took over Detroit's Woodward Avenue. The women in this project recognize they now have the opportunity to participate in muscle car culture in a manner forbidden to them during the era's heyday. As Walsh notes, during the 1960s, "women were being accepted as drivers but they by no means had automotive equality" ("Equality" 31). Whereas young women were discouraged from driving fast and powerful automobiles during the muscle car era, women today have the ability to make their own decisions on the type of car they drive and how they use it. Speaking of women in the muscle car hobby, a 54-year-old 2009 Dodge Charger owner remarked, "They want to get that thrill ride; they want to be able to do just the same [as men] and why not." A 60-year-old 2002 Camaro Z/28 owner exclaimed, "[it] could be that a lot of women are finally coming out from behind men and want to have the same degree of fun and are finding that they really can afford the extra 'toy.'" Although some are satisfied to share a car with husbands, most desire to drive muscle cars of their own. Whether behind the wheel of a 1966 Plymouth 'Cuda, 1992 Pontiac Firebird, or 2013 Ford Mustang, these women view the muscle car as a vehicle of gender equality.

In "Women with Muscle," my original investigation of women and classic muscle cars, I considered women's participation in classic muscle car culture through the lens

Rose Mrosewske's award-winning 1973 Plymouth Road Runner was featured in the special "Women of Michigan Mopar Muscle" display at the 2017 Detroit Autorama, often referred to as "America's Greatest Hot Rod Show." Rose chose the car for its rally red exterior, good price, and its association with the fast-running *Looney Tunes* character. As she remarked, "[I] always liked it when the Road Runner won out over the coyote" (courtesy Rose Mrosewske).

of conservative feminism. I chose this framework because it most appropriately explained the dichotomy between the conservative woman's quest for gender equality and her focus on traditional family and community. In this current project, in which I expand the population of participants to include a broader range of "generations"—both human and automotive—I found this contradiction to be even more pronounced. While the women adhere to, and are supportive of, cultural gender roles that endorse and promote identities of wife, mother, and accommodating partner, they claim women's presence in muscle car culture as evidence of growing gender equality. Opposed to an ideology—feminism— often misrepresented as "anti-male,"[5] married women in particular acknowledged that access into muscle car culture was dependent on male support or permission. Thus rather than define equality in the liberal feminist sense, i.e., the opposite of hierarchy, this population of women called upon other means to establish themselves as equal participants in muscle car culture. Such methods included calling upon the conservative construction of individualism to claim ownership of a muscle car, displaying automotive knowledge and savvy, and poking fun at men in the muscle car hobby.

> *Usually guys are thought as driving muscle cars. But why can't women have fun with muscle cars, too?*
>
> —60-year-old 1993 Ford Mustang owner

MY CAR

The conservative feminist, Kersten points out, values the rights of individuals; in muscle car culture individual rights often translate into a woman's prerogative to drive a car of her own choosing. Although the majority of married women who contributed to this project participate in muscle car culture alongside husbands, they were quick to point out that the car they drive belongs to them and take immense pride in personal ownership. As a 62-year-old Wimbledon White 1964½ Mustang owner remarked, "Before I had my own car I tagged along with my husband, but I changed my attitude when I got my own car. Cause then he had his and I had mine and I could say this is mama's car. I could take pride in something that was actually mine." A 58-year-old 2014 Dodge Challenger SRT owner exclaimed, "I'm one of the luckiest women in the world. [My husband] steps back and lets me have my car. It is mine. We do what I want to do to it." The women emphasized they were instrumental in car selection as well as any modifications made to the vehicle—i.e., paint color, engine, interior—after purchase. Noted a 54-year-old 2009 Dodge Charger R/T owner, "you personalize it to your taste. Nobody can tell you I don't like it. I like it; that's the main thing."

While some women acquiesced to the automotive preferences of spouses, others rejected their husband's ambivalence or recommendations regarding car models and held steadfast until they took ownership of a particular automobile. As a 60-year-old 1971 Dodge Charger Super Bee owner exclaimed, "My husband tried to tell me 'why don't you buy a GTO.' And I said if you want a GTO you buy a GTO." When her husband vacillated over the purchase of a 2010 Mustang GT, a 49-year-old paraprofessional "got really mad." As she exclaimed, "I'm like this is the one I want; this is the body style I like. And so we finally got it. I went through hell to get it." To this group of women, the ability to claim automotive ownership on their own terms was an important indicator of gender equality within the muscle car community.

As was mentioned in a previous section, the women who contributed to this project often personalize their cars in some manner as a means of identification. They also mark their Mustangs and Chargers to avoid any misconception of auto ownership and to deter husbands from driving them. Vanity license plates were cited as an effective way to tag a car as female. The plates on a 1965 Ford Mustang convertible contain the childhood nickname of its owner. As the 47-year-old analyst noted, the reason she chose to identify her car in this manner was "so when my husband hops in the car they'll know it's not his. And my husband doesn't even make the mistake of saying that it's his, or ours. It's always my car." A "sparkly" Frost Blue 1968 Plymouth Barracuda has a princess license plate with the owner's name prominently displayed. As the 50-year-old school bus driver asserted, "I have this thing about owning something. When I own it I like to mark it."

The license plate on a 1966 Dodge Charger reads "Mrs. Hemi" to distinguish it from the vehicle owned by the "Mr." As the 64-year-old nurse remarked, "I think it just tells you who you are." Other methods of identification were called upon to make sure there is no question as to who owns the car. Of her 2011 Camaro SS/RS convertible, a 42-year-old manufacturing analyst declared, "I had fairies painted on it so most people would know it was owned by a girl." As Marsh and Collett write, "to owners who have christened their cars in this way, what they drive has a very special significance for them" (13). As these actions suggest, recognition as owners in their own right was extremely important to this group of female muscle car enthusiasts. Not only does marking a vehicle in this manner serve as a form of identification, but allows women to construct the muscle car as an expression of gender equality.

Although married women often assume roles in muscle car culture that conform to cultural gender prescriptions of family, they do not consider themselves as unequal participants. Rather, through the personal choices they make about cars, and the ways in which they identify individual vehicles as their own, married women claim their own spaces in the muscle car community. The 46-year-old CAD drafter who suggested that the next Firebird her husband purchased should be a convertible; the 1971 Dodge Challenger owner who insisted on the high-impact color of "Panther Pink" as a way to honor her mother and other breast cancer survivors; the 29-year-old auto industry product manager who created her own Transformer-themed 2010 Camaro SS/RS; the woman who "earned" a 1967 Plymouth Satellite through the completion of a nursing degree after her children were grown; and the 41-year-old mother of two who not only insisted on a 1970 Dodge Charger R/T but who had it restored, painted, and equipped to her exacting specifications all demonstrate how individual car ownership allows women to consider themselves equal participants in the muscle car hobby.

Women Auto Know

When a muscle car is on display at a car show or other automotive event, the common assumption is that the owner is male. Although the car owner's name is displayed prominently on a display card in the front window, spectators and fellow exhibitors invariably ask a husband, male companion, or whatever man happens to be in the vicinity, about the automobile. A 51-year-old 1969 Mustang Mach I owner remarked, "I got pulled over in Frankenmuth because the guy didn't think it was my car. He thought it was a man's car."[6] A 31-year-old 1991 Firebird owner had just met a male friend at a car show, when a man came over and started asking the friend about the car's engine. As she explained, "I said it has [a] 3.1 V6. And he looked at me and he goes, 'I'm talking to him.' And I said, 'yeah, but it's my car.' And he shook his head with a nasty face and walked away." Although she participates in the muscle car hobby with her husband, a 55-year-old small business owner makes certain that fellow car enthusiasts understand that the black 2012 Dodge Challenger R/T is all hers. As she asserted, "it's funny, the first question I'm asked is, 'is this your husband's car or is this your boyfriend's car?' I get that all the time. And when I start pointing out things that are on the car, that are obviously not stock and are performance-related, men are stunned. That I'm that knowledgeable." Because women are relative newcomers to muscle cars, acquiring automotive knowledge while gaining the confidence to speak intelligently and knowledgeably about the cars they drive becomes an effective way to demonstrate that they are equal participants in muscle car culture.

While women remain the exception rather than the rule in the muscle car community, the women in this project expressed the belief that car savvy, respect for the American muscle car, a willingness to listen and learn, and unbridled enthusiasm for all things automotive are all that are necessary for acceptance as equals. Many of the women conduct historical research to become better informed about the cars they drive, as well as to answer automotive questions intelligently and confidently. Some scrapbook the vehicle restoration process step by step to demonstrate how the cars became their own. They frequent car shows and swap meets to uncover old sales brochures, print advertisements, repair manuals, and historical documents pertinent to their muscle car of choice. After acquiring a silver 1965 Mustang, noted a 67-year-old office manager, "we bought all the manuals, the old manuals for them, and all the spec sheets and all that other stuff." Others pride themselves on their ability to perform basic automotive maintenance and repair. Of her 1965 Mustang convertible a retired occupational therapist remarked, "I have had to learn quite a bit about how it was put together because I am frequently inundated with questions when I am out." The common assumption that women are generally uninformed about cars is both acknowledged and challenged by these female muscle car owners. Most make it a point to become thoroughly educated about the cars they drive and enjoy demonstrating that knowledge among interested spectators, as well as other muscle car enthusiasts. As a 1968 Plymouth Firebird owner declared, "I think it impresses people. People are surprised to know I know what I do."

The women who participated in this project understand that gender equality within the muscle car community is often dependent on the acceptance and approval of men in the hobby. Thus they must often walk a fine line, displaying enough knowledge to gain legitimacy, but not so much as to appear arrogant. Married women often rely on the support of husbands to gain respect as equal participants within the muscle car community. Many were quick to point out that, rather than answer questions from interested spectators about their wives' cars, husbands will redirect those spectators to their spouses. As a 53-year-old black 1973 Dodge Challenger owner remarked, "the car is always showed [*sic*] with my name on it and he always lets people know the car belongs to me not him." A 58-year-old 2014 Challenger SRT owner noted, "Guys will walk up and look at [my husband] and start asking him questions about the car and he'll say, 'ask her, it's hers.' You know then they look at me like 'it's yours?' Yeah, it's mine." While there are doubters and detractors among spectators as well as fellow exhibitors, the women believe that increased car savvy among female participants will contribute to respect and recognition as equals within the muscle car hobby. As a 49-year-old 1969 Dodge Charger owner notes, "I hope that when people come up to the car and especially now that it's just my name on it, and if they would talk to me and realize yeah I've worked on it I don't just get in the car and drive it. It makes them reconsider the image of women and cars." To the women who participated in this project, the acquisition of automotive knowledge eases their entry into muscle car culture, offers them legitimacy in a traditionally male dominated pastime, and furthers the possibility of gender equality within the muscle car community.

HOW GUYS THINK

While this expanded study included women who did not fall within the dominant demographic of muscle car culture, the majority who participated identified as white, Christian, middle-class, heterosexual, and either moderate or conservative. Consequently, most women did not openly criticize or question the patriarchal construction of the culture; rather, they often called upon creative strategies to bring attention to women's growing presence within it. A common tactic was teasing men about their attitudes toward women drivers with the hope of changing their collective mindsets. The women who contributed to this project often make lighthearted generalizations about male behavior and poke fun at "the way men think." This strategy allows them to address male resistance to female participation without challenging men's position of power within the culture itself. When a 56-year-old auto dealership biller is behind the wheel of her black 1973 Dodge Challenger, guys who pull up beside her assume it's her husband's car. As she laughingly remarked, "It's kind of like how men think." Of her 1969 Mustang Mach I, a part-time automotive tester explained, "men don't think that women should have a car like that." As a 56-year-old business analyst recalled, while at a local show with her husband and two other couples, one of the men mentioned how his wife would occasionally "help" him polish the car. As the 1971 Pontiac Firebird owner recalled, "and they both looked at my husband and expected him to pipe in something similar. And I said something to the effect of 'please don't get me started.' You know because they instantly assume that the car is my husband's and that he does all the work." A 55-year-old 2010 Challenger SRT owner noted, "Every few shows I get some old coot making a comment about 'my husband's car.' I'm not always polite in correcting them but I guarantee they will never make that comment again! I guess you could say I take an active part in changing that perception." Equality for the women who participated in this project is not about breaking barriers or destroying gender hierarchies within the historically masculine confines of muscle car culture. Rather, it's concerned with changing "the way guys think" to acknowledge women's growing automotive interest and knowledge and to become more accepting of women as enthusiastic and well-informed muscle car owners and drivers.

Writing about the change in women's status as drivers over the past 50 years, Margaret Walsh notes, "before women could negotiate automotive equality, they needed to be more confident about their gender equality" ("Equality" 31). Although the contributors acknowledge that societal changes over the past half century have created equal opportunity for women in many aspects of American life, as women participating in a conservative, historically masculine culture they must often negotiate how that gender equality is realized and expressed. Through individual car ownership, the acquisition of automobile knowledge, and the gentle teasing of male peers, the women in this project have constructed the American muscle car as a vehicle of gender equality.

The Muscle Car as a Vehicle of Respect

In a 1970 print advertisement, the headline accompanying a double-paged image of the Pontiac GTO reads, "After a few moments of respectful silence, you may turn the page."[7] The original American muscle car—produced from 1964 to 1973—was a vehicle

Theresa Newbauer enjoys her 2010 Dodge Challenger SRT not only for the way it makes her feel while driving it, but also for the friendships and experiences it has made possible. As a member of multiple car organizations and automotive forums, Theresa has found solutions to various car problems, shared and received knowledge from other muscle car enthusiasts, gotten ideas for improvements and modifications, received leads on product availability and discounts, and as she remarked, discovered a group of car guys "I just want to hang around with" (courtesy Theresa Newbauer).

that commanded and demanded a great deal of respect. Fast, powerful, colorful, and obnoxiously loud, the muscle car was a dominating presence on city streets and back-country roads for nearly a decade. Of this iconic group of automobiles, auto writer Andy Holloway notes, "their concealed power was awesome, like muscle bound guys straining out of their tight t-shirts, and they could top 100 miles per hour with ease." The respect awarded the muscle car was often returned to the young man who owned it. While adults were likely to consider car crazy teenagers as immature and irresponsible gear-heads, a young man's possession of a Dodge Charger or Plymouth Barracuda garnered a fair amount of respect from his likeminded peers. Guys who could handle a crazy fast, unpredictable, "fully equipped, practical street machine" were held in high esteem (Campisano

29). And guys who dared to engage in illegal street racing—and lived to brag about it—became neighborhood legends. As Jim Campisano writes, "[the muscle cars] were boulevard bruisers, pure and simple. If you didn't have the horsepower, you stayed out of the way" (8). Peter Henshaw adds, "muscle cars could be crude, rude, and [...] unsafe, but many buyers, no sense denying it, liked it that way" (23). The respect granted a muscle car owner was also a valuable tool for attracting young female admirers who gathered at parking lots, street corners, and drive-in restaurants to catch a glimpse of cool guys in hot cars. As a 51-year-old 1970 Plymouth Superbird owner reminisced, "Every guy wanted to have a muscle car. And in high school the girls wanted to be with the guys who had the muscle cars."

Whether demonstrating good automotive savvy through the acquisition of a loud and powerful machine, participating in illegal racing to acquire important street cred among peers, or cruising on urban and rural thoroughfares to impress teenage girls, these young men in muscle cars gained respect not only as savvy consumers, skilled drivers, and desirable boyfriends, but as models of a youthful, tough, and reckless masculinity as well. While often dismissed as ne'er-do-well troublemakers by the adults in charge, adolescents on the brink of adulthood gained the respect often missing from their young lives through ownership of an American muscle car.

Much like the car-crazy teenage boys of 50 years ago who took to the streets in powerful GTOs and throaty Mustangs, the women who contributed to this project view the muscle car as a vehicle that both demands and bestows respect. Yet the ways in which modern-day women reflect and call upon that respect differ considerably from those of their young male predecessors. While young men regarded the muscle car as a rousing and raucous means to masculinity, women today respect the muscle car for its significant role in automotive history, its imposing presence on the road, and its status as an icon of American strength, power, and style. And as female auto enthusiasts have discovered, the respect granted to the muscle car is often transferred to the woman who drives it. Whether gunning the engine of a classic 1966 Charger, a 1983 Mustang pony car, or a retro 2011 Challenger, these women earn respect as they demonstrate confidence in themselves and their abilities, secure legitimacy as skilled and knowledgeable muscle car owners, and through mastery of a high powered performance machine, alter common perceptions of the woman driver.

> While she is a beautiful car, she also has a badass engine which rocks the neighborhood. I feel proud to own such an awesome car and, I have to admit, I like the attention I get from driving her.
> —54-year-old 2014 Camaro 2SS/RS owner

PRESENCE

The muscle car is a vehicle with presence. Its sleek body style, distinctive stance, playful color palette, and rumbling sound sets it apart from other vehicles on the road. What distinguishes the muscle car, writes Keith Naughton, is its "defiant stance, low roof, slab-sided doors, snarling snout, and rubber-burning rear-wheel drive" ("Muscles"). The muscle car is a vehicle with attitude. It has been described by advertisers as well as bona fide car enthusiasts as bold, charismatic, strong, hot, assertive, untamed, and mean. The physical presence of the muscle car, as well as the aura that seems to surround and is generated by it, qualifies it as a vehicle worthy of respect within automotive circles. Among the women who contributed to this project, this indefinable presence was an important factor in the decision to own a muscle car. When asked why she chose a 2010 Camaro SS/RS, a 29-year-old auto industry product manager replied, "It's got to have road presence. And by that I mean when anybody looks at it they've got to go 'ooh.'" Of her Panther Pink 1971 Dodge Challenger convertible, a 53-year-old auto industry engineer exclaimed, "it's bright, it's fast, and it's not afraid to say 'look at me.'" The automotive requirements for a 41-year-old 2006 Dodge Charger owner were "a car with some presence. I didn't want a bland color. I like to quietly stand out from the crowd." Presence— a combination of physical properties as well as an intangible essence or aura—not only influenced women's decision to purchase a muscle car, but also contributed to its reputation as a vehicle of respect.

As was intimated by many of the project participants, driving a car with presence has the ability to change the perception of the woman behind the wheel. When an individual commonly regarded as quiet and unassuming in her everyday life roars up in a Plum Crazy Challenger or Yellow Jacket Charger, she is considered in a new and respectful light. A 72-year-old retired storeowner suggested that ownership of a 1973 Mustang— affectionately referred to as "White Thunder"—causes others to alter their opinions about her. As she was told by a fellow church member, "when you walk into a room, people look at you and say 'wow,' I'd like to get to know her." Of her Vitamin C Orange 1970 Plymouth Superbird Road Runner, an auto industry manager exclaimed, "it's a very unique car; it does get a lot of attention. And people are kind of surprised to find out that you have one." Of course, such notice has both positive and negative repercussions. As explained by a 58-year-old 1970 Pontiac GTO owner, "more attention is paid to you. Including by the police." And as a 58-year-old modified 1969 Dart Hemi owner revealed, "I've had a lot of marriage proposals because of this car!" Presence is not only a part of the muscle car's make-up, but is a quality awarded to the woman bold enough to own a strong, wild, assertive, and untamed machine. It is quality that rewards her with respect on the road as well as among family, friends, church ladies, and fellow car enthusiasts.

STRENGTH, POWER, AND STYLE

Auto writer David Newhardt notes, "Over the years, muscle cars have been threatened with extinction, yet they come back stronger than ever" (165). The qualities that have contributed to the American driver's 50-year fascination with the muscle car—and that set the muscle car apart from its more mild mannered competitors—are strength, power, and style (165). The strength of the muscle car is often reflected in its reputation as the bully of the road. Described by former *Car and Driver* editor David E. Davis as "a violent, virile catalyst car," the muscle car is pushy, obstinate, obnoxious, and brash (qtd. in Mueller 17). During the '60s and early '70s, mental and physical strength were necessary for taking on the crude steering, undependable braking, poor handling, and temperamental manual gearboxes of fast and furious GTOs and Chargers. While the retro muscle car has the benefit of new and improved technology, handling a car of such weight and power requires concentration, mental toughness, and a strong constitution.

The original muscle car was a lightweight vehicle stuffed full of big-block V8 potency. As auto writer and former muscle car owner Jim Campisano asserts, muscle cars are about "power that pins you to your seat" (8). Today's muscle cars, while safer and more fuel-efficient, are even more powerful than their predecessors. In referring to modern day muscle as "testosterone fueled," auto journalist Mike Tolson writes, "for the first time in several generations, American car buyers are presented with a handful of high-octane, high powered vehicles that rival any for performance." The style of the early cars could be described as colorful, stripped down, lean and mean performance machines. As Falconer recalls, "the cars often displayed a real playfulness in colors, including bright oranges, lime greens, and deep purples, and fun graphics based on cartoon characters" (233). The distinctive style of the original Dodge Chargers and Ford Mustangs set them apart from the family sedans and station wagons favored by parents, professionals, and other respectable adults of the day. Today's muscle cars are sleek and smooth updates of the earlier models. As *Carfax* blogger Aaron Turpen notes, "many of these reintroductions use nostalgic throwbacks in body design to elicit more interest and to solidify their muscle car heritage." And like their predecessors, modern day muscle cars are wrapped in colorful exteriors that include Redline Red, Plum Crazy, Blue Velvet Metallic, and Top Banana. Strength, power, and style—the qualities that distinguish all generations of muscle cars from the majority of vehicles on the road—contribute to the American muscle car's reputation as a vehicle of respect.

The women in this project often called upon these qualities to describe themselves as well as the cars they drive. When speaking about her 1969 Camaro Z/28, a 65-year-old retired beautician exclaimed, "It gives me a different feeling when I drive this car. It's like I'm a strong woman, look at me. This is me; this is my car." When behind the wheel of her black 2012 Challenger R/T, a 55-year-old small business owner remarked, "I feel alive, powerful, and I feel like I'm a part of something." Traditionally, the characteristics of strength and power have had negative connotations when connected to women, particularly within conservative circles. To the social conservative, strength and power are qualities long associated with masculinity. As Rebecca Klatch notes, the fear within this population is that, in the pursuit of strength and power, women will not only be neglectful of family duties, but also will "ultimately become like men" (129). However, through participation in muscle car culture, women's expression of these characteristics is both accepted and welcome. Describing themselves as strong and powerful in this context demonstrates an understanding, appreciation, and respect for the muscle car and for themselves as muscle car drivers. It acknowledges that mastery of a muscle car is dependent on the strength and power of the individual who takes the wheel. As a 63-year-old 1970 Dodge Challenger owner exclaimed, "we like having power. You know, it's power we can control and we enjoy it." A 62-year-old registered nurse declared, "I like speed and the feel of power." Of her 2015 Dodge Challenger Scat Pack, a 47-year-old IT engineer remarked, "it says I am a no-nonsense person that can appreciate the power and capability of a muscle car." The women in this project acknowledge the strength and power of the muscle car and take agency from it. Through ownership of a Mustang or Camaro, they are awarded the opportunity to demonstrate power and strength in an acceptable manner within the conservative, male dominated muscle car community.

Women are often attracted to the muscle car for its distinctive design, colorful palette, and eye-catching appearance. Ownership of a muscle car, therefore, was often cited as validation of a woman's sense of design and personal style. Recalling the purchase of her 1967 Mustang GTA fastback, a 45-year-old pharmacist explained, "After seeing the car in person, I immediately fell in love with the color and style and the 'coolness' of it all." Of her 1966 Chevrolet Impala, a nonprofit executive director remarked, "it is beautiful; it has beautiful lines. My car reflects my sense of style." A 62-year-old retired registered nurse acquired a 1967 Plymouth Satellite because, as she noted, "I love the style and color combination. Females enjoy speed, clean lines, and style." A 47-year-old analyst spoke of the connection between her 1965 Mustang convertible and her individual style more directly. As she remarked, "I want people to look at the car and think that I fit in the car. That the car and I are a good couple; a good match."

Marsh and Collett argue it is impossible to look at a car without making unconscious assumptions of the kind of person who would own it. These assumptions, in turn, influence how we feel about particular cars and what we choose to own. As they write, "when the impression we have made about the typical driver of a car matches the one we have of ourselves, or how we would like to be, then we want to buy the car" (44). A sales brochure featuring a photo of a young blonde woman posed next to a Plum Crazy 1970 Dodge Charger convinced a now 63-year-old retired retail support manager to purchase the exact same vehicle when she was 19 years old. As she recalled, "I was just a kid then. I figured well here's a car, a beautiful looking cool car and a girl even has it. I figured it was for me." When she was 21, a middle-aged schoolteacher purchased a 1989 Camaro RS. As she explained, "I liked the style; I liked the looks; I liked the thought of it." A 29-year-old auto industry product manager had her eyes set on a 2010 Camaro SS/RS. She took ownership of it, "for the way it looks. Its design. And, another reason I chose yellow is because it's a kind of look at me color and I think it's very appropriate for [the] Camaro. And mine in particular." The uniquely eye-popping colors of the muscle car guarantee that it will stand out among a sea of black and silver sedans and crossovers. Many of the contributors to this project—unassuming and even reticent in their daily lives—embraced the vibrancy and eccentricity of the muscle car's colorful palette as a means to be recognized as an individual with panache, bravura, and an exceptional sense of style. In drawing attention to itself, the muscle car—and the woman who owns it—demands and is rewarded with respect.

Confidence

The muscle car is a vehicle that exudes confidence. Like a self-assured individual, it stands its ground, holds its head high, looks you in the eye, and flexes its muscle. It is assertive, bold, open, cocky, arrogant, and never shows fear. It swaggers, sashays, struts, flaunts, and teases. In advertising past and present, bulky and burnished muscle cars stare their headlights defiantly into the camera accompanied by pronouncements such as "No Shrinking Violet," "Nothing Holds It Back," "Only the Strong Survive," "Its Closest Competition Is Its Shadow," and "Born Great."[8] Marketing during the muscle car era carried a promise that a bold Barracuda or rough and tough Road Runner would instill confidence in the young male driver. As Russell Belk writes, "a powerful engine gives the owner who controls it a feeling of enhanced power […] and high performance handling makes the man feel capable of high performance as well" (273). Geeks could become gods; the meek could become mighty; the reserved could become risk takers; and the small in stature could become larger than life when behind the wheel of an American muscle car.

One of the earliest criticisms of women as drivers was that they lacked confidence. The original woman driver stereotype—promoted in the years following World War I as a means to limit women's mobility—depicted women as incompetent, accident prone, distracted, and overly cautious. During the late twentieth century women drivers as "cautious, timid, and concerned mostly with safe point-to-point passage via straight, wide roadways" was the standard representation in car advertising and popular culture (Kraig "Liberated" 388). Driving behavior that exemplified passivity, attention to safety, and strict adherence to traffic regulations was considered appropriate for motorists whose main driving purpose was the transportation of children and the performance of household tasks. As Beth Kraig remarks, "implicit in the image of women as cautious drivers is the suggestion that a woman is perhaps not a truly qualified driver, but she at least knows just enough to avoid potentially dangerous circumstances" ("Liberated" 388). Confidence in driving was often associated with masculinity and risk taking, considered appropriate in young men but dangerous in women. Thus throughout women's driving history, confidence was a characteristic neither recognized nor rewarded in the woman behind the wheel.

Certainly there are women intimidated by the muscle car. As a 2014 Challenger owner and online administrator noted, "On the forum we've had a few guys that will say that their wives are afraid of the cars. They're afraid of the size; it's more car than they want to drive." Women with classic Mustangs and Superbirds are often concerned that the temperamental engines and aging brakes of the old cars will let them down. As the 52-year-old owner of two classic muscle cars remarked, "the Road Runner and Super Bee, there's no power steering or power brakes. No air bags. So you're nervous because they're perfect and you don't want anything to happen to them." However, to the majority who participated in this project, ownership of a muscle car contributed to a newfound sense of self-assurance. Because the common assumption is that women do not have the ability to handle a fast and powerful vehicle, demonstrating acumen behind the wheel increases and inspires women's confidence. A 43-year-old 1966 Dodge Charger owner stated, "most of the women that I talk to, friends and stuff, they're just, you know, aren't you scared and I'm like, no. You just learn how to do it." Of her 1991 Mustang, a 50-year-old auto industry project coordinator declared, "I think guys don't expect a chick to be driving a hot car like that, or know how to handle it."

The women who own and drive muscle cars are not, by nature, timid drivers. They understand the capabilities of the cars they drive as well as the skills necessary to handle a fast and powerful machine. While they have a greater concern for safety than the young men of 50 years ago, they do not allow fear to influence their driving experience. Rather, getting behind the wheel of a "thrill machine"—sometimes referred to as "not a car for the faint of heart"—provides these women with the opportunity to demonstrate they are skilled, knowledgeable, and confident drivers (Marsh and Collett 182).

Calling upon the writings of French cultural theorist Jean Baudrillard, Ian Woodward suggests that the possession of objects is not just about having, but being. "To talk about 'my car,' and so on," Woodward writes, "is to bring objects into our own possession and domination, projecting our own feelings onto a particular object that we use in order to be who we are" (141). The women who contributed to this project constructed the muscle car as a vehicle of respect as a means to transfer that respect to themselves. Relatively new to the muscle car experience, the women have appropriated traditional meanings associated with fast and powerful cars and reconfigured them for their own use. During the muscle car era, young men called upon the muscle car's physical properties—power, performance, and noise—to assert themselves as masculine and garner respect among their young male peers. Women today, however, are more likely to cite such intangibles as presence, strength, style, and confidence as means to construct the muscle car as a vehicle of respect, and to establish themselves as legitimate muscle car owners and drivers.

The Muscle Car as a Means of Escape and Empowerment

In the early twentieth century, the growing popularity of the gasoline-powered automobile among female motorists created a crisis in American households. Women's entry into the public sphere behind the wheels of noisy, dirty, and powerful automobiles not only disrupted social conventions regarding women's proper place, but also challenged popular notions of mobility, manners, and morality. Writes Michael Berger, "the implied conflict between women's desire to expand their social and economic horizons, and society's fear that such a development would lead to an abandonment of women's traditional roles in society was very real" ("Drivers" 257). This distress was accompanied by an underlying fear of bad behavior, recklessness, and promiscuity among the auto-liberated

Michele Dozeman's 1971 Hemi Orange Metallic Dodge Charger Super Bee is a former racing car that became a year-and-a-half restoration project. Under its impressive RamCharger hood sits a 440 engine and 727 slap stick transmission (courtesy Michele Dozeman).

female population. As Domosh and Seager assert, the idea that women might be able to take independent control of their mobility—and of powerful machines—"was seen by many commentators as a threat to family stability, good social order, and women's sexual purity" (123).

However, as it became clear that women had no intention of abandoning automobility, it was necessary to redirect the female motorist's growing passion for driving into a new, more gender appropriate direction. This "gendering" of the automobile experience was accomplished not only through the assignment of particular types of automobiles as male or female, but also through the creation of gender guidelines as to how and for what reasons the vehicles were to be used. As Scharff suggests, the question of how people used cars rested on the "common, longstanding assumption that men and women, quite naturally, would have different expectations and desires" (119). Men were expected to drive for excitement and exhilaration. They got behind the wheel to experience independence, recklessness, and mastery of the car and the road. From its very beginning, writes Jennifer Berkley, the automobile was presented in mass culture "as offering its male drivers freedom, power, and control" (1). Women, on the other hand, were assumed to drive not for the excitement such an action might provide, but simply as a means to perform prescribed tasks and fulfill gendered roles. A woman's natural caretaking role was reflected in the car she drove and how she used it. Rather than consider an automobile built for power or performance, women were directed toward vehicles that were reliable, economical, practical, and safe. Driving was not to be enjoyed, but rather, became a duty to be performed, a means to get from here to there, a practice rather than an experience. While a man's driving was often viewed as an escape from domesticity, women's use of the automobile tied her more closely to it. As Seiler writes, the primary function of the woman's car was to be "the wife's helpmeet in the fulfillment of her daily tasks" (60). As the car became a part of an increasing number of households, it was marketed to the woman of the house as a domestic technology. Rather than a "path to public power," the woman's car became an extension of the private sphere (Scharff 163).

There can be little argument that functional vehicles—which over time have included the station wagon, minivan, hatchback, small SUV, and crossover—have proven indispensible to women, particularly to those with family responsibilities. Many of the women who contributed to this project have owned or continue to drive such methods of transport in their roles as wives and mothers. However, while these women unequivocally honor and value the caretaking role, they view ownership of a muscle car as an opportunity to leave familial obligations—either temporarily or permanently—behind. The ability to drive away from domesticity in a fast and powerful automobile often transfers to a feeling of empowerment in muscle car owning women. Time spent alone roaring down the road in a modern Charger or classic GTO provides women with time for reflection, introspection, mindfulness of the world around them, and renewed confidence in their abilities—driving and otherwise. To many of the women in this project, the physical properties of the muscle car, as well as the visceral experience of driving it, presented the possibility of both escape and empowerment.

> When I drive it on the expressway, there always has to be a point and time that I take my hands off the wheel and throw them up in the air and scream really loud. It is that kind of wind-blowing-in-your-hair sense of freedom; I can go anywhere and do anything.

All I need is this car. That's the feeling. It makes me feel like God has a special place for cars like this.
—47-year-old 1965 Ford Mustang convertible owner

ESCAPE

The interior of a family vehicle contains all of the necessary options to keep children occupied, contained, and safe. These minivans, crossovers, and small SUVs are roomy, quiet, and comfortable. Many offer features such as noise cancellation technology that guarantee a "peaceful cabin experience" to passengers, and include a number of "clever storage spots" for holding cups, coloring books, games, and tablets (Pacifica). These vehicles often come equipped with vacuum cleaners, conversation mirrors, automatic sliding doors, built-in entertainment centers, built-in refrigerators, and a plethora of safety features. They are commonly described as an extension of the home or a family room on wheels. These safe, comfortable, and quiet vehicles project the feeling that although you are on the road, you never left the comforts of home.

The muscle car, be it classic, pony, or retro, has very few of these qualities. The antithesis of the family automobile, it is loud, fast, minimal, and powerful. Rather than reminding an individual of home, it has the ability to take one away from it physically, mentally, and experientially. To the women who contributed to this project—of whom the majority identify as mothers—the muscle car not only serves as a getaway vehicle, but also as an intimate and personal space in which to temporarily escape from domesticity and the problems of daily life. While most of her days are devoted to transporting kids in a crossover, a 43-year-old optician spends precious minutes of alone time in a 1998 Pontiac Trans Am affectionately referred to as "Goldie." As she explained, "you know, that's mine; that's my space. That's my individuality." Of her 2010 Mustang GT, a 49-year-old paraprofessional related, "that's the one place I can go to get away from everybody." The use of a muscle car for "me time" was mentioned repeatedly by the women in this project. As the 31-year-old owner of a 1991 Pontiac Firebird noted, "It's like an individuality thing: my time, my space, I can do what I want. It's just that part of my day or time that I can just be myself and remind myself that I'm my own person." A 32-year-old 2013 Mustang Boss 302 owner noted, "There is definitely nothing like being able to be alone with your thoughts with the radio on or off and just having that uninterrupted time." The interior of an automobile often serves as a woman's personal sanctuary, a room-of-her-own on wheels that is hers and hers alone. It is where she can be alone with her thoughts, to reflect, create, remember, or to simply think of nothing at all. What is important is the car exists as a secure space under woman's control. It is a place where she can be a new person. While universally celebrated as a fast and powerful machine, to this group of women, the muscle car is also valued as a personal and private space.

The possibility of becoming a new, different, and changed individual when behind the wheel of a muscle car was a common theme among female motorists. Because the muscle car contrasts so radically from the family vehicle—in form, function, power, and decibel level—it encourages women to think of themselves in an alternative light. As a 49-year-old 2010 Mustang GT owner declared, "I feel better about myself; I feel younger; I feel more alive when I'm in the Mustang compared to when I'm in my mom car." When asked how she feels when "cruising into town with the windows down, and rock music playing" in her 2013 Dodge Challenger R/T, a 65-year-old rancher responded, "like a million bucks! And maybe a lot younger than I am!" The muscle car was often presented as the antidote to an ordinary, uneventful, and predictable existence. It offers women the opportunity to engage in new experiences, make new friends, and participate in new adventures. As a 59-year-old 1965 Mustang owner remarked, "you're just constantly branching out with meeting different people from different walks of life; it kind of broadens your horizons." As was expressed over and over again, ownership of a classic, pony, or modern day muscle car allowed this group of women to escape societal expectations and domestic obligations while having the time of their lives.

To the women in this project, driving a muscle car was the number one cure for problems at work, stress at home, or simply a bad day. The muscle car often serves as a mood changer; when gunning the engine of a Mustang or Camaro, all seems right with the world. As a 54-year-old 2014 Camaro owner explained, "Even a bad day gets better when I get in her and just drive." Of her 1970 Dodge Charger R/T, a 41-year-old accountant declared, "If I'm really down, one of the good things to do is hop in my car and go for a ride. Just driving it around the block, or driving it to church. Just getting it out and driving for a little bit." A 53-year-old store manager purchased her 1977 Pontiac Trans Am as a graduation present to herself 40 years ago. As a vehicle that has always been in her life, its familiarity serves as a source of comfort and rejuvenation. As she noted, "I can go for a ride; we can just go out and cruise in it; it's wonderful to have." Escape in a muscle car, noted the female Charger, Camaro, and Firebird owners, can change one's perspective from sad to happy, from disillusioned to hopeful, from disenchanted to empowered. As a 55-year-old 2012 Challenger R/T owner professed, "I could be having the worst day, and get in that car. And for just 15 minutes, even if it's down the road and back, feel wonderful."

EMPOWERMENT

The opportunity to escape from everyday situations and cultural expectations serves as a source of empowerment to this group of women. The ability to drive off in a fast and powerful automobile to clear one's head or get away from it all is a privilege that was not often available to past generations of female motorists. As a 56-year-old 1971 Pontiac Firebird owner noted, "our mothers were more stay-at-home moms. Our age group was a lot more independent than what our mothers were." And while the majority of the female participants did not self-identify as feminists, they acknowledged that women today have more opportunities, rights, and freedoms than those that came before them. And although—as primarily conservative women—they link the ability to purchase a muscle car to their own financial success, fortitude, and hard work, they also appreciate that they are able to do what women before them, and many women today, cannot. Thus the empowerment they experience is not only reflective of the physical and visceral experience of driving a muscle car, but also stems from the realization that women's present day participation in muscle car culture remains unusual and unprecedented. A 59-year-old 1965 Mustang owner remarked, "I guess it's a nice pleasure to be able to do it, this thing; I can afford it." A 73-year-old 1973 Mustang owner added, "now I can afford it, so it's just the thrill of it, of driving and it's the power behind that surging that I just love." And as a 71-year-old retired schoolteacher, who inherited her 1994 Camaro Z/28 convertible after her husband's passing, explained, "I think women are empowered to do whatever they want to do. I just think that women want to have fun and I think it's just a more fun time to be in a car like the Camaro than it is with your old soccer mom vans." As women who overwhelmingly claim a conservative or moderate ideology, the participants in this project do not frame empowerment in feminist terms; i.e., as a rejection of gender boundaries or as a challenge to men. Rather, they call upon the muscle car to present themselves as individuals who are strong, confident, and empowered to live their own lives.

A 50-year-old bus driver explained how her "sparkly and flashy" frost blue 1968 Plymouth Barracuda came to be known as "Pearl." As she remarked, "Cause it's a blue pearl, like in I'm the captain, like Jack Sparrow did for his ship."[9] Of her 2006 Dodge Charger TorRed Daytona, a 41-year-old homemaker noted, "when I am behind TorCher's wheel I am the head of an autocracy. Absolute power. Absolute control. Absolute freedom." As they drive off in their retro Chargers, Mustang ponies, and classic GTOs, these female motorists are very much the captains of their ships. They have the freedom to escape from domesticity and the expectations of their daily lives to seek excitement, adventure, opportunity, or just a good time. They have power under the hood and the power of their convictions to do what they want to do and be what they want to be. They have control over their driving lives, as they get behind the wheel for pleasure rather than purpose. While any vehicle offers the possibility of escape, the muscle car—as the epitome of brute strength, power, and speed—encourages and enables freedom and flight. As a 43-year-old business consultant noted, when behind the wheel of her 1974 Plymouth Barracuda, she feels "empowered and free with adrenaline pumping and a big smile."

Ian Woodward writes, "far from being a sign of human weakness, self-deception or oppression by the dead hand of a malevolent social system, the patterns of relationships between people and objects suggest people actively seek out—and require—these bonds with objects" (175). Women's relationship to the automobile has long been framed within the context of women's caretaking role. Consequently, the meanings ascribed to the family vehicle—which center on its function as a safe and reliable means of child transport—are considered fixed and nonnegotiable. However, while the women in this project acknowledge that the station wagon, minivan, and crossover have and in some cases continue to serve them well in their capacity as wives and mothers, they demonstrate that, despite proclamations to the contrary, the meanings women ascribe to the automobile are both fickle and fluid. This is perhaps nowhere more evident than in the observation of women's connection to the muscle car. While women's relationship to the family vehicle establishes their legitimacy as caretakers of children, this group of women calls upon the muscle car to demonstrate they will not be tied down to one role. When behind the wheel of a Mustang, 'Cuda, or Superbird, women have the authority and ability to break away from domesticity and present themselves as skilled, intelligent, and empowered woman drivers.

4

The Woman Driver
and the American
Muscle Car

As demonstrated in the preceding chapters, women have developed inventive and effective strategies to gain acceptance into the muscle car community as legitimate muscle car drivers. In doing so, women have changed the conversation about who the woman in muscle car culture can and should be, and have challenged longstanding perceptions of the woman driver. On the surface, these accomplishments by unassuming boomer and post boomer women may seem interesting but not particularly significant. However, the embeddedness of the association of the original muscle car with masculinity in American culture, the pervasive notion that women's car interests are limited to vehicles associated with motherhood, as well as women's traditional roles in the muscle car community as ornaments or cheerleaders suggests that the ability to contest and reconfigure the gendered landscape of muscle car culture is both meaningful and extraordinary.

From the time when the Model T replaced the electric car as the popular vehicle choice, women have confronted a barrage of negative stereotypes regarding their suitability to operate the gasoline-powered automobile. And from the time when the first Pontiac GTO rumbled down Detroit's Woodward Avenue, women have been specifically and emphatically instructed as to what their role in muscle car culture should be. A brief introduction to the stereotypes that have dogged the woman driver over the past 100 years, as well as a review of the gendered roles assigned to women within the muscle car community over the past half century, will not only allow for a greater understanding of just what this group of women have quietly and effectively accomplished, but will ultimately bring legitimacy and respect to the woman who dares to get behind the wheel of an American muscle car.

[Stereotypes] are always going to be there. You just can't do anything about that. [But] we can change how we react to it. And we can change if it's actually true or not."
—47-year-old 1969 Mustang 302 owner

The Woman Driver as Cultural Stereotype

The woman driver stereotype is often considered an anachronism. While jokes about women drivers were popular during the early motor age as means to curtail women's automobility, women's current status as over half the U.S. driving population would suggest that woman driver humor is no longer relevant and serves little purpose. Women are highly valued as automotive consumers, and as statistics continually demonstrate, are considered safer and more conscientious drivers than their male counterparts. Yet despite women's reputation as an important automotive market share, there is an underlying suspicion that women are inferior drivers. This is alluded to in a recently published study in which Zachary Estes and Sydney Felker claim that a lack of confidence as drivers contributes to women's poor performance on mental rotation tasks such as parking the car and reading maps.[1] It is suggested in advertising and marketing in which the woman driver is linked with safety and practicality rather than power, performance, and driving skill. And it is reflected in jokes, memes, and comics such as that pictured here, taken not from late–nineteenth-century cartoons or funnies, but from a news publication produced in the twenty-first century.

Mona Domosh and Joni Seager write, "The car has been an especially powerful vehicle of women's liberation, both literally and metaphorically. And yet, because of that, women's relationships to cars have been contested and controversial" (123). One of the ways in which that contestation has been expressed is through the circulation and maintenance of the woman driver stereotype. The original stereotype, which portrays the female motorist as nervous, inept, and absentminded, rose to popularity after the First World War with the intention of dissuading women from getting behind the wheel. The current stereotype, which links the woman driver to domesticity, came into prominence after World War II as a means to qualify

"A Modern Driving Test." A modern take on the traditional stereotype replaces the woman driver as inept, confused, and scatterbrained with a distracted multi-tasker (copyright Andy Singer. www.andysinger.com).

women's automobility. Although women have participated in American car culture for over a century, the stereotypes about women and cars remain potent, shaping popular culture representations and auto industry decisions. As Domosh and Seager note, "in the US, which arguably has the most deeply entrenched social commitment to the car, jokes about 'women drivers' still resonate; automobile makers and dealers still treat women as secondary car consumers; women are still outsiders at garages, auto shows, racetracks, and car dealerships—all consummate 'men's spaces'" (125). The longstanding and ongoing association of the automobile with masculinity, coupled with the reluctance to concede women's equality as car owners and drivers, has sustained a cultural climate in which the woman driver stereotype is not only maintained, but continuously cultivated. As Peter Freund and George Martin remark, "This stereotype lives despite its lack of empirical support" (52).

Over the past century, numerous studies have been conducted to disrupt or dispel common perceptions of the woman driver. In 1925, the *Los Angeles Times* published an announcement by the American Automobile Association (AAA) that "tests had proved conclusively that women drivers were just as competent as men and even less variable" (Brilliant 40). Thirty years later, the AAA produced a new study with similar results. As Jeremy Packer notes, "this study not only disproved the claims about how inadequate women were as drivers but went one step further in asserting their dominance over men in this most masculine of enterprises" (47). These and other insurance studies were accompanied by reports from auto safety experts with the claim that "women in general are more law abiding than men and have better attitudes toward traffic ordinances" (Packer 55). Accident statistics have been a common means to cite women's superior driving habits. According to estimates by researchers at Carnegie Mellon University, men die at substantially higher rates per mile than women behind the wheel. As Tom Vanderbilt asserts, "Men may or may not be better drivers than women, but they seem to die more often trying to prove that they are" (255). These various reports rely on driving statistics to establish women as equal or better drivers than their male counterparts in order to problematize the woman driver stereotype.

Yet while driving statistics indicate that women are, in fact, superior drivers than men in a number of categories, they do little to alter the common perception of the woman behind the wheel. While a concern for safety is considered an important attribute for women in their caretaking roles, it is not—particularly in the masculine world of muscle cars—considered indicative of skilled driving. Rather, it is risk taking and aggressiveness that is most often celebrated in the male driver. Car chases are central to American popular culture; fast-driving men are romanticized in film and literature; thousands gather annually at racetracks all over the country to satisfy a vicarious "need for speed." Men are expected to embrace the thrill that accompanies high velocity and aggressive driving. To the male driver, writes Sarah Redshaw, "the car is promoted as the means and emblem of individual expression through aggression and performance" ("Articulations" 129). While society may superficially revile the reckless male driver, he is more often than not awarded "wistful respect" (Kraig "Wheel" 212).

As safe drivers rather than aggressive drivers, women's driving behavior will always be considered less than that of their male counterparts. The singular focus on safety not only reinforces gender stereotypes on the road and in society at large, but also has the potential to discourage the woman driver from exploring other driving experiences. However, the women who drive muscle cars engage in driving behavior that while not necessarily masculine, challenges cultural gender roles. While they consider themselves safe drivers, the women pride themselves on new driving skills acquired through alternative driving behaviors. Women in muscle cars challenge gender expectations as they gun rumbling engines, burn rubber, and participate in track days at local speedways. They unsettle gender stereotypes through the accumulation of automotive knowledge, historical data, and mechanical expertise. Through the denial, confrontation, and disruption of common representations of the female motorist, these muscle-car-driving women reimagine the woman driver as something positive and powerful.

The Woman Driver (or Not) as Representation

Women's participation in muscle car culture from 1964 to 1973 is, for the most part, undocumented in scholarship as well as popular culture. Historian Margaret Walsh suggests that young women took part in cruising culture as observers or passengers. Their main objective, Walsh contends, was to be seen, "thereby enhancing their status with their female peers" ("Home" 9). Robert Genat argues that during the 1960s and 1970s, the average young woman had very little interest in the high-powered muscle car. As Genat writes, "the majority of women seen at the drive-in restaurants were in their parents' car. [...] The young women just wanted to be there" (44). Other accounts of the muscle car era rarely mention young women at all.

Due to the absence of narratives from female participants in muscle car culture, other sources must be relied upon for information. One of the more accessible resources is advertising. As Deborah Clarke writes, "Given the extent to which ads become engrained in our heads, they seem to have the widest and strongest impact in shaping our awareness of cars and car culture" (7). However, rather than indicate how young women participated in muscle car culture, advertisements are more indicative of what the auto industry, and American culture at large, thought women's role in muscle car culture should be. As Jennifer Wicke, author of *Advertising Fictions*, observes, "Advertisements are cultural messages in a bottle" (qtd. in Clarke 8).

In muscle car print ads produced from 1964 to 1973, young women are presented in one of four roles. The most common is that of "prop." Young women called upon to fulfill this role were often positioned strategically to attract the male buyer as well as to associate the automobile with sex. While automobiles from the 1950s were often considered feminine in form, their curves reminiscent of the female body, the muscle car, as long, lean, powerful, and fast, suggested another form of sexual conquest. Stephen Bayley in *Sex, Drink and Fast Cars*, argues that in the mind of the male driver, a fast car demonstrates sexual prowess. As Bayley contends, "Driving cars fast is an act of recklessness which [...] recaptures some elements of the thrill of adolescent sex" (32). The young woman in a 1968 Chevy Camaro print ad leans against the passenger side of the vehicle so as not to be confused with the driver. The ad copy does not refer to her in any way; her presence is merely decorative.

While the possibility of sexual conquest is alluded to when women appear as props, the role of the young woman as "prize," demonstrated in an ad for the 1969 Dodge

Camaro advertisement: "Customizing the Camaro." This advertisement reflects a common and oft-repeated strategy called upon by auto manufacturers to market cars to men. In advertising from the past as well as the present, notes automotive blogger Kyle Johnson, women are included as accessories "that make cars appear more attractive to male car shoppers" (*Popular Mechanics*, May 1968).

Mother warned me...

that there would be men like you driving cars like that. Do you really think you can get to me with that long, low, tough machine you just rolled up in? Ha! If you think a girl with real values is impressed by your air conditioning and stereo . . . a 440 Magnum, whatever that is . . . well—it takes more than cushy bucket seats to make me flip. Charger R/T SE. Sounds like alphabet soup. Frankly, I'm attracted to you because you have a very intelligent face. My name's Julia.

Join the fun . . . catch **DODGE** *fever*

Watch AFL football and the Bob Hope Comedy Specials on NBC-TV.

Dodge Charger R/T Advertisement: "Mother warned me that there would be men like you driving cars like that." The woman in this advertisement is not a driver, but is presented as a reward for owning a fast automobile. As automotive blogger Kyle Johnson writes, in order to appeal to men, women in automotive advertising often appear as "objects that male car buyers want to accumulate" (*Motor Trend*, May 1969, from the Collections of The Henry Ford).

Charger, removes any question. The attractive blonde, placed in front of the automobile, lifts her skirt as both an invitation and a promise. The copy reads, "Do you really think you can get to me with that long, low, tough machine you just rolled up in?" The answer, of course, is "yes." Witzel and Bash, students of the California cruising scene, assert that the young men who participated in muscle car culture understood that driving a fast and racy car was the most effective way to attract young women. "Without a doubt," write Witzel and Bash, "a cool car was a prerequisite to get girls and get laid" (23).

Automotive scholar Margaret Walsh suggests that the most common and preferred role of the young woman in muscle car culture was that of passenger. Understanding that only boys could raise a girl's status among teenage peers, young women sought out young men in cool cars as a means to do so. As a 45-year-old 1967 Mustang GTA Fastback owner recalled, "the women fell for the guys with the fast cars and watched them work on cars and race them." A 65-year-old 2013 Dodge Challenger R/T owner added, "My girlfriend hung around guys with cool cars, so of course, I did, too!" Muscle car advertisements, such as that promoting the red Mustang convertible, often show attractive young women in the passenger seat. However, while the woman looks back to make sure she has been "seen," the intent of such advertising is not to raise the status of the woman, but rather, that of the young man behind the wheel.

Mustang advertisement: "Mustang hits the starting line full bore!" Published in a variety of car magazines with primarily male readership (*Road and Track, Car Craft, Car and Driver, Motor Trend, Car Life, Hot Rod,* and *Sports Car Graphic*), this advertisement combined "a long, long list of [automotive] goodies" and an attractive woman along-for-the-ride as selling points for the male car buyer (*Car and Driver,* June 1964, courtesy Fordimages.com).

In advertising from the muscle car era, women are rarely presented as drivers. While Mustang ads occasionally featured women in the driver's seat, it was to promote the non-muscle, low-performance, V6 engine models. In period ads for the Dodge Challenger—Chrysler's entry into the "pony car" market—the position of the young woman on the driver's side alludes to, but does not confirm, that the vehicle might be attractive to the female driver. The availability of the Dodge muscle car in "high impact" colors—such as Plum Crazy and Panther Pink pictured here—has made Dodge vehicles a very popular choice among today's female classic muscle car owners. The owner of a classic Panther Pink 1971 Dodge Challenger convertible revealed that when growing up, she had coveted the Challenger owned by her boyfriend's older sister. Her comments suggest that while young men may have perceived the attractive woman in the Challenger ad as one of the spoils of owning such a vehicle, young women, in fact, may have seen in her the possibility of themselves as competent and capable muscle car drivers. As teenagers, muscle car ownership was beyond the means of most participants in this project. However, as a 19-year-old fresh out of high school working at her first job, a now 63-year-old retired store manager saw herself in the photograph and purchased a 1970 Plum Crazy Dodge Challenger on the spot. As she recalled, "I didn't even know what I was looking for; I just

Dodge Challenger advertisement: "Our plum crazy Challenger R/T is no shrinking violet." And neither, perhaps, was the young woman who saw herself as the potential owner of this "Haulin' Hemi" machine (*Motor Trend*, January 1970).

Dodge Charger advertisement: "Charger is tickled pink over its new lower price." As Diego Rosenberg notes, inspired by the psychedelia craze that followed San Francisco's 1967 "Summer of Love," Chrysler offered several 1970–1971 Hi-Impact colors "complete with punny names" such as Plum Crazy, Sassy Grass Green, and Panther Pink (19). Fifty years later, many of the colors have taken on new meanings, particularly among female muscle car enthusiasts. As a 53-year-old 1970 Dodge Challenger convertible owner remarked, "[Panther Pink] wound up being kind of a power color, I think when it was associated with breast cancer awareness. And my mom was a survivor. So pink is a good color" (*Hot Rod*, April 1970).

opened the brochure and there it was." Thus while images of young women as props, prizes, and passengers assume women occupied peripheral roles, the Dodge Challenger and Charger ads suggests that women may have also been considered potential customers, i.e., "prospects."

Once the muscle car lost its luster during the 1980s, and thus loosened its ties with masculinity, advertising for pony cars occasionally featured women as drivers. Heon Stevenson suggests that the change in images of female motorists during this time can be attributed to women's liberation. As he writes, "housewives continued to load groceries and children into station wagons, but women were habitually portrayed at the wheel of other types of car, without a man in sight, and their body language grew noticeably more confident" (160). However, the vehicles in these advertisements and promotional brochures were celebrated for sportiness, spirit, style, and affordability rather than power or performance. Potential buyers quickly caught on to the lack of muscle in these pony cars; consequently, as male consumers fled, auto makers called upon qualities often associated with women's vehicle preferences—style and economy—to market the powerless pony cars to women. A dealer catalog for the 1983 Mustang features a "free-spirited" young woman—complete with braided headband and ruffled dress—driving what the copy describes as a car with "high spirits." A spread in a 1990 Camaro catalog—which highlights a young professional woman picking up videos on her way home from work—suggests that it is the Camaro's legendary style, rather than performance, that will "make your heart race." While women's presence behind the wheel increases during the non-muscle car era, the female consumer is most often positioned as an individual more interested in style than substance. However, at the turn of the twenty-first century, once power is returned to the Camaro, Challenger, Charger, and Mustang, women all but disappear from muscle car advertising. The good news is, so do men.

When soliciting car advertising for the start-up *Ms.* magazine during the 1970s, editor Gloria Steinem noted the uncomfortable relationship between auto manufacturers and the woman driver. Critical of the ways in which women were represented in auto industry advertising, Steinem sought to include gender-neutral ads in her magazine, images which, she lamented, were in very short supply. As Steinem remarked, "*Ms.* readers were so grateful for a routine Honda ad featuring rack and pinion steering, for instance, that they sent fan mail" (qtd. in Clarke 79). It took 40 years, but manufacturers of modern

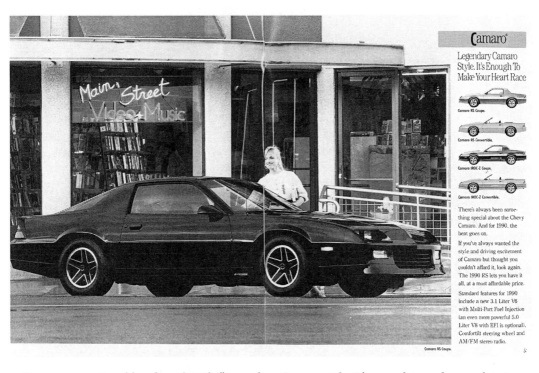

Camaro promotional brochure (1990): "Legendary Camaro style. It's enough to make your heart race." In 1950s automotive advertising directed toward the women driver, writes Heon Stevenson, "there emerged a distinct style of feminized copy which emphasized color and trimmings and the automobile's potential as a fashion accessory" (150). During the 1990s, as a means to address the single working woman who had not yet succumbed to motherhood and a minivan, automakers returned to style, comfort, and economy to attract the woman driver.

day muscle cars seem to have gotten the message. Advertisements for the Ford Mustang, Dodge Challenger, and Chevrolet Camaro focus on qualities such as power, performance, automotive heritage, and American patriotism while effectively hiding the gender of the individual behind the wheel. Whether referring to the Challenger as an "adult toy," calling upon the Mustang to reclaim America's coolness, or promoting the Camaro as a lean and mean "0 percent body fat" machine, auto manufacturers have cleverly maintained the masculinity associated with the muscle car without specifically excluding the female motorist.[2] Recognizing that women are a significant component of their consumer base, yet fearful of losing the male customer through the association of the muscle car with the woman driver, automakers have developed advertising in which any individual—male or female—can imagine themselves behind the wheel.

As Deborah Clarke suggests, advertising has had a significant impact in shaping our perceptions of women's place in muscle car culture. As she notes, the message of these ads is so important because "it does not sell goods: it sells meaning" (79). The women who contributed to this project have found ways to see themselves in muscle car advertising. No longer satisfied in the role of passenger, they have taken ownership of classic, pony, and retro muscle cars and established themselves as legitimate drivers. While they may be physically absent in current Camaro, Challenger, and Mustang advertising,

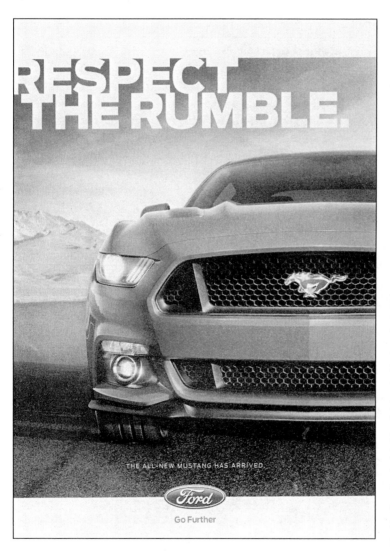

Mustang advertisement: "Respect the Rumble." The unique sound of a muscle car—throaty, roaring, and rumbling—has an appeal that knows no gender. When describing the qualities that make a muscle car a muscle car, a 56-year-old 1971 Pontiac Firebird owner proclaimed, "I like the rumble of them. I like the sound" (*Car and Driver*, January 2015, courtesy Fordimages.com).

these women—through creative and effective strategies—have made themselves visible and viable within the muscle car community.

Challenging Representations

The participants in this project ranged from 20-something women relatively new to cars to aging baby boomers in their 60s and beyond who came of age during the 1950s and 1960s, often considered the golden age of American automobile culture. Although

Growing up in Dearborn, Michigan—the birthplace of Henry Ford—Caryn Janssen would look longingly at the Mustangs owned by the boys across the street. As she exclaimed, "My entire life, I've only wanted a Mustang. It's the only car I've ever wanted." With the purchase of a 2010 Mustang GT, Caryn's dream has finally been realized (courtesy Caryn Janssen).

most of the older participants were aware of women's peripheral role in the muscle car era, as well as the cultural stereotypes surrounding the woman driver, many of the younger motorists were not. Yet while not all participants were familiar with the particulars of each stereotype, the majority acknowledged that women's driving is a subject of criticism in American car culture. And all were in agreement that ownership of an American muscle car is an effective tool to challenge existing stereotypes as well as to reinvent women's role in the muscle car community.

As should be expected, the women in this project had varying opinions regarding the woman driver stereotype and offered numerous strategies to disrupt, combat, replace, or take ownership of it. Many professed that "woman driver" is not an actual category, but rather a derogatory term used to point to an individual's lack of driving ability. As a 43-year-old 1998 Pontiac Trans Am owner exclaimed, "It's like a bad thing, you know. You see someone doing something wrong; oh it's just a woman driver." A 49-year-old 2010 Camaro owner remarked, "I feel any person, male or female, could fit the description of a woman driver." A 54-year-old 2009 Dodge Charger R/T owner added, "I think it's referring to most of the time like a bad driver, unfortunately. I know my husband always teases me about, oh that's probably a woman driver, when somebody makes a mistake." Philosophy scholar Lynn Tirrell—in her early work on language and power—discusses how sexist language works to trivialize and devalue women. As she argues, one of the primary ways in which women are oppressed through discursive practices is "marking." Tirrell writes, "marking draws attention to women's femaleness and carries implications of inferiority" (143). Referring to something as female—throws like a girl, cries like a woman, chick flick, woman driver—is not only considered the ultimate insult, but also implies that what women do and how they do it is somehow less. While "woman driver" may be gender neutral in that it is often applied to both men and women, its repeated use perpetuates attitudes and beliefs about women's inferiority in driving and any other action or activity with a deep-rooted association to masculinity.

While some participants considered "woman driver" a term used to describe any individual with questionable driving skills, others viewed it as an insult and an affront to women. A 72-year-old 1973 Mustang owner declared, "I think that's a derogatory; when somebody's saying 'woman driver' it's like saying 'my old lady.' It's a putdown. It's like we're inept, inadequate." Of the woman driver stereotype, a 46-year-old 1996 Mustang owner remarked, "[I feel] resentment. That people still use that term. It sounds like an old comedian." A 62-year-old 1964½ Mustang owner replied, "I think sometimes when you hear that it's kind of a, almost kind of a slap on the face." Many participants viewed "woman driver" as an attempt to set up women's automotive skills in opposition to, and therefore less than, those of men. As a 63-year-old 1970 Dodge Challenger owner remarked, "I think it's in men's heads. They got this thing, I think it's a guy thing, they have a thing about women drivers and how bad they are." The 31-year-old owner of a 1991 Pontiac Firebird added, "It helps men maintain their sense of empowerment. It's mostly sexist guys, I've found, who say that." A number of participants viewed use of the term as a means to disparage women not only as drivers, but also as a gender. As a 62-year-old auto body shop receptionist exclaimed, "Sometimes I get upset depending on the conversation, because some people like to assume I'm not a very good driver. And some people say women aren't good drivers. It's kind of putting all women into one category."

A 53-year-old accountant replied, "Someone is assuming that a poor driver must be female. Gender identification is biological and there is something biologically that makes me a poor driver." Stated a 37-year-old 1974 Chevy Nova owner, "I get teased so much about it. Everybody makes fun of women drivers, you know. All my friends, oh, girl driver there, women drivers, they can't drive." This automotive division, between men and women, superior and inferior, was both recognized and disputed by the contributors to this project. The woman driver stereotype, asserted a 65-year-old 2013 Dodge Challenger R/T owner, "[suggests] we are somehow inferior, make poor decisions, can't handle driving a muscle car and just a negative connotation. I know just as many very poor men drivers!"

While many participants took strong objection to the woman driver stereotype, others viewed it through a historical lens, suggesting the term is simply a relic from a time when the majority of women drove seldom or not at all. Although statistics on women's driving prior to 1963 are nonexistent, auto historian Margaret Walsh estimates that in the years prior to World War II, only a quarter of women had driver's licenses.[3] As a 60-year-old 1971 Dodge Charger Super Bee owner replied, "I know a lot of women that have never drove." An 82-year-old retiree, who transferred ownership of a 1970 Plymouth Superbird Road Runner awarded in a divorce to her 51-year-old daughter, noted, "I don't know, for me it's, when I was young, most of your women didn't drive. In fact, I didn't learn to drive until 1958." And as a 47-year-old 2015 Dodge Challenger Scat Pack owner explained, "At some point, there were enough women that were on the roads that had poor driving skills. However, this is the chicken vs. the egg scenario. Women were relegated by gender role to be 'less than' by men. Ergo they had fewer opportunities to learn how to drive, and when they did, I believe that women were perceived (unfairly) that they didn't have the capability to drive." These women suggest that the stereotype, while inappropriate today, is reflective of an earlier era when women had neither the driving experience, nor the opportunities to develop automotive skills, as their male contemporaries.

Some participants—particularly those in their 20s and 30s—dismissed the existence of the "woman driver" altogether. A 22-year-old 1966 Mustang owner noted, "I actually do not hear the term woman driver very much. But typically I just think of it as a classification and not necessarily anything more than that." However, others conceded there are female motorists who, as the 58-year-old owner of a 1970 Dodge Challenger proclaimed, "give the rest of us women a bad name!" A 50-year-old 1993 Mustang GT owner declared, "I get frustrated with the women that I see. It's like, didn't anybody show you how to drive?" Women who drive below the speed limit, who text or use cell phones while driving, who attend to their hair and makeup at stoplights, who know nothing about the car other than where to put the gas, or who are distracted by small children in the backseat were repeatedly mentioned as stereotypical woman drivers. Still other women took ownership of the stereotype, admitting that they occasionally acted in ways that inadvertently confirmed the woman driver label. A 45-year-old 1969 Mustang Mach I owner confessed, "I think there are times when we all have those feelings of uncertainty. We have all had stressful moments when we were preoccupied that we made poor driving decisions." A 27-year-old 1971 Pontiac GT-37 owner added, "There are days where my driving isn't as good and I become the stereotypic 'woman driver,' but for the most part I'm the annoyed driver wanting the 'woman driver' or 'Prius driver' to get out of my way." Yet while some admitted they had woman driver moments, most of the women strongly and adamantly distanced themselves from the stereotype. As a 47-year-old Mustang owner declared, "If it's true, that women are not as good drivers as men, I'd like to consider myself excluded from that stereotype." And as the 31-year-old owner of a 1991 Pontiac Firebird exclaimed, "I'm proud to be a woman driver that can drive well, and not be some crazy woman getting into accidents [and] backing into people." While distancing oneself from pejorative stereotypes can give the appearance of reinforcing expectations regarding the typical woman driver, the majority of women who participated in this project sought to replace existing representations with new gender scripts based on their own experience with cars. They accomplished this by using identities as muscle car owners to disrupt the stereotype as well as to set themselves up as examples of what the woman driver should and can be.

Disrupting Stereotypes

Whether they viewed the woman driver stereotype as a descriptive category, an insult, an anachronism, or an unfortunate truth, the women in this project viewed ownership of a muscle car as an effective means to disrupt enduring stereotypes and to replace prevailing representations of women in muscle car culture with constructions of their own making. While the women developed a number of strategies to reinvent the woman driver category, those mentioned most often were mastery of the muscle car, confidence behind the wheel, automotive acumen equal to that of men, and passion for driving.

The American muscle cars produced during the mid–1960s and early 1970s were rough and fast performance machines. As automotive writer Andy Holloway notes, classic muscle cars are "fast by definition," but they are also a "tougher and louder ride than today's cars" (73). While vehicles from the muscle car era had notoriously poor handling, they delivered powerful straight-line acceleration for optimal street racing success. Today's muscle cars, while safer, more reliable, and technologically superior to those from the classic era, are also bigger, faster, better, and more powerful. Auto journalist Mike Tolson, writing about the modern day Dodge Challenger Hellcat, exclaims, "[It] promises to live up to its name—every inch a challenge—so driving it well means proving something." As these auto writers assert, whether classic or modern day, the American muscle car requires driving skill, automotive knowhow, and a fair amount of moxie to operate successfully, confidently, and with panache. Mastery of the muscle car, therefore, allows women to present themselves as a new kind of woman driver.

The women demonstrated automotive acumen in a number of ways. Because the majority of muscle cars have manual transmissions, mastery of the stick shift was often mentioned as an example of exceptional driving ability.[4] As a 47-year-old 1965 Mustang owner noted, "I can tell you that everybody's impressed that I can drive a stick shift." A 59-year-old 2005 Mustang convertible owner remarked, "it makes me feel more in control when I have a stick shift." A 41-year-old 1970 Dodge Charger R/T owner exclaimed, "I really enjoy driving a stick shift. There's just not very many stick shifts out there." While less than seven percent of automobiles sold in the United States have manual transmissions,

Cherie Karcher is pictured with her award-winning 2002 Camaro Z/28 at the Camaro SuperFest in Ypsilanti, Michigan. Cherie had longed for a Camaro ever since high school. She chose a "newer-older" model for its easy maintenance and reliability. Ownership of the light pewter Camaro, noted Cherie, "means that a long time dream of mine has finally come true" (courtesy Cherie Karcher).

nearly half of the participants made a point of mentioning they drive cars with stick shifts.[5] Shifting gears, the women asserted, allowed them to focus on driving, feel the road, and more thoroughly enjoy the driving experience. Of her 2010 Ford Mustang GT, a 49-year-old paraprofessional confessed, "I just feel more in control. I don't know if it's because it's a stick shift but I just feel [*whispers*] better."

The ability to deftly handle a car with 50-year-old technology without the benefit of power steering or disc brakes was often repeated by the classic muscle car owners as an example of driving proficiency and skill. As 49-year-old office manager explained, "A modern car may have smoother handling capabilities compared to the muscle car. But there's still nothing that can compare overall to getting into that Charger and knowing the horsepower capabilities that they have." The ability to handle classic muscle cars, described by Darwin Holmstrom as "lightweight cars stuffed full of big-block V8 power" with crude handling and "virtually no braking power," was often cited by participants as a demonstration of women's driving acumen (8). Women with later model pony cars also boasted proficiency behind the wheel. As a 60-year-old 1995 Mustang GT owner remarked, "I need more self-control in this car. I really do. If I'm not careful taking off from a light it will go sideways on me. So you have to be a much more alert driver." Of her 1991 Mustang, a 50-year-old auto industry project coordinator declared, "I know how to handle

Why see a marriage counselor?
Get a Select Shift.

You want a stick shift. *She* wants an automatic. And your budget says: "one car!"
No problem anymore. Get *one* car. And get it with a Ford Motor Company Select Shift.
The Select Shift is standard equipment with every automatic transmission.
Comes on the steering column or on the floor. Works like this:
Shift the Select Shift into first or second gear; it works like
a *manual shift*. Real control in snow or mud. Assists braking on
hills—helps handle heavy trailer loads. Shift the Select Shift
into automatic. It's *automatic*. The Select Shift. *You* get your way.
She gets hers. Ford has a better idea . . . Shift for yourself!

...has a better idea

FORD MOTOR COMPANY JOB #110-00-051
THIS ADVERTISEMENT APPEARS IN
TIME—DECEMBER 23, 1966
NEWSWEEK—JANUARY 9, 1967
U.S. NEWS & WORLD REPORT—JANUARY 23, 1967
SPORTS ILLUSTRATED—JANUARY 2, 1967
NEW YORKER—JANUARY 28, 1967
PLAYBOY—FEBRUARY, 1967
SUNSET—FEBRUARY, 1967
1 PAGE 4 COLOR

GREY ADVERTISING INC.

Mustang advertisement: "Why see a marriage counselor? Get a Select Shift." While the Select Shift doesn't, in fact, qualify as a true manual transmission, this ad reinforces the notion that women prefer the ease of driving of an automatic, whereas men—assumed to be more attuned to the total driving experience—are more inclined to favor a stick shift (*Playboy*, February 1967. From the Collections of The Henry Ford).

it, I know how to do a burn out, I know how to get it, when I need to, I'm not afraid to make it perform for me." A 54-year-old 2014 Camaro 2SS/RS owner declared, "I love to get on the gas and make my Camaro scream." The women repeatedly emphasized that mastery of the skills exclusive to the muscle car experience unequivocally demonstrated they were not, by any stretch of the imagination, stereotypical women drivers. Through driving performances that include "boilin' the hides," "burnin' rubber," "doin' a brodie," and "poppin' the clutch," these women illustrate there is more than one way to consider the woman behind the wheel.[6]

Ownership of a muscle car—no matter what the generation—provided women with the confidence often considered lacking in the female motorist. Criticism of the woman behind the wheel has often centered on her presumed passivity, apprehensiveness, and cautiousness. The notion of the woman driver as fearful and self-doubting was promoted and propagated in the early years of automobility by the male press. As Scharff writes, "women, the men point out, suffer from natural impulsiveness and timidity, inability to concentrate and single-mindedness, indecisiveness and foolhardiness, weakness and utter estrangement from things mechanical" (26). It should come as no surprise, therefore, that many women have internalized this longstanding criticism so much so that that it has often become, in fact, a self-fulfilling prophecy. Thus another way that muscle car ownership alters common perceptions is by instilling and encouraging confidence in the female motorist. Of her 2005 Mustang, a 59-year-old advertising copywriter remarked, "it may say I'm a person who is in control, I know what I'm doing. I mean I felt like it gave me a little extra confidence as a driver." A 43-year-old 1974 Barracuda owner exclaimed, "I do not feel I'm a typical 'woman driver' so to speak. I am very comfortable and confident driving. I have lots of experience driving and I personally love to drive." Getting behind the wheel of her 1994 Z/28 Camaro, noted a 71-year-old retired school-teacher, demonstrates that she is "just as adept and capable of driving carefully and also confidently as a male." As these participants suggest, ownership of an American muscle car—as well as the acquisition of skills necessary to operate it effectively and purpose-fully—has the potential to instill confidence in the woman driver.

In order to alter the perception of the woman driver, many of the participants compared their driving behavior to that of men, often claiming that it was, in fact superior. As a 42-year-old 1982 Mustang owner remarked, "I think we concentrate a little bit better, we pay attention a little bit better maybe." The 56-year-old 1973 Dodge Challenger owner added, "I think that women have faster reflexes [than men]; most women I think pay real attention to the road. We're not as quick to fly off the handle; the men seem to be hot tempered sometimes when it comes to driving." Focus, levelheadedness, and atten-tiveness to the road and to others were often mentioned as qualities lacking in the male behind the wheel. Comparing the female motorist to her male counterpart, a 62-year-old 1971 Ford Gran Torino owner pronounced, "I think more considerate, because usually the ones who are letting you out, like at a light, or getting out of a gas station or something, usually are going to be women." In an automotive culture that has historically linked superior driving ability with masculinity, it is understandable that female classic muscle car owners would compare their driving behavior to that of men in order to validate their identities as exceptional drivers. In her own research into various driving cultures, Redshaw discovered that women are often "keenly aware of being excluded from what was seen as a 'more authentic' experience of driving because they were women" ("Driving" 84). The women in this project are not suggesting that they drive like men, but rather, that in many situations their driving ability is, in fact, superior to that of their male counterparts. Using the male driver as the standard not only allows these women to construct themselves as exceptional drivers, but also provides them with the opportunity to distance themselves from existing stereotypes. As a 65-year-old 1970 Chevelle owner noted, "I would say [women are] more conscientious and probably a lot more alert of what is going on."

As the participants in this project demonstrated, ownership of a muscle car can alter the perception of the woman driver from one who drives purposefully and passively to an individual with a passion for driving. From the earliest days of the auto industry, notes Ella Howard, "automotive manufacturers had characterized specific vehicles as appropriate for the woman driver" (143). These vehicles—which metamorphosed from station wagons to hatchbacks to minivans to crossovers—have been commonly promoted as functional, practical, economical, reliable, and safe. They are endorsed as having all of the qualities, accessories, options, and properties desired by and necessary for the woman driver. The marketing of these vehicles assumes that a woman's interest in cars is centered in its function as a practical but necessary domestic technology, a tool that will aid her in her primary role as wife and mother. (88). As Deborah Clarke asserts, "Automotive maternity situates mothers as both essential and cultural, a woman who drives the right car" (77).[7] While advertising promotes these verifiable women's cars as winners of five star safety tests, built to help mom with her chores and errands, family rooms on wheels, and a supermom's sidekick, descriptors such as fun, fast, powerful, exhilarating, and pleasurable are reserved for cars marketed to the man behind the wheel.[8]

The participants in this project recognize that many women have been conditioned to think of the automobile as a functional necessity rather than a source of pleasure. As a 50-year-old auto industry project coordinator noted, because many women are often "stuck" with the family car, "they don't ever get to experience having a fun car or something that makes them feel good." A 54-year-old 2009 Dodge Charger R/T owner remarked, "a lot of women drive because they have to. Because they need to rather than they like driving." And as a 55-year-old 2012 Dodge Challenger owner added, many women "really don't care about cars. Their cars are more for practicality. So they're not really focused on the actual experience of driving." Ownership of a muscle car, the women collectively argue, provides the opportunity for a different, more exhilarating driving experience. It encourages female motorists to try new things, participate in racing and track days, develop new skills, take challenging road trips, and test their limits. It helps to change perceptions of the woman driver from passive to passionate. Noted a 54-year-old 2014 Camaro owner, "So many people are impressed with the fact that I can drive such a high-powered automobile." A 29-year-old 2010 Camaro SS/RS owner understands that what she drives has an influence on how she is perceived as a woman behind the wheel. As the auto industry project manager noted, "at the end of the day, if people see me driving a four-door sedan, they might think of me as a woman driver. But I feel in my muscle car, I would like to think that people might expect I'm a better driver."

The women who use the muscle car as a means to drag race and participate in track events not only enjoy the rush and exhilaration that comes from competition, but also how they disrupt gender expectations in these hypermasculine environments. As a 50-year-old 1969 Mustang 429 Cobra Jet owner declared, "They probably think that I'm more of a risk taker maybe because I have drag raced before. They might think that I've got, I don't know, sometimes when I tell people that I go in at 120 miles an hour they think I'm crazy." A 51-year-old 1969 Mustang Mach I owner enjoys the thrill of racing as well as beating the men at their own game. As she exclaimed, "when you're sitting out there and like, you look around and all of the sudden you beat them off the light. They're telling you, you ain't no pussy at the light, that's for sure. You push and you just punch out the light so you're going um hm she's not your typical female um hm." While it was common for young men to engage in illegal drag racing during the muscle car era, young women's participation was most often limited to cheering from the sidelines. Nearly 50 years later, women not only have the means to own these fast and powerful cars, but now have the chance to use automobiles in ways that were once off limits to the young female motorist. In doing so, they are recreating the woman driver in their own image.

Despite the attempts of automakers and marketers over the past 100 years to direct women toward a specific category of car, the woman driver of the twenty-first century often has her own ideas about what kind of vehicle she should own and drive. The participants in this project alter perceptions of the woman driver through ownership of cars that are not particularly family friendly as well as driving experiences that are not practical, economical, or necessary. Through muscle car ownership, these women have not only disrupted how the woman's car is used, but how the woman driver feels when behind the wheel. While the women in this project acknowledge that the cars they drive are most often associated with the male driver, most do not perceive themselves or their automobile choices as masculine. Rather, they consider themselves as individuals who have made vehicle choices based on their own desires, driving ability, identity, and lifestyle. While they may have driven family cars in the past, or foresee doing so in the future, at this particular point in their lives they have opted to select vehicles that identify them as something other than mother or caretaker. In doing so, they have, in the context of Vannini's theory of objectification, formed a "reciprocal relationship" to a car. They have ascribed new meanings to the muscle car and in turn, have assumed new identities from old and new technologies. As they get behind the wheel of a Charger, GTO, or Mustang, these female motorists convincingly demonstrate that women's automobile use is not limited to transportation work, workplace commuting, or the performance of household tasks.[9] As they take part in road rallies and driving tours, participate in car shows and cruises, or test their automotive acumen on dragstrips and race tracks, they provide endless new ways to consider how women enjoy and employ cars.

While women's automobile use has been historically constructed as a means to "do gender" in a conventional and culturally prescribed manner, the women of this project refuse to be defined and confined by such narrow gender norms. By engaging in unexpected and unconventional automotive activities and driving practices, displaying confidence behind the wheel, demonstrating automotive acumen and mastery of the muscle car, and exhibiting a passion for driving, they expand the notion of what a woman driver is and how an automobile might be used. Through their vehicle choices, the women in this project challenge assumptions about what women can drive in order to reinvent the persona of the woman driver. In this way, they are following the lead of early female motorists who, as Clarsen writes, "produced their own enabling stories and material sites, creating the conditions for their participation in worlds otherwise denied them" ("Dust" 3).

Developing Strategies

The image of a woman behind the wheel of an American muscle car unsettles much of what has long been assumed about the muscle car driver, muscle car culture, and the female motorist. The muscle car experience in the media, popular culture, historical archives, and automotive scholarship has traditionally and overwhelmingly been considered through a male lens. The muscle car's status as powerful, fast, and loud, and its reputation as rough, risky, and a little bit ostentatious, has tied it to masculinity in persistent and impenetrable ways. Muscle car culture has endured as a space where men gather to talk about projects and modifications, trade car stories, network for parts and resources, and bond with other like-minded car enthusiasts. For the past 50 years, woman's relationship to the muscle car has been ambiguous at best. While during the classic muscle car era, a few young women had the opportunity to borrow the cars of brothers or boyfriends, the majority were relegated to secondary and non-participatory roles. In muscle car advertising of this time period, writes Heon Stevenson, the woman was most often portrayed as the "seductive passenger." As Stevenson writes, "was she the car's owner, or

Lynn Plummer Trestrail and her late husband purchased a 1966 Mustang in 1989 as an homage to their high school mascot—the Mercer High Mustang—and her husband's graduation year. Her husband worked painstakingly on the car's restoration until his death in 2002. Not wanting to give up the car that had such sentimental value, Lynn found a restorer through the local Mustang club who helped her return the "Blue Beauty" to its original state. Lynn's second husband added a 2006 Mustang to the stable so that he could join Lynn in Mustang club events. As Lynn exclaimed, "I honestly feel like a million bucks when I drive either car but especially the '66. I am so proud that I helped restore that vehicle!" (courtesy Lynn Plummer Trestrail).

the owner's partner, or [...] the kind of girly that a male buyer of the automobile in question might attract if he drove the new car?" (156). Despite their growing interest in a variety of automotive offerings, women as drivers continue to be considered primarily as married moms or single consumers in search of a practical vehicle. In the twenty-first century, notes Stevenson, attempts to attract the female motorist most often include "references to shoes, coffee, handbags, and relationships, individually or in combination [...]" (245). Although women have become a growing presence in classic muscle car communities, and compose nearly one third of modern muscle car buyers, old stereotypes and outdated representations continue to influence how the woman driver is regarded in American muscle car culture.

This project was undertaken to shake up common assumptions about the muscle car, muscle car culture, and the woman driver. The objective was to rethink what we know about women and cars, and to consider the ways in which women relate to automobiles outside of cultural conventions. The intent was to suggest that yes, many women do look for qualities such as safety, economy, reliability, and functionality in an automobile (as do a good number of male consumers), but there are a growing number of female motorists for whom practicality is just not enough. As evidenced in this project, a good number of women desire something more in an automobile than mere transportation. They are searching for a vehicle that offers excitement, adventure, thrills, and pleasure. They are pursuing a driving experience that throws them back in their seat, gets their heart rate pumping, and provides an adrenaline rush. These women are looking for an automobile in which they may reinvent themselves and take on new identities as women drivers. And in the process, they are seeking ways to become accepted as legitimate muscle car owners in both online and on-site muscle car communities.

The classic muscle car era came to a close in the mid–1970s just as the women's movement was gaining steam. Since that time, locations once closed to women have slowly opened their doors. Women have entered historically male dominated professions—medicine, law enforcement, engineering, and computer technology—with varying degrees of success. Women in the military currently account for ten percent; that number is expected to rise over time due to the 2013 lifting of the female combat ban. Women now have a higher profile in sports, as athletes, trainers, and through positions in various sports media. In each of these locations, women have had to employ specific strategies as a means to gain access and acceptance. Women who seek non-traditional career paths in the professions, for example, have relied on networking, advanced education, membership in professional organizations, internships, and mentors. Those who hope to enter the traditionally male realm of blue-collar work or trades often depend on vocational training, apprenticeships, or the good word of a current employee.[10] Women's entrance into such spaces becomes increasingly difficult the more strongly these places are associated with masculinity. It is not surprising that blue-collar professions that include physical labor in settings that can be "dirty, dusty, and otherwise suboptimal, a combination of factors that read 'masculine'" provide specific challenges for women who choose to enter them (Perry-Sizemore and MacLaughlin). Careers associated with the automobile—i.e., automotive service technicians and mechanics, automotive body and related repairers, tool and die makers, drafters, and mechanical engineers—are still overwhelmingly male dominated.[11]

The muscle car's blue-collar history—i.e., its earliest association with young Detroit gear-heads taking apart engines and street racing on Woodward Avenue—as well as the muscle car's current status as a "remedy to the threat of emasculation posed by women and bureaucracy," suggests that women's attempts to integrate into the muscle car community are most often fraught with significant obstacles (Duerringer 137). While women in professional, political, and educational locations have often relied upon legal means to level the playing field, those who desire to gain access into traditional male activities must consider alternative and more inventive tactics. The women in this project understand that those who hold the keys to their acceptance are primarily aging conservative men who hold traditional values. Thus rather than confront the men head on with demands of gender inclusion and equality, the women create acceptable—and invaluable—roles for themselves within the muscle car community. As women who identify as moderate to conservative, the women are not looking to resist the status quo or rock the boat in any manner. They do not take the advice of experts who offer strategies such as "take risks; take action; be authentic; and empower yourself" (Newman). They do not take recommendations from the feminist playbook. These women do not engage in old-fashioned consciousness raising; they do not write opinion pieces; they do not carry signs or banners nor do they hold protests or marches. As 61-year-old 2012 Camaro owner remarked, "I'm not women's lib."

Kersten's criticism of liberal feminism rests on what she describes as "a chip on the shoulder disguised as a philosophy." Contemporary feminism, Kersten argues, is too quick to cite patriarchy as the cause of women's inequality. The majority of women who contributed to this project share Kersten's viewpoint. They recognize that in order to gain acceptance into the muscle car community, it is in their best interest to work with the men in charge rather than against them. While they view the inclusion of women as an important and necessary goal, and consider themselves equal participants in the muscle car hobby, they also acknowledge that their objectives cannot be reached by provoking men. By assuming noninvasive roles within the muscle car community—as caretakers, organizers, club officers, forum administrators, and automotive historians—and by supporting male partners in the muscle car hobby, these women are able to take part in an activity heretofore closed to them. And by framing muscle car ownership through conservative values—i.e., the protection and promotion of conventional social forms, expressive individualism, attention to family and community, patriotism, and celebration of traditional gender roles—these women create an important place for themselves in the muscle car community. Since the earliest days of automobility, writes Clarsen, women have grappled "with fraught questions of how to fashion themselves into females who could feel properly at home within a domain in which being male had been construed as the norm" ("Dust" 52). This project not only reveals the meanings women ascribe to a particular automobile in a specific context but also demonstrates how women construct themselves as important actors in a historically masculine culture while keeping conservative values intact.

Why Women and Muscle Cars?

The automobile has had a monumental impact on the American way of life since its introduction in the early twentieth century. Yet, although women make up nearly half of car owners, what we know about the woman driver is based primarily on what automakers choose to tell us. Industry-generated constructions of the woman driver fail to address women's complex relationship to cars; they do not consider the automobile's role in women's reconstruction of self; they do not reflect upon ability of cars to take women's lives in new directions; they do not understand how ownership of a particular automobile has the potential to transform the woman driver in a myriad of ways.

Traditional representations have constructed the female driver as an individual whose interest in the automobile is focused primarily on reliability and functionality. The efforts of automakers over the past one hundred years to construct the "woman's car" as a form of domestic technology has resulted in the prevailing notion that women have little interest in the automobile outside its ability to carry kids and cargo. This research adamantly questions such presumptions. Through the determined selection of vehicles that are loud, fast, powerful, and difficult to handle, the subjects of this project disrupt the persistent association of the female driver with safety and practicality. Through their participation in muscle car culture these women, as Clarsen would argue, provide new meanings and human

Cindy Gillespie-Lena—aka "GT Cindy"—grew up in a car family. As a second-generation Ford employee, she has a special affinity for Mustangs. One Mustang is never enough; consequently, Cindy owns both a 1993 and 2012 Mustang GT. As she noted, "My cars are all red. I guess I like to have a hot little fun car to play with" (courtesy Cindy Gillespie-Lena).

contexts for the cars they drive, generating "unexpected and heterogeneous ways of moving and connecting to others across distances" ("Mobility" 237).

Investigating the woman driver outside of dominant cultural constructions contributes to automotive and feminist scholarship in a number of ways. First, it brings long overdue attention to women's relationship to the automobile. Due to the automobile's longstanding association with masculinity, automotive scholars have most often considered the automobile in American culture through the perspective of male automakers, marketers, and drivers. In these traditional accounts, women are considered through the lens of patriarchy—as objects to be seduced by male drivers, or as consumers of cars and household goods. Women's relationship to the automobile is cited not to reflect on the car's importance to women, but rather, as a means to reinforce cultural gender stereotypes and claim male—automotive and otherwise—authority. This project shifts the focus to consider women as independent actors in American car culture. It regards the woman driver as actively engaged in meaning—making through consideration of what a particular car is and how it might be used. It investigates the process by which women reinvent themselves through rejection of hegemonic woman driver constructions. It focuses on a specific location in which women call upon the automobile as a source of autonomy and identity formation as well as a means to negotiate historically masculine spaces.

Secondly, as it acknowledges the validity of the woman-car relationship, this project encourages women to become more auto-centric. While women's relationship to the automobile has been traditionally expressed as little more than resigned dependency, exposure to new car experiences, coupled with the acquisition of automotive knowledge, has the potential to alter the role of the automobile in women's lives and offer new possibilities for the woman driver. In their work focused on women and racing, Dani Ben-Ari and Susan Frissell assert that a cultivated interest in automobiles at an early age, particularly through involvement in motorsports, has the ability to build self-esteem in young women. In "Women Auto Know," an article recently published in *Feminist Media Studies*, I argue that the automotive knowledge and negotiation skills gleaned from women's car advice websites empower women to become more effective car consumers and more skilled drivers. The accumulation of automotive knowledge, inspired by an interest and attachment to the automobile, is likely to result in a self-assured individual who takes pleasure in the driving experience and who is better equipped to hold her own in auto dealerships and service establishments, traditional bastions of hyper-masculinity.

Thirdly, attention to women whose interest in the automobile exceeds its function as reliable transportation suggests there are employment and recreational opportunities for women with a passion for cars. As the interviews garnered for this project suggest, women's involvement with cars is often effectively channeled into auto-related areas such as racing, automotive sales and repair, and automotive journalism, as well as auto industry careers in engineering, design, marketing, and development. The connection between automotive interest and career was most recently demonstrated in the promotion of Mary Barra—a self-confessed "car gal"—to chairperson of General Motors, becoming the first woman in automotive history to head a major car manufacturer. As Barra has quickly demonstrated, women's influence in the auto industry has the potential to shift priorities and to influence how things are done.[12] Women's auto industry participation provides the opportunity for fresh and innovative perspectives to the car manufacturing practice. As Dale Spender infers, when women become part of the automotive development process, female drivers are no longer "restricted to working with a product that men designed to fit men's lifestyles and hobbies" (169).

In addition, this project suggests new avenues of research to further explore the meanings women ascribe to automobiles. In 1983 Charles Sanford challenged scholars to remedy the lack of literature addressing the relationship between women and the automobile. As Sanford wrote, "what is needed is both an intimate feminine viewpoint from several perspectives about women's experience with cars and fairly objective, even statistical, studies of the same experience" (140). While there has been a determined effort by historians and literary scholars to incorporate the woman driver into scholarship, the majority of existing research draws its analysis primarily from secondary sources, i.e., literature, film, newspapers, advertising, and various printed material. This ethnographic project provides an important new dimension to the current automotive literature through the inclusion of real women's experiences. As Daniel Miller argues, ethnography used in the study of material culture "tends to emphasize careful observations of what people actually do and in particular do with things" ("Why" 12). As it focuses on women's car ownership and driving experience within a particular population of women, this research not only troubles common perceptions of the woman driver, but also suggests the possibility of relationships between women and cars in other locations and thus encourages new areas of investigation.

In her research on girl racers, Karen Lumsden notes, "despite the proliferation of studies focusing on car cultures, the role of women within these subcultures remains largely undocumented" (143). Due to the dearth of research on the woman driver and women's driving cultures, the potential for future projects is limitless. Possibilities include women who are active in various racing cultures; women who participate in all-female car organizations; women who work in auto related fields such as auto mechanics, auto journalism, or car advice; professional female truck drivers; professional female bus drivers; and women who own hybrids, electrics, luxury sedans, small sporty "chick" cars, high-end performance cars, rat rods, and other non–minivan crossover SUV—aka "mom"—vehicles. This short listing of alternative car cultures populated by women not only reveals the multiplicity of women drivers, but also suggests how women relate to and derive meaning from vehicles in countless different ways. This project has the potential to encourage others—in scholarship, auto journalism, and within the auto industry—to explore the diverse experiences of women drivers in whatever location they happen to find them.

This project also contributes to existing scholarship through the production of new knowledge about women and cars. It augments the work of feminist historians—including Virginia Scharff, Ruth Schwartz Cowan, and Margaret Walsh—who have interrogated the cultural construction of the "woman's car" as a form of domestic technology. It continues the scholarly conversation—instigated by Kathleen Franz, Georgine Clarsen, Judy Wajcman, and Julie Wosk—regarding women's reconfiguration of masculine machines and active engagement with male technologies. It draws attention to the gendering of automobiles and the automotive experience—as argued by Scharff, Cotten Seiler, and Deborah Clarke—and reveals women's determined efforts to appropriate a masculine technology in order to create a legitimate space for themselves in American car culture. It moves away from representation and historical analysis to consider how real women in contemporary America consider the automobile and their relationship to it. It uncovers evidence of women's relationship to the automobile in new and unusual places and behind the wheels of very different vehicles. It calls upon an alternate construction of the woman driver to suggest the multiple meanings women ascribe to cars and the driving experience. It disrupts, challenges, reconfigures, and reimagines dominant representations of the woman driver through the narratives of real women. It calls upon my own previous work with alternative car cultures—chick cars, classic cars, pickup trucks, and the Lambda International Car Club—to suggest the limitless possibilities of the woman driver. And perhaps most importantly, it recognizes and promotes women as "authentic" drivers and legitimate actors in American car culture.

This project also argues for the inclusion of conservative feminism in traditional feminist scholarship. Liberal feminists have long refuted the plausibility of the conservative feminist. As Judith Stacey has argued, the repudiation of sexual politics in conservative feminist thought "represents a great leap backwards for feminists and other progressives" (560). Conservative feminism's "pro-family" stance, its celebration of traditionally feminine qualities, particularly those associated with mothering, and its dismissal of the struggle against male domination puts it in conflict with many of the foundational tenets of liberal feminism. This ingrained mode of liberal feminist thinking, coupled with a common association of conservatism with the radical religious right, has resulted in a scarcity of scholarship devoted to the conservative woman as a legitimate feminist voice. However, as the examination of this particular group of muscle car owners suggests, the incorporation of feminist values into a conservative worldview is possible. As Amy Baehr, in her analysis of the conservative feminism of Elizabeth Fox-Genovese, asserts, "feminism is committed to listening to the voices of women, including conservative women" (118). Thus, this examination of a particular group of muscle car owners provides the opportunity for women who identify as moderate or conservative to demonstrate how they are able to embody and practice a particular ideology in all aspects of their lives.

Finally, an investigation of women and muscle car culture—past and present—provides a voice for the female auto enthusiast that has been historically silenced. The majority of women interviewed for this project grew up during the golden age of car culture— the late 1950s to the early 1970s—in locations strongly associated with the automobile. They understand the importance of the automobile and the auto industry to Southeastern Michigan and neighboring states. They appreciate that in auto-centric environments such as those in which they live and work, the automobile is a significant factor in the formation of identity and community. They acknowledge that auto history and car culture have traditionally been written from the perspective of the male driver. And they also recognize that until very recently women were deterred from participation in muscle car culture as drivers. While they do not self-identify as feminists, the women who participated in this project view the opportunity to own and drive classic muscle cars as an indication of women's equality. As a 41-year-old 1970 Dodge Charger R/T owner remarked, "I think it's great that girls can be in the car hobby as well."

Power Under Her Foot

This research begins to fill a significant gap in the current literature by turning to the voices of real women. It provides insight into the meanings ascribed to the automobile by those who often participated in muscle car culture by standing on the sidelines. It provides an alternate interpretation of the muscle car by those once forbidden to drive it. It presents an alternative framework to classic feminism as a way to consider women's lives. The focus on a specific category of vehicle—the American muscle car—brings attention to how the longstanding association of powerful cars and masculinity has served to limit women's car use, impede women's recognition as legitimate car enthusiasts, and reinforce gender stereotypes about the woman driver.

As cultural studies scholar Dick Hebdige notes in his groundbreaking work on subcultures, consumption is not just about buying goods but often involves "a highly productive and creative appropriation of those goods which transform them over time" (qtd. in "Consumption," Miller 348). Social-cultural anthropologist Webb Keane suggests that

Layna Parker's love of muscle cars started with the 1971 Pontiac Firebird she purchased from her dad as a teenager, and developed into her role as administrator on a national online car forum. As she exclaimed, "I love muscle cars. There's nothing like the sound of those going down the road. You hear one and your ears just perk up. Your head gets turned around backward" (Christopher J. Crandall I photograph).

subjects do not just realize themselves through objects; rather, such objects "may allow subjects to make real discoveries about themselves" (201). Through the appropriation of an American automotive icon for their own use, the women in this project have not only forever changed the meaning of the muscle car, but in the process, have reimagined what it means to be a woman driver.

Over the past half-century, the American muscle car has had a significant impact on American auto manufacturing, auto-related industries, baby boomer youth culture, popular film and media, and the young American male. In the twenty-first century, 50 years after John DeLorean's Pontiac GTO screamed down Woodward Avenue, the women who have patiently and quietly harbored a passion for high-powered Challengers, Camaros, and Mustangs, as well as those of younger generations who have recently discovered them, have the opportunity to become recognized and celebrated as authentic muscle car enthusiasts. It's about time.

Ladies, start your—roaring and rumbling, thunderous and throaty—engines.

Chapter Notes

Acknowledgments

1. In a historical context, "automobility" is defined as the utilization of automobiles as the major means of transportation. However in *Republic of Drivers*, cultural studies scholar Cotten Seiler equates "auto mobile" to self-mobility or self-governance. Automobility, asserts Seiler, is a marker of republican citizenship and modern American identity; in the United States, the act of driving represents what it means to be free. Historian Kathleen Franz defines automobility as "the association of personal mobility with the automobile and ideas of independence" ("Automobiles" 55).

Preface

1. While there have been recent attempts to present the woman driver as an individual who enjoys the driving experience, it has been carried out through predictable scenarios; i.e., consumerism or sex. Ford, for example, promotes the Escape and its peppy EcoBoost engine by interviewing "Competitive Owners" (some of them paid actors) taking a test drive on a winding test track (http://www.ispot.tv/ad/7I4A/ford-eco-boost-challenge-motor-trend). However, as a crossover driven primarily by women (66.1 percent), the Escape's "Fun to Drive" aspect can be considered a marketing strategy to separate it from the Toyota RAV4, its strongest competitor. In 2008, Cadillac endorsed its CTS luxury sedan by featuring *Grey's Anatomy* star Kate Walsh behind the wheel (http://www.youtube.com/watch?v=jkEw1rsBUak). When she asks, in her sultry voice, "When you turn your car on, does it return the favor?" it could be argued that Walsh (and Cadillac) is directing the question to male, rather than female, drivers.

2. The demographics of enthusiast vehicles published by Hedges & Company, a SEMA-member market research and database marketing firm, indicate that women make up 32 percent of 2005–2013 Ford Mustangs buyers, 28 percent of 2010–2013 Chevrolet Camaro buyers, and 22 percent of 2008–2013 Dodge Challenger buyers. http://www.digitaldealer.com/demographics-of-enthusiast-vehicle-owners-revealed/

3. See Laura Behling, "The Woman at the Wheel: Marketing Ideal Womanhood 1915–1934" and Jennifer Berkley, "Women at the Motor Wheel: Gender and Car Culture in the USA, 1920–1930."

4. See Chris Lezotte, "The Evolution of the 'Chick Car' Or: What Came First, the Chick or the Car?"

5. Examples include Roy Furchgott, "In This Auto-Shop Class, Life Lessons Were Part of the Curriculum" and A.J. Baime, "Somewhere in Time: A Search for an Antique Car Leads to True Love."

Introduction

1. The Ford Mustang—considered the original pony car—was introduced in 1964 shortly after the Pontiac GTO to take advantage of the new market created by postwar baby boomers approaching driving age. Initially marketed as a stylish, sporty, and fun-to-drive car, performance packages were added to certain models (GT, Mach 1, Boss) in order to compete in the growing muscle car market. As Leffingwell writes, "Pony cars proved to be even more acceptable because they made muscle cars acceptable, turning them into vehicles their owners could drive to work through the week, to the market on Saturday morning, and to the drag strip or movies on Saturday night" (37).

2. "Inexpensive" is somewhat misleading. The muscle car was produced and promoted as affordable and therefore attainable to young middle-class men.

3. As most auto journalists and historians would attest, the official era of the American muscle car began with the introduction of the Pontiac GTO in 1964, and ended "when the last Super Duty 455 Firebird rolled off Pontiac's assembly line in 1974" (Holmstrom 8). The popularity of the muscle car grew exponentially; as Heitmann notes, "The GTO was a hit from the beginning, with sales of 31,000 in 1964, 64,000 in 1965, and 84,000 in 1966" (177).

4. During the 1950s and early 1960s, working-class Detroit youths could be found on Woodward Avenue street-racing hot rods of their own construction. Automotive executives such as John DeLorean, who traveled from the affluent Northwest Detroit suburbs to the downtown General Motors headquarters, would often stop along Woodward to talk cars with the blue-collar "gear heads." These conversations were the inspiration for the next generation of hot rods—the American muscle car—

and the next generation of car owners, "tens of millions of young white middle-class baby boomer men entering the auto market each year" (Holmstrom 8).

5. Chris Lezotte, "Women and Car Culture in Cyberspace: Empowerment and Car Talk in the Internet User Group."

6. Examples include Virginia Scharff's groundbreaking *Taking the Wheel: Women and the Coming of the Motor Age*; Ruth Schwartz Cowan's framing of the automobile as a form of domestic technology in "More Work for Mother" and "Less Work for Mother," and numerous articles by Margaret Walsh focusing on women's car use in the post World War II era including "At Home at the Wheel?" and "Gender and Automobility."

7. See Marie T. Farr, "Freedom and Control: Automobiles in American Women's Fiction of the 70s and 80s"; Deborah Clarke, *Driving Women: Fiction and Automobile Culture in Twentieth-Century America*; Deborah Paes De Barros, *Fast Cars and Bad Girls: Nomadic Subjects and Women's Road Stories*; Alexandra Ganser, "Roads of Her Own: Gendered Space and Mobility in American's Road Narratives, 1970–2000"; Katie Mills, *The Road Story and the Rebel: Moving Through Film Fiction, and Television*; Jennifer Parchesky, "Women in the Driver's Seat: The Auto-Erotics of Early Women's Films."

8. See the Elinor Nauen edited collection *Ladies Start Your Engines: Women Writers on Cars and the Road*.

9. Notable works include Iris Woolcock, *The Road North: One Woman's Adventure Driving the Alaska Highway 1947–1948*; Joanne Wilke, *Eight Women, Two Model Ts and the American West*; Curt McConnell, *A Reliable Car and a Woman Who Knows It: The First Coast-to-Coast Auto Trips by Women, 1899–1916*; and Georgine Clarsen, "Machines as the Measure of Women: Colonial Irony in a Cape to Cairo Automobile Journey, 1930."

10. Examples include Lesley Hazleton, *Driving to Detroit: Memoirs of a Fast Woman*, and Denise McCluggage, *By Brooks Too Broad for Leaping: Selections from Autoweek*.

11. See Kathleen Franz, *Tinkering: Consumers Reinvent the Early Automobile*; Georgine Clarsen, *Eat My Dust: Early Woman Motorists*; and Cotten Seiler, *Republic of Drivers: A Cultural History of Automobility in America*.

12. Karen Lumsden's *Boy Racer Culture: Youth, Masculinity, and Deviance* and Sarah Redshaw and Greg Noble's *Mobility, Gender, and Young Drivers* include interviews with young women racers.

13. Work includes "Evolution of the Chick Car"; "Women and Car Culture in Cyberspace"; and "Have You Heard the One About the Woman Driver?"

14. Generation or "Gen" in the context of automotive manufacture refers to a major design evolution that persists for a period of time. For example, one of the participants referred to her 1991 Pontiac Firebird as "Third Generation."

15. See "Women with Muscle: Contemporary Women and the Classic Muscle Car" and "Have You Heard the One About the Woman Driver? Chicks, Muscle, Pickups, and the Reimagining of the Woman Behind the Wheel."

16. The participants in this project were recruited primarily through car events such as shows and cruises, local car club meetings, and online forums devoted to a particular automobile. Consequently, they were generally more "car savvy" and more likely to be immersed in muscle car culture than the typical muscle car owner.

17. Term used by Ruth Rosen in *The World Split Open: How the Modern Women's Movement Changed America*.

18. It should be noted that I never used the "F" word when interviewing the participants. Feminism is a loaded and often misinterpreted term; consequently, I kept silent regarding my own ideological leanings. The conservative feminism mentioned throughout this book is a theoretical interpretation rather than an acknowledged position voiced by the women in this project.

19. See Judy Wajcman's *Feminism Confronts Technology* and her more recent work *Technofeminism*; Phillip Vannini's *Material Culture and Technology in Everyday Life*; and Ruth Schwartz-Cowan's *A Social History of American Technology*.

20. "The Woodward Dream Cruise, a Detroit Classic." *Absolute Michigan*, http://www.absolutemichigan.com/dig/michigan/the-woodward-dream-cruise-a-detroit-classic/ (accessed July 10, 2010).

21. For this project, I believed it was more important to consider how the participants defined the muscle car rather than depend on strict interpretations. (For an example of such strict interpretations, see http://www.musclecarclub.com/musclecars/general/musclecars-definition.shtml)

22. These forums included but were not limited to chargerforumz.com; challengerforumz.com; firebird nation.com; mifbody.com; detroit5thgen.com; camaro5.com; stangnet.com/mustang-forums; michianamustangs.com; modernmoparforum.com.

Chapter 1

1. Although labeled 326 CID, the 1963 Tempest V8 was actually 336 CID due to a 3.78 inch bore. The 1964 Tempest V8 was 326 CID due to a .060 reduced 3.72-inch cylinder bore to conform with GM restrictions of no more than 330 CID in midsized vehicles.

2. The HP difference is based on a comparison of the GTO 325 HP vs. Tempest 280 HP, both with 1×4 barrel carburetor. If considering the optional GTO 348 HP with 3×2 barrel carburetors, the difference would be 68HP.

3. Veteran automotive journalist Joe Oldham attributes the GTO's success to its marketing as a complete package. As he explains, "the difference with the GTO was you got the trim, emblems, buckets, big engine, and image; it was the whole package. That concept was the game-changer. It was the first car that came prepackaged like that" (qtd. in Rosenberg).

4. A comprehensive listing of classic muscle cars can be found at http://www.musclecarclub.com/muscle cars/general/musclecars-definition.shtml.

5. "Avid spectator" is a term borrowed from Robert Genat in *Woodward Avenue: Cruising the Legendary Strip*.

6. Classic car buffs—especially those who worked for, or whose family is affiliated with, a domestic auto company—are extremely loyal to a particular manufacturer (i.e., Ford, General Motors, Chrysler).

7. Mopar (Motor Parts) refers to Chrysler's parts and service division. It has since passed into broader usage as a reference to all Chrysler products.

8. Chevrolet, or Chevy muscle cars included the Camaro, Chevelle, Impala SS, and Nova SS. The 'Cuda, Duster, GTX, Road Runner, and Superbird were the Plymouth (a former division of Chrysler) muscle car offerings.

9. General Motors. Other General Motors vehicles in the classic muscle car category were the Oldsmobile 442, Pontiac Firebird, and Pontiac GTO.

10. Chrysler product. Other popular Chrysler muscle cars during the 1960s and '70s included the Dodge Charger, Dodge Dart, Dodge Daytona, Dodge Super Bee, Plymouth Barracuda and 'Cuda, Plymouth Duster, Plymouth Road Runner, and Plymouth Superbird.

11. Ford products considered classic muscle cars include the Mustang (GT, Boss, and Mach 1), Gran Torino, and Galaxie as well as the Mercury Comet, Cyclone, and Cougar.

12. Refers to automakers Ford, General Motors, and Chrysler.

13. As referenced on the City of Auburn homepage, http://www.ci.auburn.in.us/.

14. American exceptionalism in this context refers to one of the many interpretations proposed by James Ceaser, who writes, "Conservatives want Americans to think of themselves as special" (3) and the idea that there is "something special about America" (6).

15. While the association of ideological conservatism with the American auto industry and ownership of a domestic automobile is "common sense" in Southeastern Michigan and the neighboring auto centric areas, scholars in a variety of locations have made the connection among American cars, patriotism, and a conservative worldview. The Gallup Poll results of car preference by political ideology during the 2004 presidential election concluded that conservatives are more likely to drive American cars. Terence Shimp and Subhas Sharma argue that patriotism and conservatism in the metropolitan Detroit area are strongly linked to ownership of an American automobile.

16. Scholars from a variety of disciplines (Olson; Federico) have convincingly linked conservatism to whiteness. Consequently, it should not be surprising that a community in which patriotism and conservatism are demonstrated through celebration of an iconic American automobile is predominantly white.

17. Classic car culture's link with conservatism also suggests that the majority of those who participate are Christian; in fact, many of the women who took part in this project mentioned they often turn heads in the church parking lot Sunday mornings when pulling up in a rumbling Dodge Charger or Pontiac Firebird.

18. Owning a classic muscle car is not an inexpensive endeavor; while many of the women save on mechanical costs by marrying men handy with a socket wrench, participation in classic muscle car culture requires a solid middle-class income.

19. Latino and African American auto enthusiasts in Southwest Detroit are often involved in lowrider culture; one example is the Majestic Car Club. See "Majestics: History of a Car Club: From the Streets to the Show, Majestics Puts It Down One Rear Bumper at a Time," Lowrider: Performance, Artistry, Pride, Culture, Dec. 2008, http://www.lowrider.com/lifestyle/0812-lrmp-majestics-history-of-car-club/. Asian Americans in the Detroit area and elsewhere are very active in the import/compact racing/tuner scene. See "Import/Sport Compact," Asian Nation: Asian American History, Demographics, and Issues, 2001–13, http://www.asian-nation.org/import-racing.shtml. Local car enthusiasts within the LGBTQ [Lesbian Gay Bisexual Transgender Queer] community participate in the Detroit chapter of the Lambda Car Club International. See "Lambda Car Club/ Detroit," Lambda Car Clubs, http://lccdetroit.org (accessed Nov. 7, 2012).

20. VIN is an acronym for Vehicle Identification Number, a unique code employed by the auto industry to identify individual motor vehicles; RPO, or Regular Production Option, is a General Motors standard coding for vehicle configuration options; date codes, parts numbers, and casting numbers are original major components and are used to qualify a classic car as "number matching," i.e., codes that match the car when it was new; transmission and rear end, or axle, tags are codes that identify and verify a car part's year of production and authenticity.

21. Fox body refers to the rear-wheel-drive, unibody construction platform used by the Ford Motor Company for various compact and midsize vehicles from 1978 to 1993.

22. "Captive import" is commonly used in automotive marketing to refer to a vehicle that is foreign built and sold under the name of an importer or by a domestic automaker through its own dealer distribution program (thelawdictionary.com).

23. As defined in dictionary.com, retrofuturism refers to "The use of a style considered futuristic in the past."

24. Bowtie is the term adopted by Chevy enthusiasts to describe the iconic Chevrolet emblem introduced by company cofounder William C. Durant in 1913.

25. The Blue Oval refers to the Ford logo that first appeared on the 1928 Model T. It is believed that the background color was chosen by Mrs. Henry [Clara] Ford. The Blue Oval was officially adopted as the company's corporate signature in 1961 (blog.caranddriver.com).

26. Of the 17,473,320 new cars sold in the U.S. in 2015, Mustangs, Camaros, Challengers and Chargers accounted for 360,941 (Cain).

27. In "Women Auto Know," I note that car advice websites such as AskPatty.com and Women-drivers.com have developed dealership evaluation systems that provide female auto customers the opportunity to certify dealer and service establishments as "female friendly."

Chapter 2

1. In her groundbreaking work on separate spheres and women's place in the rhetoric of women's history, Linda Kerber notes that perceptions of what constitutes women's work are founded on the premise that "when women venture out of the home they are best suited to doing work that replicates housework" (28).

2. One of the more common definitions of nostalgia, write Pickering and Keightley, is longing for a past time or "for what is lacking in a changed present" (920). In "Nostalgia for What? Taking America Back from Whom?" John Garvey links conservatism to false nostalgia, i.e., the belief that everything would be fine if things could only return to the way they were. While classic muscle car owners have little desire to go back to the days before power steering, disc brakes, and modern technology, men's participation in muscle car culture can in some ways be considered a longing for a time in which American men and American cars had more power.

3. "Ford Blue" refers to the color found in the Ford logo—a blue oval with Ford spelled out in distinctive

white script lettering—one of the most recognizable corporate logos in the world. A more detailed description of the logo and its history can be found at http://www.car-brand-names.com/ford-logo/

4. http://www.autotrader.com/car-shopping/buying-a-car-how-long-can-you-expect-a-car-to-last-240725.

5. Iris Woolcock, *The Road North*; Joanne Wilke, *Eight Women, Two Model Ts, and the American West*; Curt McConnell, *A Reliable Car and a Woman Who Knows It*.

6. Todd McCarthy, *Fast Women: The Legendary Ladies of Racing*; Elsa A. Nystrom, *Mad for Speed: The Racing Life of Joan Newton Cuneo*; Miranda Seymour, *The Bugatti Queen: In Search of a Motor Racing Legend*; Steven Overman, Jr., and Kelly Boyer Sagert. *Icons of Women's Sport: From Tomboys to Title IX and Beyond.*

7. As an example, Michigan Mopar Muscle, an organization that describes itself as "The Friendly Car Club," honored its female members at the 65th Annual Detroit Autorama with a special display. "The Cars of Mopar Women" was awarded outstanding club display; three of the women were singled out for individual awards.

8. Examples include *Car Club Memories: Personal Stories from Three Dynamic Decades of Cruisin', Competition, and Cool Cars* compiled by Fred Thomas; Ambrosio and Luckerman's *Cruisin' the Original: Woodward Avenue*; *Gone in Sixty Seconds*; *Vanishing Point*; *Dirty Mary Crazy Larry.*

9. Examples include *Ladies Start Your Engines: Women Writers on Cars and the Road*, a collection of car stories edited by Elinor Nauen, and Marilyn Root's *Women at the Wheel: 42 Stories of Freedom, Fanbelts, and the Lure of the Open Road.*

10. Hill, Moulton, and Burdette argue that while many religious groups wrestle with the issue of homosexuality, "the strongest and most consistent opposition has come from conservative Protestants" (59). Brint and Arbrutyn suggest that factors including religiosity, moral standards traditionalism, gender and family ideology, class culture, and cultural geography contribute to a conservative intolerance toward homosexuality (328).

11. In my master's thesis—"Women and Car Culture in Cyberspace: Empowerment and Car Talk in the Internet Automotive Group"—over 100 female motorists were asked to reflect on their experiences in online car forums, blogs, mailing lists, and bulletin boards.

12. Literature that explores this connection further includes Joel Olson's "Whiteness and the Polarization of American Politics"; "Whitewashing Race: A Critical Perspective on Whiteness" by Margaret Anderson; "Whiteness: A Strategic Rhetoric" by Thomas K. Nakayama and Robert Krizek; "Ideology and the Affective Structure of Whites' Racial Perceptions" by Christopher M. Federico.

13. Halberstam defines female masculinity as "women who feel themselves to be more masculine than feminine" (xi). Familiar presentations of female masculinity include the tomboy, butch, and drag king.

14. See also Terrence Hill, Benjamin E. Moulton, and Amy M. Burdette, "Conservative Protestantism and Attitudes Toward Homosexuality"; Robert Anderson and Tina Fetner, "Cohort Differences in Tolerance of Homosexuality"; Steven Brint and Seth Arbutyn, "Who's Right About the Right?"

15. In a study comparing the attitudes toward homosexuality in Canada and the United States, Anderson and Fetner conclude that acceptance of homosexuality

is negatively related to age, and that changes in attitude from 1981 to 2000 reflect the influence of widespread cultural and political change.

Chapter 3

1. Alisa Priddle of the *Detroit Free Press* notes that the average age of Mustang buyers is 48. *Automotive News* writer Vince Bond, Jr., reported that the average age of the Charger buyer is 46.8 years.

2. From the "Distinction: A Possession to Prize" display noted by the author on a 13 May 2017 museum visit.

3. "Bowtie" is the common term used to refer to the Chevrolet logo.

4. From the display "Making It Mine," noted by the author at a 13 May 2017 museum visit.

5. In an interview at the 2017 Conservative Political Action Conference, special assistant to the president—and self-identified conservative feminist—Kellyanne Conway described classic feminism as "very anti-male" (Blake).

6. Frankenmuth Auto Fest, held every September in Frankenmuth, Michigan.

7. 1970 Pontiac GTO *Motor Trend* December 1969.

8. 1970 Dodge Challenger R/T *Motor Trend* January 1970; 1970 Mercury Cougar Eliminator *Car and Driver* October 1969; 1973 Plymouth Road Runner *Hot Rod*, January 1973; 1982 Chevrolet Camaro Z/28 *Sports Illustrated* February 8 1982; 1969 Pontiac GTO Judge *Hot Rod* March 1969.

9. Refers to a line spoken by Captain Jack Sparrow [played by Johnny Depp] in *Pirates of the Caribbean*. "The seas may be rough, but I am the captain! No matter how difficult I will always prevail" ("15 Most Important *Pirates of the Caribbean* Quotes").

Chapter 4

1. "Confidence Mediates the Sex Difference in Mental Rotation Performance" in *Archives of Sexual Behavior* (2012) 41: 557–570.

2. 2009 Dodge Challenger ad: "Now, This Is an Adult Toy"; 2005 Ford Mustang ad: "One of the Top Five Reasons America Is Cooler than Any Other Country"; 2002 Chevrolet Camaro Ad: "0% Body Fat."

3. Noted in Walsh's "Gender and Automobility: Selling Cars to American Women After the Second World War."

4. According to Aaron Cole, managing editor of *The Car Connection*, fewer than one in five drivers know how to drive a car with a manual transmission. http://www.thecarconnection.com/news/1110531_teaching-the-classics-how-young-drivers-are-discovering-manuals#src=10065.

5. Noted in "Driving a Stick Shift? Pros and Cons of Cars with Manual Transmissions" in the *New York Daily News*, January 25, 2013. http://www.nydailynews.com/autos/driving-stick-pros-cons-manual-transmissions-article-1.1247896.

6. These are slang terms often used in drag racing, hot rod, or muscle car cultures. "Boilin' the Hides" refers to smoking the tires during a drag race. "Burnin' rubber" is "to run a car engine so fast that one spins the tires so that rubber is left on the street" (http://dictionary.reference.com/browse/burn+rubber). "Doin'

a Brodie," also known as a " Doughnut," is a maneuver that "entails rotating the rear or front of the vehicle around the opposite set of wheels in a continuous motion, creating (ideally) a circular skid-mark pattern of rubber on a roadway" (http://en.wikipedia.org/wiki/Doughnut_(driving)). "Poppin' the Clutch" is a method of starting a car by "engaging the manual transmission through the motion of the vehicle" (http://en.cyclopaedia.net/wiki/Popping-the-clutch).

7. Clarke defines automotive maternity as "a condition in which one's role as a mother relies, at least in part, on one's place in car culture—as driver and as vehicle" (77).

8. 2001 Ford Windstar advertisement: "Why wish on a star when you can rely on five?"; 1978 Dodge Omni advertisement: "Mom's Omni"; 2000 Oldsmobile Silhouette advertisement: "Tree forts. Family rooms. Even remodeled basements can't compete"; 2003 Dodge Caravan advertisement: "Some superheroes use a phone booth. Moms have this."

9. In her dissertation "Who's Got the Keys to the Minivan," Kelley Hall characterizes "transportation work" as a form of childcare closely associated with women's family work. As Hall writes, "transportation work

is symbolically linked to heterosexual womanhood and motherhood through women's responsibility for these different transportation tasks" (22).

10. As noted in "Non-Traditional Careers for Women: Opportunities and Benefits for Women in Male-Dominated Professions." Compiled by Elizabeth Perry-Sizemore and Nina MacLaughlin in LearnHowToBecome.com.

11. See the 2014 U.S. Department of Labor Women's Bureau report on women in non-traditional occupations https://www.dol.gov/wb/stats/nontra_traditional_occupations.htm.

12. Chris Woodyard, in *USA Today*, notes that Barra is able to "project a sense of change in what has been known as a hidebound organization." Responding to the repercussions surrounding a design flaw before Congress, Barra vowed to change the corporate General Motors culture "from one where the primary focus was cutting costs to one where the primary focus is the customer" (Lebeau and Pohlman). Three and a half years after taking over the helm of General Motors, writes *Detroit Free Press* auto critic Mark Phelan, Barra is creating a company "that's more sensitive to its customers and more focused on profits than ever before."

Bibliography

Ainsworth, Susan. "The 'Feminine Advantage': A Discursive Analysis of the Invisibility of Older Women Workers." *Gender, Work & Organization* 9.5 (November 2002): 579–601.

Ambrosio, Anthony, and Susan Luckerman. *Cruisin' the Original: Woodward Avenue.* Charleston, SC: Arcadia, 2006.

Anderson, Margaret L. "Whitewashing Race: A Critical Perspective on Whiteness." *White Out: The Continuing Significance of Racism.* Eds. Ashley W. Doane and Eduardo Bonilla-Silva. New York: Routledge, 2003. 21–34.

Anderson, Robert, and Tina Fetner. "Cohort Differences in Tolerance of Homosexuality: Attitudinal Change in Canada and the United States." *Public Opinion Quarterly* 72.2 (2008): 311–330.

Atkinson, Robert. *The Life Story Interview.* Thousand Oaks, CA: Sage Publications, Inc., 1998.

Baehr, Amy R. "Conservatism, Feminism, and Elizabeth Fox-Genovese." *Hypatia* 24.2 (Spring 2002): 101–124.

Baime, A.J. "Somewhere in Time: A Search for an Antique Car Leads to True Love." *The Wall Street Journal* 28 June 2016. Web. 23 Feb 2017. http://www.wsj.com/articles/somewhere-in-time-a-search-for-an-antique-car-leads-to-true-love-1467125439

Balkmar, Dag. "On Men and Cars: An Ethnographic Study of Gendered, Risky, and Dangerous Behavior." Dissertation. Linkoping University, 2012.

Balkmar, Dag, and Tanja Joelsson. "Feeling the Speed—the Social and Emotional Investments in Dangerous Road Practices." *Gender and Change: Power, Politics and Everyday Practices.* Eds. Maria Jansdotter Samuelsson, Clary Krekula, and Magnus Aberg. Karlstad, Sweden: Karlstad University Press. 2012. 37–52.

Banks-Wallace, Joanne. "Storytelling as a Tool for Providing Holistic Care to Women." *American Journal of Maternal Care Nursing* 24.1 (1999): 20–24.

Bayley, Stephen. *Sex, Drink, and Fast Cars.* New York: Pantheon, 1987.

Behling, Laura L. "'The Woman at the Wheel': Marketing Ideal Womanhood, 1915–1934." *Journal of American Culture* 20.5 (1999): 13–30.

Belk, Russell. "Men and their Machines." *Advances in Consumer Research* 31 (2004): 273–278.

Ben-Ari, Dani, and Susan Frissell. *Girls Go Racing: Driving to Esteems.* Bloomington, IN: AuthorHouse, 2009.

Berger, Arthur Asa. *What Objects Mean: An Introduction to Material Culture.* Walnut Creek, CA: Left Coast Press, 2009.

Berger, Michael. "The Car's Impact on the American Family." *The Car and the City: The Automobile, the Built Environment, and Daily Urban Life.* Eds. Martin Wachs and Margaret Crawford. Ann Arbor: The University of Michigan Press, 1992. 57–74.

_____. "Women Drivers! The Emergence of Folklore and Stereotypic Opinions Concerning Feminine Automotive Behavior." *Women's Studies International Forum* 9.3 (1986): 257–263.

Berkley, Jennifer Elizabeth. "Women at the Motor Wheel: Gender and Car Culture in the United States of America, 1920–1930." Dissertation. The Claremont Graduate School, 1996.

Blake, Aaron. "Kellyanne Conway's Uniquely Feminist Opposition to Feminism." *The Washington Post.* 23 Feb 2017. Web. 31 Mar 2017. https://www.washingtonpost.com/news/the-fix/wp/2017/02/23/kellyanne-conways-uniquely-feminist-opposition-to-feminism/?utm_term=.a0f137d14010

Bond, Vince, Jr. "Dodge, Land Rover, Lamborghini Draw Youngest New-Vehicle Buyers, HIS Report Says." AutoNews.com. 05 May 2014, 31 March 2017 http://www.autonews.com/article/20140505/RETAIL03/140509907/dodge-land-rover-lamborghini-draw-youngest-new-vehicle-buyers-his

Boudette, Neal E. "Powerful Nostalgia—To Prop Up Sagging Sales, Detroit Returns to Muscle Cars That Recall the Glory Days." *The Wall Street Journal* B1 10 Jan 2006.

Bowles, N. "Story Telling: A Search for Meaning Within Nursing Practice." *Nurse Education Today* 15.5 (1995): 365–369.

Bright, Brenda. "Heart Like a Car: Hispano/Chicano Culture in Northern New Mexico." *American Ethnologist* 24.4 (1998): 583–609.

Brilliant, Ashleigh. *The Great Car Craze: How Southern California Collided with the Automobile in the 1920s.* Santa Barbara: Woodbridge Press, 1989.

Brint, Steven, and Seth Arrutyn. "Who's Right About the Right? Comparing Competing Explanations of the Link Between White Evangelicals and Conservative Politics in the United States." *Journal for Scientific Study of Religion* 49.2 (2010): 328–350.

Brodsky, Warren. *Driving with Music: Cognitive-Behavioural Implications*. New York: Routledge, 2015.

Bukszpan, Daniel. "Modern-Day Muscle Cars of 2014." *The Car Chasers*. 25 Oct 2013. Web. 6 Jun 2015. http://www.cnbc.com/2013/10/24/hottest-new-modern-day-muscle-cars-of-2014.html

Byrnes, Nanette. "Blowing Blue Chips Off the Road." *Business Week* 3807 11 Nov 2002: 16.

Cain, Timothy. "2015 Year End U.S. Vehicle Sales Rankings—Top 288 Best-Selling Vehicles in America—Every Vehicle Ranked." *Good Car Bad Car*. 7 Jan 2016. Web. 8 Jun 2016. http://www.goodcarbadcar.net/2016/01/usa-vehicle-sales-by-model-2015-calendar-year-december.html

Campisano, Jim. *American Muscle Cars*. New York: MetroBooks, 1995.

Cantor, Daniel. "From the Director." Program for *Anne Washburn's* Mr. Burns: A Post-Electric Play at the Lydia Mendelssohn Theater, Ann Arbor. University of Michigan School of Music, Theater, and Dance, 2017.

Caperello, Nicolette D., and Kenneth S. Kurani. "Households' Stories of Their Encounters With a Plug-In Hybrid Electric Vehicle." *Environment and Behavior* 44.4 (2012): 493–508.

Ceaser, James W. "The Origins and Character of American Exceptionalism." *American Political Thought: A Journal of Ideas, Institutions, and Culture* 1 (Spring 2012): 1–25.

Cheney, Peter. "In Pictures: The Most Over-the-Top Chick Cars and Macho-Mobiles on the Road." *The Globe and Mail* 16 May 2013. Web. 9 April 2014. http://www.theglobeandmail.com/globe-drive/culture/in-pictures-the-most-over-the-top-chick-cars-and-macho-mobiles-on-the-road/article11951098/?from=12424797

Clarke, Deborah. *Driving Women: Fiction and Automobile Culture in Twentieth-Century America*. Baltimore: The Johns Hopkins University Press, 2007.

Clarsen, Georgine. *Eat My Dust: Early Women Motorists*. Baltimore: The Johns Hopkins Press, 2008.

_____. "Gender and Mobility: Historicizing the Terms." *Mobility in History: The State of the Art in the History of Transport, Traffic, and Mobility*. Eds. Gijs Mom, Gordon Pirie, and Laurent Tissot. Switzerland: Editions Alphio—Presses Universitaires Suisses, 2009.

_____. "Machines as the Measure of Women: Colonial Irony in a Cape to Cairo Automobile Journey, 1930." *The Journal of Transportation History* 29.2 (2008): 44–62.

Clor, John M. *The Mustang Dynasty*. San Francisco: Chronicle Books, 2007.

Cole, Aaron. "Teaching the Classics: How Young Drivers are Discovering Manuals." TheCarConnection.com 17 May 2017. Web. 20 May 2017. http://www.thecarconnection.com/news/1110531_teaching-the-classics-how-young-drivers-are-discovering-manuals#src=10065

Coontz, Stephanie. *The Way We Never Were: American Families and the Nostalgia Trap*. New York: Basic Books, 1992.

Cooper, Baba. *Over the Hill: Reflections on Ageism Between Women*. Freedom, CA: Crossing Press, 1988.

Cowan, Ruth Schwartz. "Less Work for Mother." *American Heritage Magazine* 38.6 September/October 1987. Web. 21 January 2011. http://www.americanheritage.com/content/less-work-mother

_____. *A Social History of American Technology*. Oxford: Oxford University Press, 1997.

_____. "Twentieth-Century Changes in Household Technology." *More Work for Mother: The Ironies of Household Technologies from the Open Hearth to the Microwave*. New York: Basic Books, 1983. 69–101.

Cruikshank, Margaret. *Learning to be Old: Gender, Culture, and Aging*. Lanham, MD: Rowman & Littlefield, 2009.

Dannefer, Dale. "Neither Socialization nor Recruitment: The Avocational Careers of Old-Car Enthusiasts." *Social Forces* 60.2 (December 1981): 395–413.

"Demographics of Enthusiast Vehicle Owners Revealed." Digitaldealer.com 9 Oct 2012. Web. 7 May 2017. http://www.digitaldealer.com/demographics-of-enthusiast-vehicle-owners-revealed/

Demorro, Chris. "Over One-Third of Sports Cars Bought by Women Were Mustangs." *StangTV* 11 Sep 2015. Web. 3 Jan 2016. http://www.stangtv.com/news/over-one-third-of-sports-cars-bought-by-women-were-mustangs/

"Distinction: A Possession to Prize." Petersen Automotive Museum. 6060 Wilshire Blvd., Los Angeles, CA, 90036. 13 May 2017.

Domosh, Mona, and Joni Seager. *Putting Women in Place: Feminist Geographers Make Sense of the World*. New York: The Guilford Press, 2001.

Donatelli, Cindy. "Driving the Suburbs: Minivans, Gender, and Family Values." *Material History Review* 54 (Fall 2001): 84–95.

"Driving a Stick Shift? Pros and Cons of Cars with Manual Transmissions." NYDailyNews.com 25 Jan 2013. Web. 3 Mar 2015. http://www.nydailynews.com/autos/driving-stick-pros-cons-manual-transmissions-article-1.1247896

Duerringer, Christopher. "Be A Man—Buy a Car! Articulating Masculinity with Consumerism in *Man's Last Stand*." *Southern Communication Journal* 80.2 (2015): 137–152.

East, Leah, Debra Jackson, Louise O'Brien and Kathleen Peters. "Storytelling: An Approach That Can Help to Develop Resilience." *Nurse Researcher* 17.3 (2010): 17–25.

Ebo, Bosah. "Internet or Outernet" in *Cyberghetto or Cybertopia? Race, Class and Gender on the Internet*. Westport, CT: Praeger, 1998.

Estes, Zachary, and Sydney Felker. "Confidence Mediates the Sex Difference in Mental Rotation Performance." *Archives of Sexual Behavior* 41 (2012): 557–570.

Falconer, Tim. *Drive: A Road Trip Through Our Complicated Affair with the Automobile*. Toronto: Viking, 2009.

Fallon, Ivan, and James Srodes. *Dream Maker: The Rise and Fall of John Z. DeLorean*. New York: G.P. Putnam's Sons, 1983.

Farr, Marie T. "Freedom and Control: Automobiles in American Women's Fiction of the 70s and 80s." *Journal of Popular Culture* 29 (1995): 157–69.

Federico, Christopher. "Ideology and the Affective Structure of Whites' Racial Perceptions." *Public Opinion Quarterly* 70.3 (Fall 2006): 327–353.

"The 15 Most Important *Pirates of the Caribbean* Quotes, According to You." OhMyDisney.com n.d. Web. 9 Apr 2017. https://ohmy.disney.com/movies/2016/01/05/the-15-most-important-pirates-of-the-caribbean-quotes-according-to-you/

Finch, Christopher. "Muscle Cars Versus Minis." *Cars:*

Examining Pop Culture. Eds. David H. Haugen and Matthew J. Box. Farmington Hills, MI: Thomson Gale, 2005: 80–89.

Flory, J. "Kelly," Jr. *American Cars, 1973–1980: Every Model, Year by Year.* Jefferson, NC: McFarland, 2013.

Foster, Mark. *Nation on Wheels: The Automobile Culture in American Since 1945.* Belmont, CA: Thomson, Wadsworth, 2003

Franz, Kathleen. "Automobiles and Automobility." *Material Culture in Everyday Life.* Eds. Helen Sheumaker and Shirley Wajda. Santa Barbara, CA: ABC-CLIO, 2008. 53–56.

_____. "'The Open Road': Automobility and Racial Uplift in the Interwar Years." *Technology and the African-American Experience: Needs and Opportunities for Study.* Ed. Bruce Sinclair. Cambridge, MA: The MIT Press, 2004. 131–153.

_____. *Tinkering: Consumers Reinvent the Early Automobile.* Philadelphia: The University of Pennsylvania Press, 2005.

Freund, Peter, and George Martin. *The Ecology of the Automobile.* London: Black Rose Books, 1996.

Frohnen, Bruce. "The Patriotism of a Conservative." *Modern Age* 48.2 (Spring 2006): 105–118.

Furchgott, Roy. "In This Auto-Shop Class, Life Lessons Were Part of the Curriculum." *The New Times* AU4, 12 Dec 2014.

Ganser, Alexandra. *Roads of Her Own: Gendered Space and Mobility in American Women's Road Narratives, 1970–2000.* New York: Rodopi Press, 2009.

Gartman, David. *Auto Opium: A Social History of Automobile Design.* London: Routledge, 2004.

Garvey, John. "Nostalgia for What? Taking America Back from Whom?" *Commonweal* 119.6 (1992): 7–8.

Genat, Robert. *Woodward Avenue: Cruising the Legendary Strip.* North Branch, MN: Car Tech, 2010.

Grassley, Jane S. "Tales of Resistance and Other Emancipatory Functions of Storytelling." *Journal of Advanced Nursing* 65.11 (November 2009): 2447–2453.

Halberstam, Judith. *Female Masculinity.* Durham, NC: Duke University Press, 1998.

Hall, Kelley J. "Who's Got the Keys to the Minivan? The Gendered Division of Child Transportation Work in Dual-Earner Families." Dissertation. The University of Akron, 1998.

Hazleton, Lesley. *Driving to Detroit: Memoirs of a Fast Woman.* New York: Simon & Schuster, 1999.

_____. *Everything Women Always Wanted to Know About Cars: But Didn't Know Who to Ask.* New York: Main Street Books, 1995.

Heitmann, John A. *The Automobile and American Life.* Jefferson, NC: McFarland, 2009.

Henshaw, Peter. *Muscle Cars.* San Diego: Thunder Bay Press, 2004

Hill, Terrence D., Benjamin E. Moulton, and Amy M. Burdette. "Conservative Protestantism and Attitudes Toward Homosexuality: Does Political Orientation Mediate this Relationship?" *Sociological Focus* 37.1 (2004): 59–70.

Holloway, Andy. "A Sweet Ride." *Canadian Business* 75.12 (24 June 2002): 73.

Holmstrom, Darwin. "Introduction: Real Muscle Cars." *The All-American Muscle Car: The Birth, Death, and Resurrection of Detroit's Greatest Performance Cars.* Eds. Jim Wangers, Colin Comer, Joe Oldham, and Randy Leffingwell. Minneapolis: Motorbooks, 2013. 7–10.

Howard, Ella. "Pink Truck Ads: Second-Wave Feminism and Gendered Marketing." *Journal of Women's History* 22.4 (2010): 137–161.

Johnson, Kyle S. "On Sexism in Car Commercials: Still Going Strong." Thenewswheel.com 22 Apr 2016. Web. 24 May 2017. http://thenewswheel.com/on-sexism-in-car-commercials/

Johnstone, Barbara. "Community and Contest: Midwestern Men and Women Creating Their Worlds in Conversational Storytelling." *Gender and Conversational Interaction* (January 1993): 62–80.

Keane, Webb. "Subjects and Objects." *Handbook of Material Culture.* Eds. Christopher Tilley, Webb Keane, Susanne Kuchler, Mike Rowlands, and Patricia Spyer. London: Sage Publications, 2006, 197–203.

Kerber, Linda K. "Separate Spheres, Female Worlds, Woman's Place: The Rhetoric of Women's History." *The Journal of American History* 75.1 (1988): 9–39.

Kersten, Katherine. "What Do Women Want? A Conservative Feminist Manifesto." *Policy Review* 56 (Spring 1991): n.p., Academic Search Complete, EBSCOhost.

"K.I.T.T." Knight-rider.wikia.com n.d. Web. 15 May 2017. http://knight-rider.wikia.com/wiki/K.I.T.T._(2000)

Klatch, Rebecca. *Women of the New Right.* Philadelphia: Temple University Press, 1988.

Kraig, Beth. "The Liberated Lady Driver." *The Midwest Quarterly: A Journal of Contemporary Thought* 28 (1987): 378–401.

_____. "Woman at the Wheel: A History of Women and the Automobile in America." Dissertation. University of Washington, 1987.

Krause, William. *Hollywood TV and Movie Cars.* St. Paul: MBI Publishing Company, 2001.

Landström, Catharina. "A Gendered Economy of Pleasure: Representations of Cars and Humans in Motoring Magazines." *Science Studies* 19.2 (2006): 31–53.

Lebeau, Phil, and Jeff Pohlman. "Can CEO Mary Barra Change General Motors' Corporate Culture?" *NBC News.* 16 May 2014. Web. 5 Dec 2014. http://www.nbcnews.com/storyline/gm-recall/can-ceo-mary-barra-change-general-motors-corporate-culture-n107521

Leffingwell, Randy. "Birth of the Pony Car." *The All-American Muscle Car: The Birth, Death, and Resurrection of Detroit's Greatest Performance Cars.* Eds. Jim Wangers, Colin Comer, Joe Oldham, and Randy Leffingwell. Minneapolis: Motorbooks, 2013. 37–66.

Lemish, Dafna, and Varda Muhlbauer. "'Can't Have it All': Representations of Older Women in Popular Culture." *Women and Therapy* 35.3–4 (2012): 165–180.

Lerman, Nina E., Arwen Palmer Mohun and Ruth Oldenziel. "Versatile Tools: Gender Analysis and the History of Technology." *Technology and Culture* 38.1 (1997): 1–8.

Levin, Hillel. *Grand Delusions: The Cosmic Career of John DeLorean.* New York: The Viking Press, 1993.

Lezotte, Chris. "The Evolution of the 'Chick Car' Or: What Came First, the Chick or the Car?" *The Journal of Popular Culture* 45.3 (2012): 516–531.

_____. "Have You Heard the One About the Woman Driver? Chicks, Muscle, Pickups, and the Reimagining of the Woman Behind the Wheel." Dissertation. Bowling Green State University, 2015.

_____. "Out on the Highway: Cars, Community, and the Gay Driver." *Culture, Society, and Masculinities* 7.2 (2015): 121–139.

_____. "Women and Car Culture in Cyberspace: Em-

powerment and Car Talk in the Internet User Group."
Thesis. Eastern Michigan University, 2009.
_____. "Women Auto Know: Automotive Knowledge, Auto Activism, and Women's Online Car Advice." *Feminist Media Studies* 15.1 (2014): 1–17.
_____. "Women with Muscle: Contemporary Women and the Classic Muscle Car." *Frontiers: A Journal of Women Studies* 34.2 (2013): 83–113.
Lofgren, Orval. *On Holiday: A History of Vacationing.* Berkeley: University of California Press, 1999.
Lumsden, Karen. *Boy Racer Culture: Youth, Masculinity, and Deviance.* New York: Routledge, 2014.
"Making it Mine." Petersen Automotive Museum. 6060 Wilshire Blvd., Los Angeles, CA, 90036. 13 May 2017.
Marsh, Peter, and Peter Collett. *Driving Passion: The Psychology of the Car.* 2nd ed. Winchester, MA: Faber & Faber, Inc., 1989.
McCarthy, Todd. *Fast Women: The Legendary Ladies of Racing.* New York: Miramax Books, 2006.
McCluggage, Denise. *By Brooks Too Broad for Leaping: Selections from* Autoweek. Santa Fe: Fulcorte Press, 1994.
McConnell, Curt. *"A Reliable Car and a Woman Who Knows It": The First Coast-to-Coast Auto Trips by Women, 1899–1916.* Jefferson, NC: McFarland, 2000.
McKinney, William Blythe. "The Classic Muscle Car Era." Thesis. Clemson University, 2009.
McShane, Clay. *Down the Asphalt Path: The Automobile and the American City.* New York: Columbia University Press, 1994.
Miller, Daniel. "Back Cover." *Material Cultures: Why Some Things Matter.* Ed. D. Miller. Chicago: The University of Chicago Press, 1998.
_____. "Consumption." *Handbook of Material Culture.* Eds. Christopher Tilley, Webb Keane, Susanne Kuchler, Mike Rowlands, and Patricia Spyer. London: Sage Publications, 2006. 341–354.
_____. "Driven Societies." *Car Cultures.* Ed. Daniel Miller. Oxford: Berg, 2001. 1–34.
_____. "Why Some Things Matter." *Material Cultures: Why Some Things Matter.* Ed. D. Miller. Chicago: The University of Chicago Press, 1998.
Mills, Katie. *The Road Story and the Rebel: Moving Through Film, Fiction, and Television.* Carbondale: Southern Illinois University Press, 2006.
Mueller, Mike. *Motor City Muscle.* St. Paul: MBI Publishing, 2004.
Nakayama, Thomas K., and Robert L. Krizek. "Whiteness: A Strategic Rhetoric." *Quarterly Journal of Speech* 81 (1995): 291–309.
Nauen, Elinor, ed. *Ladies Start Your Engines: Women Writers on Cars and the Road.* London: Faber & Faber, 1997.
Naughton, Keith. "Detroit Muscles Up." *Newsweek* 147.11 13 Mar 2006: 40–42.
_____. "In Car Buying, Baby Boomers Surpass the Young." *Bloomberg.* 30 Aug 2013. Web. 2 June 2017. https://www.bloomberg.com/news/articles/2013-08-29/in-car-buying-baby-boomers-surpass-the-young
Naughton, Keith, Joanna Broder, Joan Raymond, Hillary Shenfeld, Margaret Nelson Brinkhaus, Patrick Crowley, and Tara Weingarten. "The Long and Winding Road." *Newsweek* 149.15 09 Apr 2007: 64.
Newhardt, David. "Modern Muscle Déjà Vu Sort of." *The All American Muscle Car: The Birth, Death, and Resurrection of Detroit's Greatest Performance Cars.*

Ed. Darwin Holmstrom, Minneapolis: MBI Publishing Company, 2013. 159–166.
Newman, Romy. "6 Strategies for Breaking Down Gender Barriers in Any Profession." Fortune.com 27 Jun 2016. Web. 3 May 2017. http://fortune.com/2016/06/27/united-state-of-women-gender-barriers/
Nystrom, Elsa. *Mad for Speed: The Racing Life of Joan Newton Cuneo.* Jefferson, NC: McFarland, 2013.
O'Connor, Christopher, and Katharine Kelly. "Auto Theft and Youth Culture: A Nexus of Masculinities, Femininities, and Car Culture." *Journal of Youth Studies* 9.3 (July 2006): 247–267.
Olson, Joel. "Whiteness and the Polarization of American Politics." *Political Research Quarterly* 61.4 (December 2008): 704–718.
Orr, Deborah. "Funky Old Women; There's a New Attitude Among Older Women. Once Expected to Fade Into Invisibility, They're Undergoing Social Reinvention. Respect, Says Deborah Orr." *The Independent* (October 23, 2004): 16–17.
Overman, Steven, Jr., and Kelly Boyer Sagert. *Icons of Women's Sport: From Tomboys to Title IX and Beyond.* Santa Barbara, CA: ABC-CLIO, 2012.
Oz, Daphne. "Women: Lead the Health Movement!" Oprah.com 30 Apr 2010. Web. 5 Jul 2016. http://www.oprah.com/health/The-Power-of-Women-Societys-Caretakers-Daphne-Oz
Packer, Jeremy. *Mobility without Mayhem: Safety, Cars, and Citizenship.* Durham, NC: Duke University Press, 2008.
Paes de Barros, Deborah. *Fast Cars and Bad Girls: Nomadic Subjects and Women's Road Stories.* New York: Peter Lang, 2004.
Palladino, Grace. *Teenagers: An American History.* New York: Basic Books, 1996.
Parchesky, Jennifer. "Women in the Driver's Seat: The Auto-Erotics of Early Women's Films." *Film History: An International Journal* 18.2 (2006): 174–184.
Passon, Jerry W. *The Corvette in Literature and Culture: Symbolic Dimensions of America's Sports Car.* Jefferson, NC: McFarland, 2011.
Perry-Sizemore, Elizabeth, and Nina MacLaughlin. "Non-Traditional Careers for Women: Opportunities and Benefits for Women in Male-Dominated Professions." LearnHowToBecome.com. n.d. Web. 3 May 2017. http://www.learnhowtobecome.org/under represented-careers-for-women/
Pflugfelder, Ehren. "Something Less Than a Driver: Toward an Understanding of Gendered Bodies in Motorsport." *Journal of Sport and Social Issues* 33.4 (2009): 411–426.
Phelan, Mark. "Mary Barra Shapes a New GM: Fast, Focused, and Decisive." *Detroit Free Press* 3 June 2017. Web. 3 June 2017. http://www.freep.com/story/money/cars/mark-phelan/2017/06/04/mary-barra-general-motors/352853001/
Pickering, Michael, and Emily Keightley. "The Modalities of Nostalgia." *Current Sociology* 54.6 (November 2006): 919–941.
Priddle, Alisa. "2015 Ford Mustang on Dealer Lots Next Month." UsaToday.com 18 Sept 2014. Web. 31 March 2017 http://www.usatoday.com/story/money/cars/2014/09/18/2015-mustang/15800057/
Prown, Jules David. "Mind in Matter: An Introduction to Material Culture Theory and Method." *Winterthur Portfolio* 17.1 (1982): 1–19.
Redshaw, Sarah. "Articulations of the Car: The Dominant

Articulations of Racing and Rally Driving." *Mobilities* 2.1 (March 2007): 121–141.

_____. "Driving Cultures." *Cultural Studies Review* 12.2 (September 2006): 74–89.

Redshaw, Sarah, and Greg Noble. *Mobility, Gender, and Young Drivers: Second Report of the Transforming Drivers Study of Young People and Driving.* Sydney: NRMA Motoring and Services. 2006. Web. 28 February 2015 http://www.uws.edu.au/__data/assets/pdf_file/0003/46353/Transforming_Drivers_Report_2_-_Mobility,_Gender__and__Young_Drivers.pdf

Reich, Holly. "Mustang Sally Nails the Female Market." Washingtonpost.com 6 June 2005. Web. 19 May 2017. http://www.washingtonpost.com/wp-dyn/content/article/2005/06/06/AR2005060601397.html

Reichert, Elizabeth. "Individual Counseling for Sexually Abused Children: A Role for Animals and Storytelling." *Child and Adolescent Social Work Journal* 15.3 (1998): 177–185.

Root, Marilyn. *Women at the Wheel: 42 Stories of Freedom, Fanbelts, and the Lure of the Open Road.* Naperville, IL; Sourcebooks, 1999.

Rosen, Ruth. *The World Split Open: How the Modern Women's Movement Changed America.* New York: Penguin Books, 2000.

Rosenberg, Diego. *Selling the American Muscle Car: Marketing Detroit Iron in the 60s and 70s.* Forest Lake, MN: CarTech, 2016.

Ross, Sally R., Lynn L. Ridinger,, and Jacquelyn Cuneen. "Drivers to Divas: Advertising Images of Women in Motorsport." *International Journal of Sports Marketing & Sponsorship* (April 2009): 204–214.

Sanford, Charles. "'Woman's Place' in American Car Culture." *The Automobile and American Culture.* Eds. D.L. Lewis and L. Goldstein. Ann Arbor: The University of Michigan Press, 1983. 137–152.

Sargeant, Jack, and Stephanie Watson. *Lost Highways: An Illustrated History of Road Movies.* London: Creation Books, 1999.

Scharff, Virginia. *Taking the Wheel: Women and the Coming of the Motor Age.* Albuquerque: University of New Mexico Press, 1991.

Sease, Douglas R. "Mad for Muscle Cars: One Man's Search for the Vehicle That Helped Define His Youth." WSJ.com 14 July 2007. Web. 5 Jun 2016. https://www.wsj.com/articles/SB118400854448461183

Seiler, Cotten. *Republic of Drivers: A Cultural History of Automobility in America.* Chicago: University of Chicago Press, 2008.

Seymour, Miranda. *The Bugatti Queen: In Search of a Motor-Racing Legend.* London: Simon & Shuster, 2004.

Shackelford, Todd K., and Avi Besser. "Predicting Attitudes toward Homosexuality: Insights from Personality Psychology." *Individual Differences Research* 5.2 (2007): 106–114.

Sheller, Mimi. "Automotive Emotions: Feeling the Car." *Theory, Culture, and Society* 21.4/5 (2004): 221–242.

Shimp, Terence, and Subhash Sharma. "Consumer Ethnocentrism: Construction and Validation of the CETSCALE." *Journal of Marketing Research* 24.3 August 1987: 280–89.

Sloop, John M. "Riding in Cars Between Men." *Communication and Critical/Cultural Studies* 2.3 (2005): 191–213.

Smart, Bridget, Amanda Campbell, Barlow Soper, and Walter Buboltz, Jr. "Masculinity/Femininity and Automotive Behaviors: Emerging Knowledge for Entrepreneurs." *Journal of Business and Public Affairs* 1.2 1997. n.p.

Spender, Dale. *Nattering on the Net: Women, Power and Cyberspace.* North Melbourne, Australia: Spinifex Press, 1995.

Stacey, Judith. "The New Conservative Feminism." *Feminist Studies* 9 no. 3 (1983): 559–583.

Stevenson, Heon. *American Automobile Advertising, 1930–1980: An Illustrated History.* Jefferson, NC: McFarland, 2008.

Svendsen, Arvid. "Authenticating Your Muscle Car." *Hot Rod Network.* 8 June 2015. Web. 8 Aug 2016. http://www.hotrod.com/articles/authenticating-your-muscle-car/

Thomas, Fred, ed. *Car Club Memories: Personal Stories from Three Dynamic Decades of Cruisin,' Competition, and Cool Cars.* Bloomington, IN: AuthorHouse, 2008.

Tilley, Christopher. "Objectification." *Handbook of Material Culture.* Eds. C. Tilley, W. Keane, S. Kuchler, M. Rowlands, and P. Spyer. London: Sage Publications, 2006. 60–73.

Tilley, Christopher, Webb Keane, Susanne Kuchler, Mike Rowlands, and Patricia Spyer, eds. "Introduction." *Handbook of Material Culture.* London: Sage Publications, 2006. 1–6.

Tirrell, Lynne. "Language and Power." *A Companion to Feminist Philosophy.* Eds. Alison M. Jaggar & Iris Marion Young. Malden, MA: Blackwell, 1998.

Tolson, Mike. "Testosterone-Fueled Muscle Cars Make a Comeback." Houstonchronicle.com 27 Dec 2014. Web. 6 Jun 2015. http://www.houstonchronicle.com/news/houston-texas/houston/article/Testosterone-fuled-muscle-cars-make-a-comeback-5969618.php

Turpen, Aaron. "How the American Muscle Car Grew Up." *CarFax.* 12 Aug 2014. Web. 6 Apr 2016. http://www.carfax.com/blog/american-muscle-car-grew/

"2017 Chrysler Pacifica—Family Minivan." Chrysler.com 2017. n.d. Web. 9 Apr 2017. http://www.chrysler.com/pacifica.html

Ulrich, Lawrence. "The $4,000,000 Plymouth." *Fortune* 15.2, 17 Oct 2005: 192–210.

_____. "What Your Car Says About You." *MSN Autos.* 2009. Web. 9 Sep 2014. http://editorial.autos.msn.com/article.aspx?cp-documentid=445065

Vanderbilt, Tom. *Traffic: Why We Drive the Way We Do (and What It Says About Us).* New York: Random House, 2008.

Vannini, Phillip, ed. *Material Culture and Technology in Everyday Life: Ethnographic Approaches.* New York: Peter Lang, 2009.

Varney, Wendy. "Of Men and Machines: Images of Masculinity in Boys' Toys." *Feminist Studies* 28.1 (Spring 2002) 153–174.

Wajcman, Judy. *Feminism Confronts Technology.* University Park: The Pennsylvania State University Press, 1991.

_____. *Technofeminism.* Malden, MA: Polity Press, 2004.

Walsh, Margaret. "At Home at the Wheel? The Woman and Her Automobile in the 1950s." The Third Eccles Centre for American Studies Plenary Lecture: Proceedings of the British Association of American Studies Annual Conference, 2006. The British Library (2007): 1–21.

_____. "Gender and American Mobility: Cars, Women, and the Issue of Equality." *Cultural Histories of Sociabilities, Spaces, and Mobilities.* 2nd ed. Ed. Colin Divall. New York: Routledge, 2016.

_____. "Gender and Automobility: Selling Cars to American Women After the Second World War." *Charm* (2009): 295–310.

_____. "Gender and the Automobile in the History of the United States." *Automobile in American Life and Society*. University of Michigan–Dearborn. 2004–2010. Web. 09 Dec 2009. http://www.autolife.umd. umich.edu/Gender/Walsh/G_Overview1.htm

_____. Review of *Republic of Drivers: A Cultural History of the Automobile*, by Cotten Seiler. Dec 2009. *Reviews in History*. 15 May 2013. Web. 5 Jan 2014. http://www. history.ac.uk/reviews/review/778

Wexler, Bruce. *The Illustrated History of Muscle Cars*. New York: Chartwell Books, 2013.

"What are Lesbians' Favorite Cars?" *Lesbian News* 12 March 2016. Web. 5 Dec 2016. http://www.lesbian news.com/what-are-lesbians-favorite-cars/

Wilke, Joanne. *Eight Women, Two Model Ts and the American West*. Lincoln: University of Nebraska Press, 2007.

Witzel, Michael Karl, and Kent Bash. *Cruisin': Car Culture in America*. Osceola, WI: MBI Publishing Co., 1997.

Woodward, Ian. *Understanding Material Culture*. London: Sage, 2007.

"The Woodward Dream Cruise, a Detroit Classic." AbsoluteMichigan.com. 12 Aug 2009. Web. 10 Jul 2010. http://www.absolutemichigan.com/dig/michigan/ the-woodward-dream-cruise-a-detroit-classic/

Woodyard, Chris. "Five Things 'Time' Revealed about GM CEO Mary Barra." *USA Today* 28 Sep 2014. Web. 2 Nov 2014. http://www.usatoday.com/story/money/ cars/2014/09/28/time-magazine-gm-ceo-mary-barra/ 16342439/

Woolcock, Iris. *The Road North: One Woman's Adventure Driving the Alaska Highway 1947–1948*. Anchorage: Greatland Graphics, 1990.

Wosk, Julie. *Women and the Machine: Representations from the Spinning Wheel to the Electronic Age*. Baltimore: Johns Hopkins University Press, 2001.

Yost, Mark. "Muscle Cars on Parade." *The Wall Street Journal* 22 August 2007 D10.

Index

Numbers in bold italics indicate pages with illustrations